Whiteness, Feminism and the Absurd in Contemporary British and US Poetry

Whiteness, Feminism and the Absurd in Contemporary British and US Poetry

Jenna Clake

EDINBURGH
University Press

Edinburgh University Press is one of the leading university presses in the UK. We publish academic books and journals in our selected subject areas across the humanities and social sciences, combining cutting-edge scholarship with high editorial and production values to produce academic works of lasting importance. For more information visit our website: edinburghuniversitypress.com

© Jenna Clake, 2025

Edinburgh University Press Ltd
13 Infirmary Street
Edinburgh EH1 1LT

Typeset in 10.5/13 Adobe Sabon by
IDSUK (DataConnection) Ltd, and
printed and bound in Great Britain.

A CIP record for this book is available from the British Library

ISBN 978 1 4744 9434 2 (hardback)
ISBN 978 1 4744 9436 6 (webready PDF)
ISBN 978 1 4744 9437 3 (epub)

The right of Jenna Clake to be identified as the author of this work has been asserted in accordance with the Copyright, Designs and Patents Act 1988, and the Copyright and Related Rights Regulations 2003 (SI No. 2498).

Contents

Acknowledgements	vi
Introduction: The Absurd, Race and Gender	1

PART I

1. Feminine/Feminist Humour and Whiteness in Contemporary British Absurdist Poetry	25
2. Miscommunication and Failure to Connect in the Absurd	45
3. The Apocalypse in the Absurd	69

PART II

4. Authority, 'White Trash' and Culture in Jennifer L. Knox's *A Gringo Like Me*	91
5. Sadness in Caroline Bird's *The Hat-Stand Union* and *In These Days of Prohibition*	113
6. Reality and Imagination in Emily Berry's *Dear Boy*	133
Afterword: Failing Better	151
Notes	159
Bibliography	173
Index	196

Acknowledgements

This book has been long endeavour, as most books are. It could only be written in earnest with a research sabbatical, and I am grateful to Victoria Bell and Natasha Vall for supporting my research in this manner, and to my colleagues in English and Creative Writing at Teesside University for covering my responsibilities during this period. To my students who have studied 'Writing Popular Culture' with me, I am grateful for your enthusiasm and perception, and for our discussions, which have given me faith in this project.

I am lucky to have many wonderful colleagues and friends who have offered guidance, advice and feedback. My special thanks go to Rachel Carroll, Jane Ford, Isabel Galleymore and Rob Hawkes. Many thanks, too, to Edinburgh University Press for their care and attention throughout the editorial and publishing process.

I would not have begun working on the Absurd without tutelage, support and mentoring from Luke Kennard and Elsa Braekkan Payne, whose encouragement from my undergraduate studies to my PhD gave me confidence, challenged my thinking, and introduced me to the work of many great poets and critics. I am grateful to Ruth Gilligan and Jack Underwood for providing thorough and incisive feedback.

My PhD thesis, where my research into the Absurd first began, features interviews with Rachael Allen, Emily Berry, Crispin Best and Caroline Bird. Though I do not reproduce or use these interviews in this book, I am grateful for these poets' time and insight, and for the generosity of their answers during my early research into the Absurd. Some of the chapters in this book have developed from conversations at the following conferences: 'Contemporary Poetry: Thinking and Feeling', 'Out of Practice', 'Great Writing', 'AWW-STRUCK: Creative and Critical Approaches to Cuteness'; many thanks to their organisers. I'm grateful to Richard O'Brien and Elizabeth O'Connor for their teamwork in organising *Poetry and TV*.

To Jamie, I owe my endless thanks – for being my champion, motivator and sounding-board, and for the practical and emotional care that comes with writing.

Introduction: The Absurd, Race and Gender

A few years prior to writing this book, I came to a realisation that twenty-first-century British and United States poetry uses characteristics of the Absurd – its captivating mixture of humour, bizarreness and emotional depth – to communicate existential dread, fear and anxiety. In an era of political and social turmoil on both sides of the Atlantic – where issues of gender, race, class and sexuality are irrevocably linked with concerns of how to survive in a capitalist society; where increasing technological abilities and our damage to the natural world dominate news stories – a new aesthetic was emerging. In critical discussions and reviews, names for a new movement or school were offered, but there was no unanimous agreement; nothing seemed fitting. There was no recognition of who was a member, what the poetics of this movement might be or defining characteristics. These discussions failed to see that this was an aesthetic, not an organised movement – that many poets, linked by publisher, mentor or writing workshops, or not, were taking the irony and nihilism of the Absurd and turning inwards, directing its anxieties and concerns in idiosyncratic ways. Most importantly, there was no acknowledgement that this emerging trend was indebted to the Absurd.

In this book, then, I aim to identify this aesthetic and explore its relationship to an Absurdist literary tradition. This new aesthetic of the Absurd is uniquely specific to a twenty-first-century disposition; it is a poetics of anxiety, one that can attempt to destabilise and ridicule established orders, poetry itself and its readers, while also reaching for emotional resonance through popular culture, apocalyptic scenarios and existential dread. It is also an aesthetic preoccupied with gender, as women poets write back against the misogyny of the literature and theatre of the Absurd. A quick survey of the literature of the Absurd indicates that its primarily recognised writers are white and male. In her analysis of the literary Absurd, Joanna Gavins identifies 'authors of prose fiction most frequently categorised as "absurd" by literary critics' (2013, p. 11): John Barth, Samuel Beckett, Albert Camus, Joseph Conrad,

2   *Whiteness, Feminism and the Absurd in Contemporary Poetry*

Joseph Heller, Franz Kafka, Daniil Kharms, Herman Melville, Thomas Pynchon, Mark Twain, Kurt Vonnegut. She also adds Harold Pinter and Jean-Paul Sartre to this list (2013, p. 20), somewhat rejecting Martin Esslin's claims that the writers did not belong to the Theatre of the Absurd (Esslin in Gavins, 2013, p. 20). Indeed, Gavins notes that 'academic analyses which approach poetic texts as manifestations of an absurd sensitivity are [. . .] scarce' and identifies poets whose work is often considered Absurd: Stephen Crane, T.S. Eliot, Robert Frost, Thomas Hardy, Ted Hughes, James Joyce, Wallace Stevens, Charles Simic (2013, p. 141). She later identifies James Tate as an Absurdist poet (2013, p. 153). Neil Cornwell further identifies the poet Russell Edson's work as belonging to the Absurd (2006, p. 174).

Women, then, rarely appear in scholarly investigations of the Absurd. Where they do – such as in Cornwell's brief mention of a 'women's absurd' (2006, p. 292), or Michael Y. Bennett's *The Cambridge Introduction to Theatre and Literature of the Absurd* (2015) and Emily B. Klein's (2022) taxonomy of a 'New Feminist Absurd' in theatre – the women are playwrights: Beth Henley, Maria Irene Fornes, Caryl Churchill (Bennett, 2015, pp. 119–22); Margaret Hollingsworth, Lyudmila Petrushevskaya and Sarah Kane (Cornwell, 2006, p. 292). As poet Alice Notley has noted, this is part of a wider cultural issue, in that 'men lead movements and argue with each other over the present and future of poetry, insuring they get a space in the so-called discourse' and 'the whole idea of a literary movement, the academy, the avant-garde, are all male forms' (in Nelson, 2007, p. 133).

While Notley's comments are not wrong, they reflect a broader trend for discussions about gender equality which eschew ideas of race. As such, there is also little discourse in these conversations about the new aesthetic around race and Absurdism. Glaringly, the above writers are all white, and conversations about representation in poetry – especially experimental or avant-garde poetry – seem to be trapped in gender politics. So, it is not possible to acknowledge this aesthetic in contemporary British and US poetry without highlighting how the Absurd – both historically and in the present – has a troubled relationship to race, and whiteness – of the poetry establishment, perceived ideas about avant-garde poetry and who poetry readers are – pervades. Indeed, in my earlier investigations into this new aesthetic in the Absurd, I too eschewed the lens of whiteness and, although my work acknowledged race and class, gender was at the forefront of my work. Yet it is impossible to truly look at modern politics and poetry without considering how social categorisations such as race, class and gender create overlapping and symbiotic systems of discrimination – what Kimberlé Crenshaw

Introduction: The Absurd, Race and Gender 3

has named an intersectional approach (1989). This book is a personal endeavour as a critic and poet: I want to explore how contemporary Absurdist poetry might interrogate whiteness so that I may undertake the endeavour myself.[1] In this book, then, I explore the politics – even if latent – of this new aesthetic in the Absurd, and its relationship to race, gender and the avant-garde.

Whiteness in the Avant-Garde, Race in Poetry

Anthony Reed writes in *Freedom Time: The Poetics and Politics of Black Experimental Writing* (2014) that we are in an 'era of official "color blindness," where now optimistic, now nostalgic "post-"'s proliferate' (2014, p. 1). He states the importance of considering 'historical gaps and erasures' but also thinking about and 'produc[ing] inhabitable futures on terms other than those of the present' (2014, p. 1). Indeed, as Reed (2014), Cathy Park Hong (2014) and Claudia Rankine and Beth Loffreda (in Rankine et al., 2016) write, most considerations of 'avant-garde' or experimental writing in English tend to neglect writing by people of colour or perpetuate the idea that writing by people of colour must be about racism. For Reed, this is due to 'granular attention to particular networks, coteries, and traditions of writers and writing', and a 'nominally color-blind methodology or the ahistorical and theoretically untenable position that "class" is somehow more important than race', and that, in most criticism, 'experimentation and race seem opposed' (2014, p. 3).

This approach is no more apparent than in Marjorie Perloff's article 'From Language Poetry to the New Concretism: The Evolution of the Avant-Garde' (2022), in which she writes: 'In recent years, ideological and identity-based movements have sometimes been labeled "avant-garde"'; she cites 'the Black Arts movement, the feminist performance art of the '70s, or the "new" Asian-American poetries' and argues that 'the "breakthrough" of such movements tends to be short-lived, the aim of the groups concerned being ironically counter-avantgarde in their drive to win acceptance within the larger public art sphere' (2022, p. 17). Perloff's argument neglects deeper reading of any such works (which she does not cite) and her only mention of poets of colour comes under a short section describing 'identity-based movements', as though all work by writers of colour can be reduced to this, and as if the reader naturally sees an issue with identity politics or identity-driven writing, however Perloff might be defining this. Indeed, during a panel in 2000 hosted by the Poetry Society of America and The New School (proceedings published by *Fence*), 'What's African about African American Poetry?', Harryette Mullen noted: 'Because poetry typically appeals to relatively small audiences, we may be in danger of becoming isolated from varieties of experience outside our own particular frame of reference' (in Alexander et al., 2000). She discussed the importance of eschewing a 'singular black experience', highlighting 'the "double consciousness" defined by W. E. B. DuBois', and how 'it is increasingly apparent that the recipe for mixing our African with our American consciousness varies with each individual' (2000).

Issues regarding representation and race pervade British poetry, as well as US poetry, as Sandeep Parmar writes in her influential essay, 'Not a British Subject: Race and Poetry in the UK' for the *Los Angeles Review of Books* (2015).[2] For Parmar, British poetry has a 'serious problem with race', because 'we are mostly locked into a semi-confessional, detached, and wary handling of the self as a stand-in for the folklore of universal human experience' (2015). In a follow-up to her essay, entitled 'Still Not a British Subject: Race and UK Poetry', published in the *Journal of British and Irish Innovative Poetry* (2020), Parmar writes that 'race and literary (though not necessarily poetry) culture is becoming a regular feature in public discourse', but notes that this is unlikely to dismantle 'the authority of whiteness' while conversations about 'authenticity' and 'craft vs. identity politics' continue. Yet, in her first essay, Parmar notes that 'there's a transatlantic conversation happening today that was missing from previous decades', and that 'aesthetic divides seem less politicized than they were in the 1970s – and this may well be because subsequent generations of poets confront the authenticity prized by their forebears with political cynicism' (2015). This leaves some space – even if it is small, contested – to challenge notions of race in British and US poetry, to bring this conversation to the front of scholarship.

In this book, then, I hope to discover how whiteness pervades Absurdism, and to also think about how its poets understand and challenge the privilege and stasis that comes with it. I also highlight the work of writers of colour, exploring how their work provides more determined, hopeful iterations of the Absurd, noting, as Jill Magi argues, that the work of poets of colour 'should not only be instrumentalized toward political aims' (2017). I argue, then, that this new iteration of the Absurd is an unacknowledged aesthetic of British and US twenty-first-century poetry; it rejects the misogynistic approaches of the Absurd, which is grounded in heteronormative, stereotypical depictions of the 'nagging', insane woman and her long-suffering husband; it grapples with ideas of race and class, to varying degrees. The argument of this book is cumulative, each chapter adding to a layered investigation into this aesthetic:

first, its techniques, characteristics, concerns; second, its attempts to grapple with race; third, how writers use Absurdism to offer prospects of hope and change; and finally, how writers of the Absurd might move away from a nihilistic acceptance and into a space of hopefulness.

The Absurd naturally engages with traditions of avant-garde poetry, but, as David Lehman writes in his exegesis of the New York School: '*Avant-garde*, like *existentialism* or *postmodernism*, is bedeviled by imprecise use and has been debased to the precise extent of its popularity' (1999, p. 283), and so there is likely crossover between what one might consider avant-garde or distinctly Absurdist. However, Lehman states:

> Any would-be avant-garde enterprise faces three built-in contradictions. An avant-garde movement needs to embody an adversarial thrust, yet when politics is given dominance, the result is often fatal for art. It must be a collective movement, though acting collectively goes against the grain of that insubordinate individual, the modern artist. Finally, it must overcome resistance, but if it does so, it must also necessarily remove an enabling condition for its own existence. This is, after all, the historical pattern of avant-garde movements, which tend to decline in artistic vitality at the exact same moment that they succeed as fashion statements, so that, as Renato Poggioli pointed out in his authoritative study, *The Theory of the Avant-Garde*, 'the whole history of the avant-garde art seems reducible to an uninterrupted series of fads.' (1999, p. 286)

Indeed, the Absurd sits outside some of these confines of the avant-garde – it is not, for example, a collective movement. Yet Lehman's claims about the short-lived nature of an avant-garde movement, and how apoliticism is vital to its survival, are worth interrogating, and I will return to these ideas throughout this book.

There is not a group of poets deliberately identifying themselves as 'Absurdists'; this aesthetic has emerged without a clear identity. I refer to the Absurd as an aesthetic – rather than a school or movement – for a number of reasons. First, a 'school' or 'movement' in poetry typically denotes a set – albeit occasionally contested – group or membership. The New York School exists in modern poetry and academic circles as one of the most prominent, well-read and well-researched schools of poetry, and yet discussions of the school are plagued by disputes surrounding its membership. Indeed, this new aesthetic of the Absurd has emerged without an existing membership, and so to apply the term 'school' to it would invite unnecessary discussions regarding membership and application of arbitrary criteria to establish affiliation.[3] The second reason for not applying the terms 'movement' or 'school' to the aesthetic is that schools or movements often establish set rules or techniques for their poetry that

6 *Whiteness, Feminism and the Absurd in Contemporary Poetry*

each adherent poet must follow in order to retain their membership. The Flarf movement, as Andrew Epstein notes in his review for the *Los Angeles Review of Books*, existed 'on a private email list', and relied heavily on a technique developed by its affiliates, referred to as 'Google sculpting' which 'calls for the poet to trawl the internet for preexisting language', typically by 'putting combinations of intentionally silly or offensive keywords into a search engine ("pizza" and "kitty," "Rogaine" and "bunny," "pussy" and "turtleneck")' and then 'creatively arranging the results into strange, funny, and unsettling collages' (2018). The Absurd has no such set of determinants.

While this new aesthetic of the Absurd applies and responds to the characteristics of earlier iterations of the Absurd, it does not do so dogmatically: poets may apply *some* of the characteristics of the aesthetic in their poems, but not all at once. Ultimately, because the Absurd is not a school or movement, it does not have a membership creating generative rules or techniques, and therefore styles and approaches differ from poet to poet. Indeed, a school or movement might exist for a short amount of time; its concerns or techniques might prove to generate a limited amount of work. Epstein notes that Flarf is 'now more a period style than a going concern', which is exacerbated by the fact that 'many of the poets themselves have moved on' (2018). A number of the poets included in this book have had mainstream success with their work, having been shortlisted for or awarded major literary prizes, or named by the Poetry Book Society as Next Generation Poets.[4] The influence of this aesthetic has, then, widened – especially in Britain – with the poets leading courses at academic institutions and teaching writing workshops at Arvon, the Poetry School and literary festivals. It is not possible to fully track this influence in this book, but I draw on a wide range of poets and poems that use Absurdist techniques – whether or not the poet employs these regularly in their oeuvre.

Much speculation about the identity of this new aesthetic has taken place in poetry criticism, particularly in British poetry criticism. In a review for *Ambit* of Jack Underwood's debut collection, *Happiness* (2015), Ralf Webb notes that there is 'a broad aesthetic in contemporary UK poetry – an aesthetic that resists succinct, unloaded description' and settles somewhat uneasily on the term 'anecdotal post-sincerity' (2015), but neglects to provide a definition or concrete set of characteristics. Webb argues that 'the as-yet-unnamed "school" that employs this aesthetic is, by now, well established rather than emergent' (2015), but cites only three white, British poets whose work he believes fits into this category: Jack Underwood, Sam Riviere and Emily Berry. Furthermore, Webb does not discuss the aesthetic's impact or naysayers.

In an essay published in 2017, Charles Whalley writes about South African poet Kate Kilalea's poem, 'Hennecker's Ditch', arguing for a similarity in style between Kilalea's poem and 'a cohort of poets for whom anxiousness is an inextricable part of their approach towards the world, particularly in the young British poets practicing the "Faber Anxious Style"' (2017). Indeed, anxiety features prominently in the Absurd, and I will explore its import in this book. However, Whalley does not acknowledge that what he perceives as a British aesthetic or trend has US antecedents and contributors. Indeed, that British poets' work bears similarities to Kilalea's highlights that the internet – particularly the rise of online poetry journals and social media platforms – has ensured that geographical location does not affect the kind of poetry to which one has access and can use as inspiration. In this book, I do not have adequate space to investigate the global reach of this new aesthetic in the Absurd, so I have chosen to focus on poetry from either side of the Atlantic, to investigate the blurred aesthetic divides between British and US poetry, as Parmar puts it.

Whalley limits the origins of what he deems 'Faber Anxious Style' to one British poetry publisher. Indeed, many of the poets in this book are published by Faber & Faber, but it is not the only publisher, and these are not the only poets writing the Absurd. This does raise the pertinent issue that the avant-garde must 'define itself in relation to tradition', while simultaneously existing 'on the verge of becoming a tradition itself, with adherents and disciples' (Lehman, 1999, p. 285), so that what is avant-garde becomes mainstream – which has certainly become the case for some contemporary poets writing Absurdist poetry. Whalley assesses that for these poets, 'the present is inflected with dread', and that 'their universes are often absurd, but more in the troublingly *unheimlich* than the playful' (2017).[5]

Fiona Moore asserts that the poets all belong to the 'School of Lumsden', named after poet and editor Roddy Lumsden, 'and his own reading of Americans including writers of the Gurlesque' (2016), which again disregards the reach of the Absurd and its history, and supposes that all poets writing the aesthetic must have studied under Lumsden's influence. This book therefore addresses an urgent need to define an aesthetic that has eluded critics thus far and establish its characteristics and history, highlighting its relationship to the Absurd while also problematising and unpacking its approaches.

The 'a-logical in a logical manner'

The Absurd originates in twentieth-century France: Martin Esslin applied the term 'Absurdism' to a group of playwrights, and his subsequent book, *The Theatre of the Absurd*, published in 1961, became an

8 Whiteness, Feminism and the Absurd in Contemporary Poetry

authority on the matter. As Cornwell writes, '*Webster's New Collegiate Dictionary* confirms the noun "absurd" as "the state or condition in which man exists in an irrational and meaningless universe"' (2006, p. 3). Thus '"absurdism" is defined as a philosophy based on this, and on the belief that "[man's] search for order brings him into conflict with his universe"' (2006, p. 3). However, Absurdism is typically considered to belong to theatre, so further discussion or implication of the Absurd in other literature has been hampered; as Esslin writes, the Absurd 'combines laughter with horror' (2023, p. 347) and, as Easterling notes, is defined by miscommunication (1982, p. 7).

In art, what might be considered Absurd is also called surreal, Dada or existentialist,[6] so that the categories are blurred, and what is Absurd remains contested. According to Albert Camus's definition of the Absurd, 'man is placed in an alien, inhuman world, which may appear characterized by "strangeness" and "denseness"' (in Easterling, 1982, p. 2). This 'inhuman' world is incongruous to humankind's expectations (Easterling, 1982, p. 3). Indeed, as Esslin notes, Camus's usage of the word pertains to the meaning 'incongruous, unreasonable, illogical', rather than 'ridiculous' (Esslin, 2023, p. 5). The Absurd 'combines laughter with horror' (Esslin, 2023, p. 347) and is defined by miscommunication (Easterling, 1982, p. 7). Esslin states that the 'Theatre of the Absurd is facing up to a deeper layer of absurdity – the absurdity of the human condition itself in a world where the decline of religious belief has deprived man of certainties' (2023, p. 339). It is clear, then, that the Absurd is concerned with unbalancing the world, or representing a world that is already unstable. It highlights that of which we are unsure, presenting the world (and human relationships) as impenetrable in a darkly humorous manner.

As Cornwell notes, the Absurd is 'born out of nihilism, existentialism, fuelled by certainty of death' (2006, p. 5), while Hinchliffe states that, in addition, 'Absurd Theatre relies heavily on dream and fantasy' (1969, p. 10). Cornwell has observed that 'satire, humour and incongruity are always potential ingredients of the absurd' (2006, p. ix), and seats the central concept, humour, between its main characteristics in the Absurd: satire and incongruity. Michel Delville has noted that, in what he deems the fabulist prose poem, 'a taste for black humour and tragicomical absurdities' is common (1998, p. 17). However, for all this humour and fantasy, Cornwell has noted that Jean Paul Richter 'seeks to differentiate between "satire, humour, irony and whimsy", while adopting the Aristotelian proposition that the ridiculous "stems from harmful incongruity"' (2006, p. 15).

Indeed, the Absurd is grounded in logic: Germaine Brée notes that in the Absurd, one relates the 'a-logical in a logical manner' that somehow adheres 'to some kind of reality' (in Cornwell, 2006, p. 92). According to Jerry Palmer, in the Absurd, a 'mixture of sense and nonsense is central to the joke process' (1987, p. 35); he argues that the 'construction of a surprise (the *peripeteia*)' is 'central to the logic of the absurd' (1987, pp. 40, 89). As Tom Stoppard writes, Absurdist works are formed from 'absurdities pushed to absurdity compounded by absurdity and yet saved from mere nonsense by their internal logic' (in Cornwell, 2006, p. 150). According to Cornwell, the following are also indicative of the Absurd: 'Digressions, inflated similes, snatches of zany dialogue, hyperbole, narrative and syntactic non-sequiturs, superfluous detail and irrelevancies, non-appearing characters and other forms of redundancy' (2006, p. 45).

The Absurd is also preoccupied with the inability to communicate effectively. Indeed, Wim Tigges comments: 'In nonsense, language creates a reality, in the absurd, language represents a senseless reality' (in Cornwell, 2006, p. 22). Giora S. Shoham also recognises the Absurd as 'a disengagement both resulting from and leading to a breakdown in human interaction' (in Cornwell, 2006, p. 24). If language becomes unstable and suspect, and we are unable to communicate effectively through speech, then our feelings, thoughts and relationships with one another become unstable and suffer. We lose the ability to be meaningful. This loss of meaning, of connection with others, is crucial to the Absurd.

Penelope Rosemont's *Surrealism: Inside the Magnetic Fields* (2019) offers a more personal account of the movement, and claims surrealism as a movement for activism and change. Yet, historically, the role of women in surrealism was, as Sabina Stent states, largely limited to Andre Breton's idea of the 'Surrealist female, one who was almost totally dependent upon her male companion and who belonged to her mate' (2012, p. 7); the woman was the 'male artist's muse' (2012, p. 7). Stent identifies Meret Oppenheim, Dora Maar, Elsa Schiaparelli, Leonora Carrington, Frida Kahlo, Dorothea Tanning, Remedios Varo and Lee Miller as key figures of women's surrealism. Moreover, in an exhibition catalogue for a solo exhibition at Newlyn Orion Gallery in 1976, Ithell Colquhoun relays how, due to her reluctance to accept E.L.T.'s Mesen's statements of allegiance to the surrealist group, she 'was neither invited to participate in the Surrealism Today Exhibition at the Zwemner Gallery in June 1940, nor to contribute to the special issue of The London Bulletin published in conjunction with the show' (2006).

It is evident, then, that space for activism in the avant-garde is highly contested. Perhaps this stems, also, from heated disagreement about what the avant-garde means, and who belongs to it. Returning to Perloff's exploration of the evolution of the avant-garde, she offers Peter Bürger's definition: 'It radically questions the very principle of art in

10   *Whiteness, Feminism and the Absurd in Contemporary Poetry*

bourgeois society according to which the individual is considered the creator of the work of art' (2022, p. 12). She also posits that 'the term avant-garde invariably refers to group formations—to those eager bands of brothers (or sisters) who collaborate to overturn the status quo of the bourgeois Establishment' (2022, p. 12). This would, then, discount the Absurd as I am defining it in this book for not being an organised movement. I contend that this is not necessary, nor a defining feature of avant-garde poetry, since relationships between contemporary poets and spheres of influence, as Parmar writes, are less contested in the twenty-first century. Perloff, then, seems to be reigniting a futile argument. Indeed, she takes this as an opportunity to erroneously point out that the New York School 'did not attack art as a bourgeois institution, nor did it call into question the centrality of painting and lyric poetry among the media' (2022, p. 16). Frank O'Hara's 'Personism: A Manifesto' (2004)[7] acts as a swift riposte to this claim; David Lehman's *The Last Avant-Garde: The Making of the New York School of Poets* (1999) provides a more thorough argument against Perloff's.

The Met's exhibition, *Delirious: Art and the Limits of Reason 1950–1980*, which ran from September 2017 to January 2018, suggests an apparent resurgence in popularity of Absurdist art. As the exhibition's description suggests:

> The years between 1950 and 1980 were beset by upheaval. Around the globe, military conflict proliferated and social and political unrest flared. Disenchantment with an oppressive rationalism mounted [. . .] Artists responded to these developments by incorporating absurdity, disorder, nonsense, disorientation, and repetition into their work.

Lexi Manatakis writes in her review of the exhibition for *Dazed*: 'Waking up in today's world feels like a fucking nightmare', and cites the following reasons: 'Trump and his bigotry are now 365 days in power, Brexit is an absolute mess, the systematic oppression of women, PoC [people of colour], the LGBT community is still incredibly prevalent' and 'our beautiful planet is decaying' (2017). At the time of writing, the USA has revoked *Roe* v. *Wade*, with severe consequences for reproductive rights, and although Donald Trump is no longer President of the United States, the consequences of his time in office are still being felt. Indeed, issues with reproductive rights are not confined to the US: in June 2023, a forty-four-year-old British woman was jailed for carrying out a late abortion. The ramifications of Brexit are being heightened by war in Ukraine, and the other issues Manatakis lists (and, indeed, several other issues and wars) have not been resolved. What place, then, does the Absurd take in times of political upheaval and existential dread? Can it do more than simply reflect that inner turmoil onto a reader, audience member or admirer of a work? If the Absurd is 'the assertion of a condition of being "nothing"' (Cornwell, 2006, p. ix), does the Absurd encourage stasis, inaction?

It is worth noting that many of these definitions of the Absurd and surrealism do not acknowledge Afro-surrealism. In a brief essay for *Black American Literature Forum* (1988), Amiri Baraka coined the term 'Afro-surreal' to define Henry Dumas's work, identifying Zora Neale Hurston, Jean Toomer and Toni Morrison as 'the giants of this genre' (1988, p. 164). For Baraka, the Afro-surreal is 'morality tales, magical, resonating dream emotions and images; shifting ambiguous terror, mystery, implied revelation' (1988, p. 164) – the latter a notable departure from the Absurd's nihilism. In her introduction to Afro-surrealism, written in 2013, Terri Francis notes that 'surrealism breaks [. . .] borders, crossing often seamlessly between animate and inanimate, conscious and subconscious', and that the Afro-surreal is defined by haunting (2013, p. 97). Francis argues that, like the Absurd, 'neither surrealism nor Afrosurrealism is a style, a set of criteria, an ideology, a genre, or even a coherent exploration. It is not a movement' (2013, p. 97). Afrosurrealism, then, recentres 'blackness at the core of surrealism and modernism', since 'Black artistic practice ignited the European avant-garde' and 'artistic movements have blended over time' (2013, p. 100).

Francis therefore contends that the idea that 'white experimental artists appropriated black art full stop' (2013, p. 100) is not necessarily so straightforward, but turning back to Parmar's and Park Hong's works, it is clear that there is a troubled relationship to race in the avant-garde. Indeed, reflecting on the criticism his 'Call it Afro-Surreal' (2009) has received, D. Scot Miller points out that much naysaying focused on the name, which some deem problematic for making the 'Afro' a prefix to the surrealist movement – thereby denying the originality of those connected to the aesthetic. Scot Miller argues that he borrowed the name from Baraka with permission (2016), which does not necessarily counter those arguments, but Aimé Césaire was as foundational a presence as Breton in the early surrealist movement; according to Jose Rosales, he 'worked with and drew from the surrealist tradition' and 'brought all the tools of the movement into explicit contact with the question of colonialism and colonized subjectivity' (2016). As such, for the purposes of this book, my definition of the Absurd in contemporary poetry contains writers of colour and white writers – not to dismiss the potential variations and approaches (since it is my aim to expose them), but to acknowledge, as Francis has, that something that is 'not a movement' needs some sense of coherence to be written about (2013, p. 97).

12 Whiteness, Feminism and the Absurd in Contemporary Poetry

While capitalisation of the term 'Absurd' when referring to the literary aesthetic or Theatre of the Absurd is generally inconsistent, I refer to the aesthetics as the 'Absurd'. As Cornwell writes: 'Textual inclusion of the word "absurd" ("absurdly", "absurdity" etc.) even when repeatedly employed, may not constitute any guarantee that a work is to be regarded with justification as fully, or solely, belonging to what we may choose to consider "literature of the absurd"' (2006, p. 100). Where I use 'absurd', 'bizarre' or 'zany', these terms will refer to a sense of strangeness in more widely understood forms, rather than being directly related to how the Absurd is created or functions. Bennett argues that Esslin's definition of the Absurd is reductive due to his focus on 'one main theme' (2015, pp. 3, 7), and contends that we might loosely group 'writers and their work' as Absurd by focusing on techniques, rather than theme (2015, p. 8). My approach synthesises Esslin's and Bennett's, drawing on thematic and technical characteristics of the Absurd, understanding that these features are a recursive framework through which to identify work that has Absurdist sensibilities.

Many of the poems I refer to in this book are prose poems, and, as Lehman writes in his introduction for *Great American Prose Poems: From Poe to the Present* (2003): 'The form of a prose poem is not an absence of form. It is just that the sentence and the paragraph must act the part of the line and the stanza' (p. 14). Indeed, scholarship has examined the relationship between the prose poem and surrealist works at length. Delville's *The American Prose Poem* (1998) explores interactions between surrealism, the Absurd and the prose poem, and is a key source for my book. Jane Monson's edited collection *British Prose Poetry: The Poems Without Lines* (2018) highlights the history of the prose poem in Britain, and Jeremy Noel-Tod's introduction to *The Penguin Book of the Prose Poem* (2018) offers a broad survey of the prose poem's history. Marguerite S. Murphy's *A Tradition of Subversion: Prose Poem in English from Wilde to Ashbery* (1992) provides crucial insight into the reader–writer relationship in prose poetry and the subversive nature of the prose poem. As Luke Kennard writes in his consideration of David Gascoyne's prose poetry: 'Prose poetry is more spacious [. . .] it allows for more incongruity and complex yet visible patterns; already at odds with the supposed purpose of prose (to convey information clearly) it is, in fact, the ideal Surrealist form' (2018, p. 253). In this book, in order to take in as many types of poetry as possible – both formalist and *vers libre* – I do not consider form a determining factor of the Absurd. Indeed, poets respond to the characteristics of the Absurd in idiosyncratic manners. To consider form as a determining factor of the Absurd would exclude crucial approaches and poets from the aesthetic

Introduction: The Absurd, Race and Gender **13**

and impose a rigid approach to the Absurd, which defies the very nature of the aesthetic and indeed its social and political concerns of inward-facing anxiety and existential dread. I undertake formal analysis where formal choices serve to enhance the tone or subject of the poem.

However, I wish to differentiate the Absurd and that which uses a central (or recurring) metaphor in a surrealist manner. In her collection *Mama Amazonica* (2017), Pascale Petit uses the Amazon rainforest as a repetend to explore her mother's mental illness and experience of sexual abuse. In the first poem, 'Mama Amazonica', Petit's mother is named '*Victoria amazonica*' (2017, p. 11), ostensibly aligning her with the rainforest. This connection becomes most evident in 'Rainforest in Sleep Room', in which Petit refigures the ECT treatment her mother receives as the destruction of the Amazon rainforest, so that a motorway runs through 'the Amazon's brain I like an ice pick through an eye socket' (2017, p. 17). Reality and image become blurred – but on a metaphorical rather than dreamlike level. All the references to medical procedures, such as the explicit mention of ECT (2017, p. 17), the mother being described as a 'patient' (2017, p. 18) and 'her stats' (2017, p. 18) constantly remind the reader that the Amazon rainforest is being used metaphorically, and the reader therefore understands the images and comparisons to the rainforest as a means of describing them.

Fundamentally, the reader understands from the beginning of the collection that the Amazon rainforest is a point of reference, illustrative of the mother and father's relationship, and the mother's mental health. Petit opens the collection with the lines: 'Picture my mother as a baby, afloat I on a waterlily leaf' (2017, p. 11). Petit places her mother, as a baby, in the rainforest, signalling that imagination is important when reading the poems: Petit has imagined her mother as part of the rainforest. The first word, 'picture', is the most important element of these opening lines. Petit provides her reader with an instruction, telling them to imagine the links between the Amazon and her mother from the very first word. Consequently, the idea of imagining, of the metaphor, is foregrounded and is therefore unforgettable: it is how we must read all the poems.

In 'Buck', a fawn 'begins to sprout I rifles, butts first, barrels', rather than antlers (2017, p. 37). The image of rifle butts instead of antlers is vivid and ostensibly is classically surreal, recalling Salvador Dali's 'Lobster Telephone' (1936) or René Magritte's 'The Flavour of Tears' (1948). However, Petit's image is also clearly in service of the political and personal aims of the collection: the mother's brutal medical treatment and the ecological concerns of deforestation and violence against nature. The baby as a fawn (a metonym for nature) grows a human-made weapon out of its head. This image is entirely logical: the deer's antlers are a weapon in the animal kingdom, and they are logically swapped with a weapon from the human world. The image reinforces the binary of nature being intrinsically good and humans being inherently bad (especially in our influence on nature). Yet, while logical, it is too essentialist to be Absurd, which refuses to provide clear answers and does not provide binary oppositions as political standpoints. Petit essentially writes in a world that *makes sense*, where the relationship between the writer and the reader is untroubled. Instead, as I will demonstrate throughout this book, the Absurd focuses on blurring imagination and reality, destabilising sense and subverting the reader–writer relationship.

'Female Insanity' in the Absurd

While I have established here that Absurdism has an issue with race, gender politics have been the central focus of debates about Absurdist writing, and it is important to consider – as I will throughout this book – how this might thwart and aid conversations about race. Celeste Derksen notes that 'male exclusivity' has been a 'defining feature of absurdism' (2002, p. 209). Carl Lavery and Clare Finburgh write that Esslin's study of the Absurd, 'for all its exhaustive comprehensiveness [. . .] analyses not a single female theatre-maker' (2015, p. 14). Indeed, Cornwell's *The Absurd in Literature* dedicates only one page to women writers, with the assertion: 'there seem to have been few women absurdist writers' (2006, p. 292). Additionally, Cornwell's work does not discuss poetry at length, and when it does, focuses mainly on male prose poets. Gavins recognises Cornwell's omissions and Derksen's comments, noting that 'academic analyses which approach poetic texts as manifestations of an absurd sensitivity are [. . .] scarce' (2013, pp. 140–1), and that 'the majority of authors whose works are identified as "absurd" . . . are white and male and writing towards the second half of the twentieth century' (2013, p. 58). However, Gavins does not cover a single writer who identifies as a woman. Her study focuses mainly on prose fiction, and when it does turn to poetry, three white, male poets are discussed: Charles Simic, James Tate and Ted Hughes.

Cornwell recognises that Derksen identifies a 'feminist absurd' (2006, p. 29), but he neglects to explore what this might mean or even look like. Bennett does identify '(later) female absurdists' (2015, p. 119): Adrienne Kennedy, Beth Henley, Maria Irene Fornes and Caryl Churchill; however, these playwrights' notable Absurdist outputs were all produced in the period 1950–80. Emily B. Klein identifies a 'New Feminist Absurd' in the plays of Sheila Callaghan, Ruby Rae Spiegel, Jackie Sibblies

Drury, Suzan-Lori Parks, Young Jean Lee, Bekah Brunstetter and Alice Birch (2022), in which 'expressions of rage [. . .] seemed to be intricately tied to questions of race, class, age, and privilege', and 'futility becomes its own form of freedom' (2022, pp. 26, 27).

In the type of Absurdism I wish to investigate, this latent sexism has played an important role, acting as a backdrop from which women writers have attempted to assert themselves as avant-gardists. As Elizabeth Evans writes:

> The past 20 years has witnessed a renewal of interest in feminist activism on both sides of the Atlantic. In part this has been a response to neoliberal and neoconservative attacks, both implicit and explicit, on the gains made by feminists during the 1960s and 1970s (Walby, 2011; Reger, 2012). Such a backlash against women has occurred at both the legislative and societal level in Britain and the US, exacerbating, inter alia: sustained violence against women; an increasingly blatant sexual objectification of women and girls; persistent attacks on women's bodily autonomy; and continued economic inequality. (2015, p. 1)

Evans highlights that the understanding that 'matrices of oppression effect power dynamics' has 'emerged from the writings of black feminists' (2015, p. 2). Despite the racial diversity of the playwrights she studies, Klein notes that 'many of their most laughable and ridiculous characters are white' (2022, p. 28). These characters remind 'audiences of the challenges of representing contemporary feminism without also representing its whiteness and white supremacy' (2022, p. 28). Such plays highlight the 'nearly two-hundred-year exclusion of BIPOC (Black, Indigenous, People of Colour) women' from American feminism, which 'still struggles with its own absurd history of negating and invisibilizing its constituents of colour' (2022, p. 28). For Klein, American feminism is also guilty of 'co-opting or occluding the work of BIPOC feminists and erasing them from its major narratives' (2022, p. 28). Klein's 'New Feminist Absurd' in theatre has several resonances with the contemporary Absurdist poetry I study in this book, yet Klein sees her new aesthetic as distinctly American, and declares that this sets it apart from Esslin's 'Eurocentric Theatre of the Absurd' (2022, p. 30). As I have demonstrated above, US and British poetry have much in common, especially when it comes to the Absurd. Throughout this book I place British and US poets' work side by side and read them in conversation with one another. Indeed, the way in which poets approach their Absurdism is idiosyncratic, responding to political climates and personal experiences (while eschewing the 'confessional'). I demonstrate throughout the book

16 Whiteness, Feminism and the Absurd in Contemporary Poetry

that both white British and white US poets begin to challenge notions of whiteness and privilege – obliquely or explicitly – through issues of gender and class.

I acknowledge Hélène Cixous's claim that 'it is impossible to define a feminine practice of writing, and this is an impossibility that will remain, for this practice can never be theorized, enclosed, coded – which doesn't mean that it doesn't exist' (1976, p. 883). The inability to define 'feminine' writing could be problematic, but Cixous is correct: 'You can't talk about *a* female sexuality, uniform, homogenous, classifiable into codes – any more than you can talk about one unconscious resembling another' (1976, p. 876). To simply define writing as 'masculine' or 'feminine' is reductive. However, Cixous notes that 'far more extensively and repressively than is ever suspected or admitted, writing has been run by a libidinal and cultural – hence political, typically masculine – economy' (1976, p. 879). Cixous claims that as a result of this repressive economy, women never have their chance to speak, and this is 'unpardonable', since writing is 'precisely *the very possibility of change*, the space that can serve as a springboard for subversive thought, the precursory movement of a transformation of social and cultural structures' (1976, p. 879).

As Toril Moi states, 'femininity' is a 'cultural construct', therefore 'patriarchal oppression consists of imposing certain social standards of femininity on all biological women, in order precisely to make us believe that the chosen standards for "femininity" are *natural*' (2001, p. 65), and indeed, social standards for femininity are also applied to transgender women, not just biological women. Moi states that it is therefore in the interest of the patriarchy to ensure that femininity and femaleness stay confused, and it is subsequently important for feminists to dispel this misconception (2001, p. 65). Mirroring Cixous, Moi writes: 'since creativity is defined as male, it follows that the dominant literary images of femininity are male fantasies too'; she argues that women are 'denied the right to create their own images of femaleness, and instead must seek to conform to the patriarchal standards imposed on them' (2001, p. 57).

However, Sandra Gilbert and Susan Gubar argue that 'much of the poetry and the fiction written by women conjures up "[a] mad creature"' (in Moi, 2001, p. 60) through which female writers 'can come to terms with their own uniquely female feelings of fragmentation, their own keen sense of the discrepancies between what they are and what they are supposed to be' (in Moi, 2001, p. 60). Gilbert and Gubar, as Moi notes, persistently use 'female' where 'feminine' should be used (2001, p. 65), and their argument is also too neat a construction to encompass all women's writing. However, the idea of a 'feminine' writing which deals with existential issues – an attempt to understand the

Introduction: The Absurd, Race and Gender   **17**

self and one's position in the world – is pertinent to understanding the Absurd's strategies of self-effacement, and so Gilbert and Gubar's definition is helpful in this context, opening up space to discuss to what end this self-effacement is deployed.

Returning to the Absurd, Delville's study of Edson's prose poems is crucial to understanding the aesthetic's previous handling of gender roles. Delville asserts that Edson's prose poems are preoccupied with the 'threat of female insanity' (1998, p. 11), and he defines 'female insanity' as:

> The ensuing prospect of the disintegration of the self, or worse – at least from the point of view of the male persona – its dissolution into a female Other whose aggressive laughter seems to represent what critics have identified as menace of uncontrolled sexuality, the castrating allegory of the *vagina dentata*, the vagina with teeth. (1998, p. 116)

Delville suggests that 'female insanity' is experienced from a male perspective and that, through laughter, emasculation occurs. Many of Edson's prose poems follow the 'modern everyday man who suddenly tumbles into an alternative reality in which he loses control over himself' (Delville, 1998, p. 110); this loss of control is typically instigated by a female character, usually the man's wife.

This 'female insanity' has evident antecedents in earlier Absurdist works, as in Albert Camus's *The Stranger* (1989). In Camus's novel, the protagonist Mersault is controversially racist, misogynistic and emotionally devoid – until this blocking of emotion becomes too much, and he murders an Arab man on the beach, shattering 'the harmony of the day, the exceptional silence of a beach where I'd been happy' (1989, p. 59). In Mersault's point of view, older women are almost grotesque. They have 'bulging stomachs', barely visible eyes, which are a 'faint glimmer in a nest of wrinkles', and 'toothless mouths' (1989, p. 10). When Mersault meets younger, more attractive women, such as Marie, he focuses on their breasts, and how women giggle and wave at him (1989, p. 24).

The women of *The Stranger* are hyperbolic and dramatic. Marie declares her love for Mersault and begs him to marry her, even as he reminds her he does not love her; Raymond's mistress, an Arab woman, whom he and Mersault accuse of cheating, is 'beaten . . . till she bled' (1989, p. 31); she screams at him in a 'shrill voice' (1989, p. 35), evidently invoking misogynistic tropes about women as desperate to marry, foolish and shrill. The only exception to this is Mersault's *maman* – who, as Ward notes, Mersault refers to with a 'child's word' throughout (1989, p. vii) – who is mysteriously silent (for he does not remember her vividly until the end of the novel) and for whom he is, it seems,

18 *Whiteness, Feminism and the Absurd in Contemporary Poetry*

sentenced for not grieving properly. Overall, Mersault lacks proper connections with women – with anyone, it seems. As George Heffernan writes, Mersault displays 'depraved indifference toward the lives of Arabs' (2014, p. 15); he is 'racist, because at first he declines to write the letter that Raymond wants him to write to his allegedly unfaithful mistress', but '[when] he discovers that the woman to whom he is supposed to write it is an Arab, he complies with Raymond's request without further ado' (2014, p. 15).

As Heffernan argues, 'the philosophical strength of *The Stranger* is not that it exhorts the readers to embrace Meursault's celebration of the alleged absurdity of life', but it instead 'challenges them to dig to a deeper level of reflection than that of which Mersault is capable' (2014, p. 3). Indeed, for Heffernan, if Mersault 'had spent more time trying to understand others and less time crying about not being understood by them' then he 'would not have fallen into the fateful failure of communication and into the vicious pattern of subalternation that are depicted by the novel' (2014, p. 7). Rightly, Heffernan notes that just because the 'protagonist is utterly bereft of any consciousness of sexism, racism, and colonialism, it does not follow that the author is too', and that Mersault is intended as a 'mirror' for the reader, 'to show the prejudices that are neither morally respectable nor socially acceptable' (2014, pp. 7–8).

Nonetheless, Mersault's view of women and his racist notions live on in Absurdist literature, and specifically in poetry, in what Robert Pinsky termed 'one-of-the-guys surrealism' (in Williamson, 2006, p. 41), and Alan Williamson has deemed a 'phenomenon' of 'cynicism' in poetry (2006, p. 41). Williamson defines this cynicism as 'a lack of passion towards experience in general, a certain blaséness, combined – and this is the crucial thing – with a basic, self-mocking distrust of the possibilities of art itself' (2006, p. 41). Williamson admits that he dislikes this kind of poetry 'intensely' (2006, p. 41) and, while his description of this cynicism is correct, that is not to say I join Williamson in his dislike of this poetry, or his sense that mocking poetry is blasphemous. What Williamson defines as a 'sycophancy toward pop culture' is, as I will argue throughout the book, very much a way to engage in a destabilisation of elitism in poetry in order to better connect with the reader. This book is a celebration of contemporary Absurdist poetry as much as it is a critique of its handling of gender and race.

Edson's poetry belongs to this 'one-of-the-guys surrealism', as Holly Iglesias claims in her investigation of women's prose poetry, *Boxing Inside the Box: Women's Prose Poetry* (2004). In Edson's 'The Father of Toads', a man's wife gives birth to a toad from her armpit (1994, p. 120), and frequently asks her husband if he loves their new child.

The crux of Edson's joke – its *peripeteia* – is that this is not the first time that the woman has delivered a toad or brought absurdity into the man's life. The zaniness of the episode continues with the woman wanting to name the new toad 'George Jr.' (1994, p. 120), when her husband reveals that they already have a child-toad named after him. Edson's joke is that the woman has descended into a kind of insanity in which her body acts strangely and her thought processes are confused. The woman sees no issue in naming the new toad 'George Sr.' (1994, p. 120), thereby asking her husband to become nameless and hide. The man is therefore resigned to a paternal role to the exclusion of any other defining characteristics or traits. While Edson's scene mirrors the narrative forced upon women who become mothers, crucially, the woman's body is responsible for the eccentricity. Edson's poem communicates anxiety about the loss of identity at the woman's hands. As the man is unable to father human children, he is emasculated by the woman's 'insanity' – her body, which does not behave as it should, and her inability to empathise with the man's distress and confusion. The joke is dark: the reader may find the woman's insanity funny, but also must appreciate her threat.

In several of Edson's poems, women become threats to normal domestic life. In 'The Rat's Tight Schedule' the man's wife accepts the disintegration of a rat's body. Her statement: 'those are pieces of rat' is matter-of-fact, as though this is an everyday experience, and is also antithetical to the husband's outrage and melodramatic response: 'But I could have flipped and fallen through the floor' (1994, p. 225). Edson blurs sense and nonsense in 'The Rat's Tight Schedule', as the absurdity of the rat's disintegration is placed in opposition to the man's exaggerated reaction. The man views the woman's reaction as a threat to his everyday life: she allows the rat to interrupt the domestic situation and potentially endanger him. The man is focused on his own well-being and not on the bizarre situation surrounding the rat, and this constructs an odd, off-kilter surprise in the way that the man and woman communicate and what they prioritise. Eventually, the man is overtaken by the woman's 'insanity' and engages with the rat too. The woman pleads with her husband to be 'patient' with the rat because he is 'thinking of turning into a marsupial', to which the husband replies: 'A marsupial? A wonderful choice!' (1994, p. 225). Again, Edson constructs a world logic based on eventually accepting absurdity. Rather than focusing on the bizarre situation, the man accepts the absurdity and engages with it; his wife's 'insanity' is contagious. In 'On the Eating of Mice', the woman roasts 'a mouse for her husband's dinner' as she has done for twenty years (1994, p. 217), while in 'The Dog's Dinner', the woman 'discovers that it is her dog that she is cooking for her dog's dinner' (1994, p. 156),

20 *Whiteness, Feminism and the Absurd in Contemporary Poetry*

and in 'The Unscreamed Scream', a woman 'thinks she must cook her cat' to 'keep herself from screaming' (1994, p. 196). In these poems, the women act strangely, unsettling the domestic setting by eating the very things that make up their domesticity: their pets (or pests).

Part I of this book highlights significant poets of this new aesthetic in the Absurd, and identifies characteristics and how these pertain to crucial ideas about whiteness and feminism in contemporary Absurdist poetry. In Chapter 1, I follow Sara Ahmed's idea of 'institutions' of whiteness (2007), arguing that we might think of the new aesthetic of the Absurd as occupying a large room, where more and more poets are wandering in. I examine how contemporary white British Absurdist poets – Heather Phillipson, Sam Riviere, Selima Hill and Luke Kennard – focus on gender in their poetry, and generally assume that their readers are white and middle class. Thinking about the British poetry establishment's problems with race, as argued by Sandeep Parmar (2015; 2020), this focus on gender is ultimately a positive move in contemporary Absurdist poetry, one which opens up space for poets to consider the intersections of race, class and gender, without problematically reifying whiteness, and using the assumed readership as a catalyst for change.

In Chapter 2, I investigate how contemporary Absurdist poetics is preoccupied with our failures to connect and communicate with one another. I argue against 'emotionally non-directive' writing, examining how white British poet Rachael Allen uses her *4chan Poems* (2014; 2016) to explore miscommunication through gender and class, and think about how she might, too, use this as a space to explore whiteness. I move into an investigation of masculinity in white British poet Crispin Best's *Faber New Poets 14* (2016)[8] and *Hello* (2019), and show how, under Best's attempts to destabilise hegemonic masculinity, lies an endeavour to destabilise the Absurd's nihilism. Chapter 3 turns to the Absurd's preoccupation with the apocalypse. In reading Samuel Beckett's *Endgame* (2006), Tom Stoppard's *Rosencrantz and Guildenstern are Dead* (1999) and Never Angeline Nørth's *Sara or the Existence of Fire* (2014), I demonstrate that death, apocalypse, repetition and 'ongoingness' are key elements of Absurdist thought. Absurdist poetry suggests that we must learn to work with the Absurd and the apocalypse, rather than trying to individually make meaning of the world, and contemporary Absurdist poets depict apocalyptic situations as symptomatic of feminist concerns of anxiety (Ahmed, 2014), and gender and racial inequality. In the work of Korean-American poet Franny Choi, Black American poet Morgan Parker and American poet Jane Yeh, the cyborg symbolises hopeful change; in white American poet Jennifer L. Knox's writing, the android can be representative of 'dangerous possibilities'

(Haraway, 2016), which invites her readers to consider their own attitudes to the apocalypse.

Part II comprises three chapters investigating three key poets, exploring their idiosyncratic responses to ideas of social change and whiteness, and how their work highlights ideas about class, gender roles and the relationship between poetry and popular culture. In Chapter 4, I analyse how Jennifer L. Knox employs a self-effacing humour to destabilise the reader–poet relationship and deflate elitist, classist approaches to poetry through direct engagement with 'high' and 'low' culture in her poems. In doing so, I explore how Knox uses popular culture to ridicule systems that extol privileged, male writers and reductive narratives for women. Knox's poetry has a complex relationship to whiteness and class, and I explore her ideas of 'punching up' and 'punching down' (Yu and Knox, 2019) to examine her grappling with cultural capital and privilege. Chapter 5 turns to the 'Sad Girl' internet movement, which is wrought with worrying fetishisations of whiteness and inertia; yet, in some guises, it demonstrates how sadness can be a site for movement and change, which in turn can be used to understand white British poet Caroline Bird's collections *The Hat-Stand Union* (2013) and *In These Days of Prohibition* (2017). Drawing on Dave Coates, Louis MacNeice and Samuel Beckett's *Waiting for Godot* (2006),[9] I argue that Bird's poems act like parables, in which Bird warns her (presumed white, middle-class) reader against their own ennui and inaction. Chapter 6 studies white British poet Emily Berry's blurring of imagination and reality in her debut poetry collection, *Dear Boy* (2013), which I here understand further through Freud's *The Uncanny* (2003).[10] Through close readings of Berry's poems, I reveal how she blurs imagination and reality to comment on gender roles, privilege, the British government and abuses of power. I compare Berry's work to an additional poem by British poet Mona Arshi to demonstrate how motherhood no longer acts as a site of empathy, and therefore how contemporary Absurdist poets can eschew empathy as a method for social change. Following on from Berry's use of the uncanny, I further develop an exploration into Berry's engagement with tropes of horror films and the Southern Gothic, with particular reference to the horror film *The Woman* (Lucky McKee, 2011) to investigate Berry's engagement with issues of gender and race.

In this book, I aim to provide a comprehensive study of contemporary Absurdist poets' work, to recognise the history of the Absurd, and its importance to poetry – which has often been overlooked – and to raise questions in regard to the influence of popular culture in poetry. I also try to grapple with the question of how poetry can be political and foster change – and what happens if its readership does not engage with invitations to assess and change. The difficulty of writing about whiteness as a white author is how one goes about this endeavour without recentring whiteness. By virtue, this book must think about whiteness in detail, and it must think about how white writers engage in and neglect interrogations of their own whiteness. As such, this book cannot provide comprehensive answers to some of our biggest questions (and the Absurd itself would perhaps resist doing so). It cannot provide a conclusive answer to the problem of whiteness or whiteness in the avant-garde. It indirectly addresses ideas of better representation and publishing practice. I hope it is a step in the right direction.

PART I

Chapter 1

Feminine/Feminist Humour and Whiteness in Contemporary British Absurdist Poetry

Sandeep Parmar declared in her 2015 essay for the *Los Angeles Review of Books*, 'Not a British Subject: Race and Poetry in the UK', that 'British poetry, like British society, has a serious problem with race'. In her influential essay, Parmar charts how 'in spite of high-profile black British poets nearing the canon, poetry in the United Kingdom wishes to remain largely and exclusively free from the "identity politics" of race' (2015). She outlines how British poetry as an institution systematically rewards 'poets of color who conform to particular modes of self-foreignizing' and leave 'the white voice of mainstream and avant-garde poetries in the United Kingdom intact and untroubled by the difficult responsibilities attached to both racism and nationalism' (2015). Parmar writes that a 'mostly white poetic establishment prevails over a patronizing culture that presents minority poets as exceptional cases – to be held at arm's length like colonial curiosities' (2015). Contemporary British avant-garde poetry has not yet come to terms with the avant-garde's reiteration of whiteness, and despite broader conversations about race in UK poetry publishing and reviewing, the Absurd has, typically, remained the territory of white writers.

In this chapter, then, following Sara Ahmed's idea of 'institutions' of whiteness (2007), I argue that we might think of the new aesthetic of the Absurd as occupying a large room, where more and more poets are wandering in. Most of these poets are white. Some will choose to stay, while others might make a passing visit. I analyse some of the key characteristics of contemporary Absurdist poetry, demonstrating how this iteration of the Absurd eschews the 'female insanity' dynamic as described in the book's Introduction and focuses on gender equality, by examining the work of white British Absurdist poets – Heather Phillipson, Sam Riviere, Selima Hill and Luke Kennard. I argue that contemporary Absurdist poetry generally assumes that its readers are white and middle class. If this remains an unchallenged position, it is deeply problematic, but the writers are, I contend, holding a mirror up to their presumed readership, and these readers' privileged and flawed thinking. This is ultimately a positive move in contemporary Absurdist poetry, which opens up space for poets to consider the intersections of race, class and gender without problematically reifying whiteness, and use an assumed readership as a catalyst for change.

British Poetry, the Avant-Garde and Race

The avant-garde is a necessary target for critique. Parmar notes that, in the past, 'there were no poets of color and few women within these avant-garde circles' (2015). Indeed, in her response to avant-garde poetry in the US, 'Delusions of Whiteness in the Avant-Garde', published the year before Parmar's essay, Cathy Park Hong writes: 'To encounter the history of avant-garde poetry is to encounter a racist tradition' (2014). Park Hong recognises that 'American avant-garde poetry has been an overwhelmingly white enterprise, ignoring major swaths of innovators—namely poets from past African American literary movements' (2014). So too is the case for British avant-garde poetry. As Jahan Ramazani writes, 'the mononarrative of innovation as belonging to the (white) avantgarde, as poetry studies is finally beginning to recognize, often misses the importance of this multiracial, multiethnic, multinational widening of formal possibilities' (2019, p. xxviii). Parmar notes that 'the divides between the mainstream and avant-garde have lessened and that overlaps do exist today between their coteries, publishing presses, poetry magazines, reading series, prize lists, academic departments, and conferences' (2015), and that 'there are more poets writing now, I would argue, who belong fully to neither camp and who write for a more international readership than the average British consumer of plain-speaking, well-mannered verse' (2015). Parmar notes the US's influence, in which 'British poets are much more receptive to and influenced by, for example, New York School, Language, and "post-Language" poetry' (2015).

In her follow-up essay, 'Still Not a British Subject: Race and UK Poetry' (2020), published as part of a special issue for the *Journal of British and Irish Innovative Poetry*, Parmar furthers her critique of the avant-garde, noting that although 'race and literary (though not necessarily poetry) culture is becoming a regular feature in public discourse, aided by high-profile writers and cultural commentators like Reni Eddo-Lodge, Afua Hirsch, and Nikesh Shukla, among others', this does not mean that whiteness is being dismantled or interrogated (2020).

For Parmar, 'conservative and regressive attitudes towards poets of colour and diversity – itself a deeply problematic term but one we are stuck with nonetheless – are still hugely in evidence in spite of an upsurge in publishing'; this is because 'experimental poetics are seen as incompatible with fixed identity politics' (2020). Indeed, Parmar argues that in such evaluations, '"identity" is a threat to critical value, which had before been neutral, and now must become secondary to the politicised position of the teller – who is, incidentally, only subject to those objectionable forces that do not apply to white men' (2020).

British avant-garde poetry, then, has a problem with whiteness. To understand this, I wish to draw on Sara Ahmed's article 'A Phenomenology of Whiteness' (2007) to demonstrate how the British avant-garde acts as what Ahmed calls 'an institution', characterised by an 'accumulation of past decisions' which, in turn, shape spaces 'by the proximity of some bodies and not others: white bodies gather, and cohere to form the edges of such spaces' (2007, p. 157). For Ahmed, whiteness might be 'described as an ongoing and unfinished history, which orientates bodies in specific directions, affecting how they "take up" space' (2007, p. 150). Whiteness is bound to be 'reproduced' because it is 'seen as a form of positive residence: as if it were a property of persons, cultures and places' (2007, p. 154), and consequently '"holds" through habits' so that 'public spaces take shape through the habitual actions of bodies' (2007, p. 156).

The avant-garde can therefore be understood as an 'institution' in which the 'bodies' are the white poets most renowned or revered. We might picture British poetry (its editors, writers, readers, reviewers) as working inside a building with many rooms: the avant-garde occupies several large rooms in this building, and the vast majority of 'bodies' in those rooms are white. Ahmed asserts that white bodies 'do not get "stressed" in their encounters with objects or others, as their whiteness "goes unnoticed"' (2007, p. 156); indeed, as Robin DiAngelo writes, '[w]hiteness' is perceived as 'universal' (2016, p. 250). Ahmed claims that 'white bodies do not have to face their whiteness; they are not orientated "towards" it, and this "not" is what allows whiteness to cohere, as that which bodies are orientated around' (2007, p. 156). In such a way, whiteness 'holds' through avant-garde poetry – through its publication, readership and authorship[1] – creating an assumption and habit of whiteness, because (past) decisions about canonisation, about who is published, who is awarded prizes, who is recognised as belonging to the avant-garde, are constantly repeated.

Developing the image of avant-garde poetry as several rooms in a building (and contemporary Absurdist poetry taking up at least one of

28   *Whiteness, Feminism and the Absurd in Contemporary Poetry*

those rooms), it follows, as Ahmed suggests, that 'spaces also take shape by being orientated around some bodies, more than others' (2007, p. 157). If we envisage that the vast majority of 'bodies' in these rooms are white, then, even if there are people of colour in the space, we will still perceive the institution – or the 'rooms', in this case – as white, because, as Ahmed suggests, 'whiteness itself is a straightening device: bodies disappear into the "sea of whiteness" when they "line up"' (2007, p. 159).[2] In this way, even if a person of colour is recognised as writing the avant-garde, their work is subsumed into a perceived tradition of white writers, and as Parmar, Park Hong and Ramazani comment, the true tradition and thread of influence and innovation is obscured.

'Female Insanity' into 'Handeyesque' Poetry

In the Introduction, I assessed how Edson's poetry creates 'female insanity', and what Robert Pinsky deems 'one-of-the-guys surrealism' (in Williamson, 2006, p. 41). In her book, *Boxing Inside the Box: Women's Prose Poetry* (2004), Iglesias notes Dana Gioia's assertion that American poetry's most 'influential form' is the prose poem, and that in 'recent' practice, it has 'mostly become a kind of absurdist parable' (in Iglesias, 2004, p. 8). Indeed, as Iglesias writes, American prose poetry has turned to a 'Surrealist influence . . . whether in absurdist fable or monologue' (2004, p. 12), and for Delville, the focus of such prose poems is 'human consciousness itself – with its endless speculations and its relentless associational imaginings' (1998, p. 131). The scope of this book extends beyond prose poetry, because, as this chapter will evidence, these characteristics are no longer confined to prose poetry alone. This book's scope also extends beyond the US, and British and US poetics are, as Sandeep Parmar writes, 'increasingly in dialogue due to high profile American poets of colour being published here [in Britain] as well as the predominance of social media networks' (2020).

Yet Iglesias is correct to highlight a tradition of male-centred poetries, and a penchant for an Absurdism or surrealism which favours a 'subset of "bruised boy" prose poems featuring icy mothers, hounding wives, provocative stepdaughters, suffocating mothers, nebulous *you*'s and *she*'s, all conspiring to send the poet's Inner Child to an early grave' (2004, p. 23). Iglesias laments this turn in prose poetry, defining it as 'male prose poetry', which is underpinned by 'anxiety, self-indulgence' where the 'focus is inward, cerebral, singular, ephemeral, anxious, insubstantial – a talking head, disembodied, laughing skittishly in isolation' (2014, pp. 13, 14). For Iglesias, then, these widely accepted characteristics 'form a barrier to the reception of women's prose poetry' (2004, p. 16).

In this chapter, I wish to explore the legacy of this 'one-of-the-guys surrealism' in contemporary British poetry; first, to demonstrate that a new type of Absurdism – prose poem not required – has become popular among poets and publishers in Britain; second, to explore how that poetry might aim to reject the latent misogyny of 'one-of-the-guys surrealism'; third, to recognise that, for all these attempts for equity in Absurdist or surrealist works, the avant-garde (and British poetry in particular) has an issue with race; finally, to consider how space might emerge for Absurdist poets to think through race. It is my contention that while poets have attempted to bring feminine and feminist humour into the Absurd and reject this 'female insanity' dynamic, there is still space for whiteness to be tackled.

One of the most renowned Absurdist poets, James Tate, wrote poems – free verse and prose poem – meeting Gioia's and Iglesias's descriptions. Tate's work is also indebted to the 'female insanity' dynamic; in his study of Tate's work, Anthony Caleshu writes that 'as with earlier surrealists [. . .] the male leer dominates in Tate's poems which are shaped according to the gaze of hetero-male speakers' (2011, p. 143), echoing Delville's statements regarding Edson. Caleshu describes Tate's poetry as 'character-laden and voice-driven' (2011, p. 2), and 'assumes the performative front of a deadpan, dramatic monologue whereby the speaker is akin to a stand-up comedian of the driest humour' (2011, p. 2). While such a speaker might be 'self-aware of his part in the drama and the ironies that give momentum to his narration', 'there's no self-consciousness that might betray him as anything but earnest' (2011, p. 2). This is particularly evident in Tate's poem 'The Bookclub', in which the speaker's wife, Bobbie, comes 'home from her bookclub I completely drunk and disheveled' (2012, p. 146). The Absurd often favours the banal (Hinchliffe, 1969, p. 10), and in this poem, Tate refigures a stereotypical (white) suburban, US, married life. Indeed, in 'The Bookclub', the speaker acts as the voice of reason, asking, 'what the hell happened to you?' (Tate, 2012, p. 146) when Bobbie returns home. Initially, Bobbie's reaction to the book seems melodramatic. From what she tells her husband of its plot ('about the girl's mother dying, I and then her baby getting sick and her husband I leaving her'), her group's assertion that it is 'corny' (2012, p. 146) might be fair. Tate does not provide any reasons or hints as to why Bobbie might have been so upset by the book, so her reaction seems hyperbolic.

Tellingly, the speaker does not comfort Bobbie about her sadness or her physical injuries but merely asks, 'So what happened?' (2012,

30 *Whiteness, Feminism and the Absurd in Contemporary Poetry*

p. 146) to prompt her to talk about the fight, and she accordingly recalls the argument:

> 'Irene was laughing and that's when I got up
> and slapped her. And she punched me in the gut
> and I grabbed her hair and threw her to
> the floor and kicked her in the face. And then
> Rosie and Tina and that bitch Sonia
> from Leverett all jumped on me . . .' (2012, p. 146)

The fight is darkly comedic in its hyperbole – it is almost ridiculous that the women would fight so violently over differing opinions of a book. This suggests that the women are volatile, and that Bobbie is unbalanced and unpredictable – she is either wild or the brunt of the joke (or both). However, the speaker again ignores Bobbie's feelings, and does not comfort her. He merely asks: 'So when did you get drunk?' which seems to defuse the situation entirely, as Bobbie explains that she and her friends went to 'Lucky 7 together and laughed and I laughed about it' (2012, p. 146). Her manner seems altered: Bobbie is no longer upset about the book or the women's reactions to it. In this way, Bobbie's response seems strange, particularly when she then describes her friends as 'pussycats' (2012, p. 146).

Indeed, Bobbie's assertion acts as the *peripeteia*; it is severely at odds with her earlier description of the fight (and perhaps the speaker's understanding of women and their relationships). The speaker, then, offers a voice of reason, and casts aspersions on Bobbie's mental well-being; he believes that she is 'badly in need of repair' (2012, p. 146). This, the final line of the poem, suggests that the speaker knows best, that his wife is acting irrationally (perhaps due to her drunkenness). Consequently, the Absurd's approach to gender has traditionally functioned in the following manner: the woman is 'insane', and inflicts this insanity on the man, typically her husband; stereotypical depictions of men and women are used to portray marriage and heteronormative domesticity as banal, yet under threat by the woman's behaviour; incongruity and dark humour are essential.

In her article, 'And Now, Deep Thoughts about "Deep Thoughts"' for *The New York Times Magazine* (2013), Kathleen Rooney does not identify these characteristics as belonging to the Absurd, but she instead suggests that there are close links between comedy and modern US poetry, particularly between comedian Jack Handey's *Saturday Night Live* segment, 'Deep Thoughts', and modern poetry. Rooney writes that 'Deep Thoughts' 'were designed to satirize the genre of the feel-good affirmation' and 'typically pair a keen observational eye with a declarative genius, a gift for the concrete utterance' (2013). Rooney provides the following examples: 'If trees could scream, would we be so cavalier about cutting them down? We might, if they screamed all the time, for no good reason' and: 'As the evening sun faded from a salmon color to a sort of flint gray, I thought back to the salmon I caught that morning, and how gray he was, and how I named him Flint' (2013).

According to Rooney, the 'Deep Thought' works because 'Handey starts with a cliché, then both punctures and reanimates it through an ostensibly gauche and accidental surrealism'; he 'assaults the convention of poetic metaphor [. . .] revealing that a lot of allegedly "poetic" writing is a fraudulent and circular game', revealing its 'trite conventions' (2013). Rooney comments that this type of humour, the 'accidental surrealism' of the everyday, is now prevalent in modern poetry, and argues that 'the conversationality, concise humor, ludicrous situations and faux-sincere profundity' of 'Deep Thoughts' 'now appear often in contemporary poetry' (2013). Rooney notes that poets who favour a 'Handeyesque style' use 'deflated language, delivered in the persona of a kooky everyman [. . .] that toes the line between the funny and serious' (2013). This style is not a far cry from Edson's or Tate's Absurdism: the 'everyman' is a central figure, as is the incongruity of the humorous and serious.

Some contemporary Absurdist poets have responded to the misogyny in the literature of the Absurd – from theatre and novels to their poetry forebears – and sexism in the reception of Absurdist works (as outlined by Iglesias (2004) and Derksen (2002)), trying to shape a poetics which takes gender equality into consideration. Indeed, not all contemporary Absurdist poetry will have adopted this stance, nor will all poetry that might be considered Absurdist belong to the aesthetic I am identifying. Yet as J.T. Welsch notes, there is a trend in British poetry for 'explicit engagement with "wider issues" and, in some cases, specific critical discourses' (2020, p. 154), such as 'feminist and queer theory, postcolonial theory, animal studies, and countless other areas that inform poetry's approach to historical and contemporary social issues' (2020, p. 155), and the Absurd has adopted this stance in a particular way.

This new aesthetic of the Absurd is, for want of a better term, 'successful': several of the poets studied in this chapter alone have been awarded an Eric Gregory Award, awarded by the Society of Authors for a collection by poets under the age of thirty.[3] In addition, Caroline Bird was awarded the Forward Prize for Best Poetry Collection in 2020, and shortlisted for the Costa Prize in 2020,[4] the T.S. Eliot Prize in 2017, the Ted Hughes Award in 2017 and the Dylan Thomas Prize twice in 2008 and 2010. Selima Hill's 1997 collection, *Violet*, was shortlisted

32 *Whiteness, Feminism and the Absurd in Contemporary Poetry*

for the Forward Poetry Prize, the T.S. Eliot Prize and the Whitbread Poetry Award; Hill received a Cholmondeley Award from the Society of Authors in 1986 and was awarded the King's Gold Medal for Poetry in 2023. Luke Kennard was also awarded the Forward Prize for Best Collection in 2021, having been shortlisted for the same award in 2007 (making him the youngest writer ever to have been shortlisted); he was shortlisted for the International Dylan Thomas Prize in 2016. Heather Phillipson's first poetry collection, *Instant-flex 718* (2013) was short-listed for the Fenton Aldeburgh First Collection Prize and the Michael Murphy Memorial Prize in 2013. Sam Riviere has been shortlisted for the Ledbury Forte Poetry Prize (2017) and received the Forward Prize for Best First Collection in 2012 for *81 Austerities*.[5] I list prizes not because I believe them to be the best indicator of 'success' or 'talent' in poetry – as Parmar (2015) and Welsch (2020) write, prize culture is bound up in its own prejudices and self-regulation[6] – but to demonstrate that this aesthetic is highly esteemed and rewarded in the institution of contemporary British poetry. No longer is the avant-garde in opposition to the mainstream – it *is* the mainstream.[7]

A Feminine or Feminist Absurd?

The Absurd is traditionally perceived as apolitical, a result of its nihilism, which is inherited 'from futurism [. . .] passed on in turn, almost intact, to surrealism' (Poggioli, 1968, p. 63). Indeed, Toby Silverman Zinman argues that 'feminism and absurdism cannot coexist because feminism necessar-ily exhibits a commitment to promoting social change, which assumes a degree of agency that is anathema to absurdist philosophy' (in Derksen, 2002, p. 222). However, Derksen argues for the existence of a feminist Absurd in theatre through her analysis of Margaret Hollingsworth's play *The House that Jack Built*, stating that in Hollingworth's version of the Absurd, 'the subject of absurdism can be constructed and read from a more overtly political, socially engaged standpoint', because Holling-sworth 'deploys absurdism in a manner that foregrounds gender concerns and so points to the exclusion – or incomprehension – of gender as a con-trolling framework of meaning in the established tradition' (2002, pp. 212, 209). Indeed, broadly speaking, contemporary British poets writing the Absurd have followed suit, using gender as an arena in which to stake a political claim and move away from 'one-of-the-guys surrealism'. This Absurd, adopting a 'Handeyesque' approach, treads a fine line between the funny and the serious; the subject of the joke and the joke itself is often complicated and uncomfortable. Speakers are self-effacing, attempt

Feminine/Feminist Humour and Whiteness in Absurdist Poetry   33

to reveal major flaws about themselves and humanity more widely, and to expose gender dynamics and roles as damaging and nonsensical. The aesthetic tries – with varying degrees of success – to distance itself from misogynistic depictions of 'female insanity'.

In her article 'Humor, Poetry and Privilege' for *Indolent Books* (no longer available online), white US poet Jennifer L. Knox focuses on 'self-effacing humour' in poetry. Knox states that such humour 'requires the ability to abdicate (or seemingly abdicate) authority' and acknowledges that 'for women, POC [people of colour], PWD [people with disabilities], LGBTQ, anyone existing/ living/ writing outside of patriarchal privilege, the idea of abdicating authority is ABSURD because authority is always at risk' (2016). Contemporary Absurdist poetry thrives on this zany self-effacement, destabilising the idea of the poet – or the speaker – as an enlightened figure. Knox recognises that, personally, her instinct is to become the target of laughter, but she 'must reclaim authority at some point in the poem' (2016). She explains that 'when people are laughing, they're vulnerable'; it is her intention to 'lead the audience into the ring, and when they're laughing their asses off, reclaim authority and cut their throats' (2016). For Knox, true privilege lies in being able to 'give it away and take it back' (2016), which, for some of the people she identifies in her essay, may not be possible at all. If Knox acknowledges that one must have authority in the first place to then be able to acquiesce it, her poetics suggests an acknowledgement of her inherent sense of privilege – perhaps, without naming it, her whiteness. However, Knox also suggests that humour is one of the few routes through which a non-privileged writer might gain power by making their audience laugh. If the privileged writer acquiesces their authority, can this hold a mirror up to the (presumably also privileged) reader, shedding light on matrices of power? What does the white, privileged poet's work *do*? Can it provoke change?

Broadly speaking, contemporary British poets have adopted two key approaches to humour in this new aesthetic of the Absurd, which I identify as 'feminine' and 'feminist' after Gloria Kaufman's definitions of female and feminist humour (1980). For Kaufman, feminist humour is underpinned by an 'attitude of social revolution – that is, we are ridiculing a social system that can be, that must be changed' (1980, p. 13). Feminist satire 'is didactic and often overtly so', so 'no matter how pessimistic it sounds, it seeks to improve us by demonstrating – through devices of irony, of exaggeration, of sarcasm and of wit – our human folly' (1980, p. 14). In Kaufman's terms, feminist satire desires reform, and so, whether or not change is stimulated, 'implicit ideals' are foregrounded (1980, p. 14). On the other hand, what Kaufman deems

34 *Whiteness, Feminism and the Absurd in Contemporary Poetry*

'female humour' intends to 'ridicule a person or system from an accepting point of view ("that's life")' (1980, p. 13); the 'nonacceptance of oppression characterises feminist humour and satire' (1980, p. 14). In the final part of this chapter, then, I wish to look at some examples of contemporary British Absurdist poetry which uses feminist and feminine humour, to demonstrate how the Absurd has attempted to engage with issues of gender equality and eschew the 'female insanity' dynamic of earlier Absurdist works.

In her poem 'Heliocentric Cosmology', Heather Phillipson uses 'mashed potato' eleven times (with one variation of 'unmashed potato'), always at the end of a line. The speaker over-explains:

> Got what?
> asked my husband through a mouthful of mashed potato.
> I was at home with my husband, eating mashed potato. (2013, p. 14)

The speaker tells us that she is at home with her husband, eating mashed potato (something the reader could have gleaned from the previous line), and this pushes Phillipson's poem into 'Handeyesque' territory, or what Paul McDonald claims is 'akin to what Mikhail Epstein terms "trans-sentimentality"', 'sentimentality after the death of sentimentality', which 'has passed through all the circles of carnival, irony and black humour, in order to become aware of its own banality, accepting it as an inevitability and as the source of a new lyricism' (2017, p. 9). The setting is inarguably domestic and banal: the characters are at home, eating dinner together, and the speaker identifies her partner as her 'husband', foregrounding a heteronormative dynamic. This, in conjunction with the mashed potato as a symbol of banality, suggests that Phillipson is examining gender roles. As Hanna Scolnicov has noted, 'gender roles are spatially defined in relation to the inside and the outside of the house. Traditionally, it is the woman who makes the house into a home' (in Derksen, 2002, p. 214), but in Phillipson's poem, the husband observes while his wife makes an important 'discovery'.

The speaker compares her discovery to that of Galileo's championship of Copernicus's heliocentric cosmology:

> It was like when Galileo dropped balls of the same material
> but different masses from the Leaning Tower of Pisa,
> except Galileo didn't use his mouth or mashed potato,
> and the ground isn't a plate of mashed potato. (2013, p. 14)

The speaker's repetition of 'mashed potato' undermines her 'discovery' by creating a comparison to Galileo's work through something domestic

Feminine/Feminist Humour and Whiteness in Absurdist Poetry   35

(and almost bland), thereby creating bathos. In her article 'Click, Click, Click: Cliché in the poetry of Emily Berry, Heather Phillipson and Sam Riviere' (2015), Edwina Attlee writes that Phillipson's poems are 'full of declaration, observation and statements of apparent fact', and the poet's use of repetition 'speaks of a resistance to meaning' (2015, pp. 2, 3). For Attlee, there is 'a persistent mood of disingenuousness' in what she deems post-internet poetry,[8] because, for these poets, 'truth and significance have a sell-by-date [. . .] and it is always fast approaching' (2015, p. 3). As such, Phillipson calls the validity of the speaker's 'discovery' into question in the final lines of the poem, when the speaker states: 'I had discovered that the earth goes around the sun. | Copernicus pre-discovered it' (2013, p. 14). Despite the speaker opining that she has made a 'discovery', the reader knows that this is not an original discovery; it is, after all, Copernicus's innovation, filtered through Galileo.

This new aesthetic of the Absurd is, as Attlee writes of Berry's, Phillipson's and Riviere's poetry, concerned with insincerity. The poets writing this aesthetic direct their insincerity towards the idea of 'significance', undermining the idea of poetry – or anything considered canonical or 'high' culture – as something to be revered (as I aim to show throughout this book). In 'Heliocentric Cosmology', Phillipson is commenting on the delusion of 'great discoveries' and the intelligence of 'great men'. Phillipson's over-explanation and unnecessary repetition undermines the perceived intelligence of the speaker precisely at the moment she is trying to convince the reader of her 'discovery'. This subsequently destabilises the relationship between the reader and poet; thereby all the speaker's sense or wisdom is lost. The husband's passivity and the speaker's faux-discovery are the subjects of ridicule. Neither the speaker nor her husband are 'true' intellectuals or geniuses, because such beings cannot exist – discoveries, Phillipson suggests, are as banal and pointless as mashed potato, and it is futile for women to try to become 'great' by mimicking men's findings.

Following Kaufman's definitions of humour, Phillipson's poem might be classed as 'feminine', ridiculing 'a person or system from an accepting point of view' (1980, p. 13). Indeed, Phillipson's poem aims to shed light on the futility and ridiculousness of patriarchal[9] 'great discoveries', but it does not offer an alternative, and the confines in which it suggests that 'discovery' is futile are at once broad and narrow: it is, at least, fruitless for this couple, who are significantly undefined so that they play 'everypeople' roles. Phillipson leaves the reader to imagine this couple: their race, their class, their whole lives, and this blankness suggests a sort of unchallenged 'universality' in which the universal is white and middle class, where an acceptance of banality and lack of meaning is ubiquitous.

36 *Whiteness, Feminism and the Absurd in Contemporary Poetry*

If, as Attlee writes, the poets of this new aesthetic in the Absurd are 'fascinated and perturbed by desire for meaning' (2015, p. 4), they *can* deconstruct this search for meaning, but can also falter when searching for an alternative. Phillipson's 'universal' characters are therefore symptomatic of a tendency in much contemporary Absurdist poetry: an assumption that the reader is white, and middle class.

Sam Riviere's *81 Austerities* (2012) might ostensibly have the most explicitly political drive of all the collections considered in this chapter. *81 Austerities* takes on the austerity measures of the Conservative-Liberal Democrat British government, creative writing as an academic discipline and the internet, in a decidedly self-effacing manner. Riviere's interest in plagiarism and forgery[10] is clear in 'It's Great to Be Here', in which a case of mistaken identity leads the speaker to consider what it would be like to masquerade as a woman who writes poetry and enter 'the mslexia comp 1 year' (2012, p. 81). Riviere creates humour partly from the speaker's meandering imagination, extending a single daydream into a bizarre scenario, where the speaker attempts to convince himself that assuming a woman's identity is ethical. However, it is an uncomfortable humour, one where the subject of the joke – and indeed the punchline – is unclear. The speaker's misogyny is apparent in the way he childishly refers to women as 'a girl' and, towards the end of the poem, invokes marriage vows – an undoubtedly historically patriarchal system – so that the 'wife' of the poem can 'thank this guy [. . .] till death do us part' and in perpetuity grant him permission to 'accept I on my behalf the prize' (2012, p. 81). Undoubtedly, the woman – even if imaginary – is duped in this poem, as is *Mslexia* (known for publishing women's writing only), the publication granting the prize.

Poetry itself is also subject of the joke: the inverted syntax of the poem's final lines harks back to a more 'traditional', rhyming poetry, or the kind of syntax a student in a creative writing class might be warned about. So, then, Riviere seems to suggest that women's prizes allow writers of sub-standard levels to win. Ultimately, the joke is not funny. VIDA counts[11] indicate that men are published far more often than women (2020), and are, according to Rachael Allen and Sophie Collins, proof of 'the pervasiveness of internalised sexist attitudes' (2012, p. 3). That Riviere would achieve more success as a woman is part of the poem's joke. The poem takes aim at the sexism of the publishing industry, but the joke also undermines women poets, or organisations for women's writing. The speaker's daydream of pretending to be a woman and winning the competition has an almost sneering tone of superiority that masquerades as self-effacement (*Isn't poetry silly?*): the speaker is better than all the women poets, sufficiently clever to fool everyone into

Feminine/Feminist Humour and Whiteness in Absurdist Poetry   37

believing that he should have won the competition and to create a plan that means he will not arouse suspicion when he reads at the award ceremony. The joke is fraught because it is not apparent how or why it is funny. Women's work is unrecognised; men's writing receives more attention and awards. Riviere continues that joke, never establishing whether the continuation is in service of promoting gender equality, by exposing the ridiculousness of this inequality, or merely laughing at it and those who suffer under the structures of publishing.

What happens once the gaucheness and ridiculousness of poetry is exposed so that, as an institution, its reverence is diminished? What can poets do then? As I will demonstrate throughout this book, the Absurd has a fraught relationship with the question of what poetry can do. Indeed, there is little to suggest in Riviere's work that the Absurd has fundamentally moved on. When Rooney writes of an 'everyman' in 'Handeyesque' poetry, is there one, ubiquitous everyman to imagine? Is he the same man who speaks in Edson's and Tate's poems? Is, unfailingly, that man white? Rooney is writing about a US poetics, but as Parmar points out, British poetry criticism fails to address the issue of race too, so Rooney's description of an 'accidental surrealism' in modern poetry is essential to understanding this new aesthetic of the Absurd as it appears in both British and US poetry. The white poet may feel that they have been placed in a bind, for as, Ahmed writes: 'If the work of critique does not show that its object can be undone, or promise to undo its object, then what is the point of that critique?'; yet she notes that the 'desire for signs of resistance can also be a form for resistance to hearing about racism' and that, 'if we want to know how things can be different too quickly, then we might not hear anything at all' (2007, p. 164). Not all poems can, or should, centre whiteness, because this perhaps recentres the white voice again (Ahmed, 2007, p. 164), but poems that are explicitly trying to undermine some system of oppression can go further in offering an alternative, and if poets are willing to examine other issues of social inequality, there is a chance also for them to reckon with race.

The aesthetic's clearest intervention is its destabilisation and refiguration of women's experiences. In the 'female insanity' version of the Absurd, male speakers and characters are permitted to embrace nihilistic dislocation and strangeness, while women exploring their own existential dread is somehow taboo, branding them 'insane'. Rather than explore 'insanity', the poets of this new aesthetic in the Absurd reject this sense of 'madness', and instead seek to depict their existential dread in more nuanced terms. Caroline Bird's poem 'Mothers', published in her 2013 collection, *The Hat-Stand Union*, features a speaker

38   *Whiteness, Feminism and the Absurd in Contemporary Poetry*

who addresses an unnamed 'you' and explores a series of shifting relationships between the speaker, her addressee and the speaker's 'future child' (2013, p. 13), Bertha. In thinking about the addressee, the speaker believes that she 'was the child in this scenario' (2013, p. 13), while her 'future child' seems to predict the death of her mother, who is perhaps also the speaker:

> my future child called me on the telephone
> and said, in a squeaky voice, 'My mum is dying,
> can you come over, I need someone to talk to.' (2013, p. 13)

Bird uses these contradictions and shifting, uncertain relationships to question prescriptive notions of motherhood. Throughout the poem, Bird suggests that adulthood and childhood are complicated, and intertwined. The speaker remembers a woman from her 'adulthood' – when the reader might expect her to say 'childhood' – who she has also seen in a 'bed-wetting dream', as 'a terrible pain ripped | through my stomach' (2013, p. 13), invoking labour pains. At once, the speaker is a child and a mother, and seems to be caught in a painful liminal space between the two: not quite child, and heading towards the pain and responsibility of motherhood.

The mother–daughter relationship becomes more complicated as Bertha and speaker swap roles. Bertha scolds the speaker like a mother: 'I told you | no more running away from hospital, didn't I?' (2013, p. 13). At the mention of the hospital, the reader questions the speaker's credibility, as it appears that the speaker is not able to report the circumstances fully or clearly. Bird's poem ends with the speaker talking to Bertha, who does not seem to be present:

> Bertha, I went straight back. [. . .]
>
>   [. . .] This is my picture of mummy:
> that is a tree because she's in a forest, those are
> mummy's pink gloves and that's an axe. (2013, p. 13)

At the end of the poem, the speaker assumes a childlike position, and the deeply sinister, violent undertones of the picture are unsettling. The speaker's voice adopts a childlike simplicity, which is uncomfortably at odds with the picture she describes. Initially, the drawing depicts an idealised version of the mother surrounded by nature. However, the axe undercuts this idealised image and presents a threat with violent connotations. In the picture, the mother is not exactly what she seems.

Bird shifts the speaker's and Bertha's roles continually throughout the poem, charting the reversal and fluidity of responsibility throughout

Feminine/Feminist Humour and Whiteness in Absurdist Poetry 39

a mother–daughter relationship. When the speaker is in hospital, she is vulnerable and her voice becomes childlike, invoking how a mother–daughter relationship inverts with age: as the mother grows older, the daughter becomes responsible for her. Throughout the poem, there is a sense of impending doom (death), and neither the future child nor the mother can mitigate this. Here, Bird rejects the 'female insanity' dynamic by demonstrating that the most painful experiences in women's lives have very little to do with 'insanity', domesticity and husbands, and are instead bound up in women and girls' relationships to one another, and the unavoidable experiences of life and death.

Selima Hill's poetry has long been thought of as surrealist (Winrow, 2013, p. 11), yet Hill herself rejects the label, writing in an exchange with Julia Copus for *Poetry London*:

> I hate the thought of being 'surreal' – i.e. whacky, arbitrary, showy-off. I feel like I am the opposite of surreal. However, I can understand how, to other people, things I say might not make sense. Why should they? It's my own sort of private synaesthesia. (2022)

Indeed, part of the issue of identifying this new aesthetic in the Absurd is its own poets' reluctance to label themselves as surrealist or Absurdist writers,[12] as though this cheapens their work, as though their work 'transcends' these labels.[13] Indeed, this might be an attempt to move away from the controversies of the avant-garde more broadly, but I would argue that being able to accept one's literary heritage (however explicit or implicit) and engage with critical conversations about this heritage and its politics might allow one to also challenge its shortcomings more clearly. Hill's poetry is characterised by 'techniques of shock, bizarre, juxtaposition and defamiliarisation' and a subversion of 'conventional notions of self and the feminine' (Rees-Jones, 2005, pp. 165, 166); her poems are rooted in familial relationships and marriage, as exemplified by her 1997 collection, *Violet*.[14]

Violet is divided into two sections: 'My Sister's Sister', which explores the death of the speaker's mother and the speaker's fraught relationship with her sister; and 'My Husband's Wife', which explores the speaker's divorce from her husband and jealousy over his new lover. Hill's work is, as Berry writes, 'suspicious' of both men and women (2022) in the domestic sphere, although in her 2021 interview with Berry, Hill claims to be afraid to be asked about feminism (and Berry does not ask her about it), which may suggest Hill's lack of confidence in speaking about feminism, rather than simply a reluctance to class her work as interacting with feminist ideas. Regardless of Hill's own ambivalence to claiming her

40 *Whiteness, Feminism and the Absurd in Contemporary Poetry*

work as surrealist or Absurd, or engage with discourses of feminism, this does not mean it is not a fruitful route of investigation.

'My Sister's Sister' begins with the poem 'My Sister's Tooth', in which the speaker watches her sister 'crossing open fields strewn with limbs' in order 'to get home safely' and give the speaker 'a human tooth embedded in a bean I and carved into the shape of a poodle' (1997, p. 11). The poem is replete with nightmarish images, which create a sense of violence and surreality that develops throughout the sequence and suggest that the speaker regards her sister at once as an idol and also as a horror to be withstood. Indeed, the poem – and many other poems in *Violet* – are written as a single sentence, which provides the poems with a sense of breathless confession, or an outpouring of emotion. The speaker is jealous of her sister, marvels in 'My Sister's Nose' at 'the way she talks to men I do not know' (1997, p. 12) and watches on as she becomes engaged to two men at once in 'My Sister Goes to Italy'. The sister is flighty, flirty and flippant, while the speaker tries to prepare herself for their mother's impending death. In 'My Sister and I Finally Arrive at the Hospital', the speaker and her mother whisper to one another: 'We both agree I it won't be long before she dies. However I my sister must be humoured till she does' (1997, p. 19).

More so than 'madness', 'My Sister's Sister' is an attempt to communicate the devastating emotions of grief, and the way it turns the sisters against one another and confuses reality. As the mother dies, the speaker longs to be alone with her, noting in 'My Sister's Shoes': 'My sister and myself are *estranged*' (1997, p. 27). The sister takes on a shifting role, someone who is, in 'My Sister Goes to London for the Day', 'out of reach, I someone years of pain had made untouchable' (1997, p. 30), and then can, briefly, be thoughtful, sliding 'a tub of ice-cream' onto the speaker's lap in 'My Sister's Horse', then driving 'away as fast as she can' (1997, p. 22), away from this moment of emotional connection and sincerity. Indeed, in 'My Sister Has Twins', the sister leaves her children 'sleeping soundly I in the nursery' while she catches 'the first bus to the sea' in 'a nightie and duffle coat' (1997, p. 15). This image of the sister escaping suggests she has issues of her own – difficulties with motherhood, with responsibility – that the speaker cannot understand or delve into. The women in 'My Sister's Sister' are complex, slippery figures, who are not 'insane', who do not torment their husbands in a domestic situation, but rather torment one another with their rivalries and the possibility of what their relationship to each other might have been. Indeed, as Winrow writes, Hill locates 'intimate relationships' as a 'source of tension for gender-identity formation where these emotions can be influential with a shaping effect' (2013, p. 1). As such, Hill's

Feminine/Feminist Humour and Whiteness in Absurdist Poetry   41

speakers frequently make reference to other women's bodies – their breasts, their tight dresses, how men appreciate their bodies – casting the speaker's sense of inadequacy and jealousy across the poems.

As Emily Berry writes in her review for the *London Review of Books* of Hill's twentieth collection, *Men Who Feed Pigeons* (2022), '"What kind of woman am I?" is one of Hill's recurring questions, and it's a question, really, about roles and the ways in which we inhabit or refuse them' (2022). At times, Hill's speaker is stereotypically and obsessively jealous, consumed by anger at her husband's betrayal and new lover. In 'Buckets', the speaker describes the new lover as 'blood' and the husband as 'the blood-stained patient | who's coughed her up | in the flightpaths of my joy' (Hill, 1997, p. 38); in 'The World's Entire Wasp Population', she daydreams about vicious revenge on the new lover. The speaker brutally reshapes her wedding ring in 'Jesu's Blood' and 'My Wedding Ring' in an act of defiance. In 'I Know I Ought to Love You', the speaker most looks like one of Edson or Tate's 'insane' wives, admitting, 'Screaming is the best I can do': 'I scream at you for such a long time | that even when I stop the scream goes on' (1997, p. 54).

Ian Gregson writes that Hill's writing should be 'regarded as a strategically overstated gender performance, which deconstructs gender assumptions by drawing attention to them through caricaturally vivid simplification' (2011, p. 20). Indeed, Hill's speakers are hyperbolic, passionate and focused on what pains them. Fundamentally, though, Hill's speakers in 'My Sister's Sister' and 'My Husband's Wife' feel more rational than Edson's or Tate's women characters can ever be, because they are speaking for *themselves*.[15] Hill's inventive, strange and surreal images provide acute metonyms for the pain her speakers experience, and the speakers seem compelled in their (often) short, tumbling poems to confess their worst feelings. Rather than acting in bizarre and incomprehensible ways, the speaker of 'My Husband's Wife' is necessarily understandable: she is heartbroken, with legitimate reason, and she is able to articulate that feeling, without it being mediated and defamiliarised by a man. Hill's surreal and visceral images work to capture the tumultuousness of heartbreak, rendering it understandable as it is devastating and reorders the speaker's perception of her world. As the speaker comes to terms to life without her husband, she sees the world as grief-stricken and strange.

Later in the sequence, in 'Following Stars', the speaker writes that she is 'myself again', and, addressing her husband, says: 'You're better off without me definitely' (1997, p. 70). She moves onto another man, another wedding dress, and the sequence ends with the speaker walking 'towards a bed piled high for him and me' (1997, p. 80). Hill's poetry does not eschew the institution of marriage or domesticity per se, but

42 *Whiteness, Feminism and the Absurd in Contemporary Poetry*

the speaker must accept her anger, work through it and come out the other side, changed and able to move on. She is not stuck in the realm of 'insane' woman, angry woman (which supposes that anger cannot be pragmatic) or heartbroken woman. The change the speaker enacts is in her own life – no longer railing against her husband and his new lover, but able to express herself and understand, whatever the future might hold for her. At the same time, Hill's poetry enacts the trope of the devastated woman to deconstruct the misogynistic stereotype: there is more than meets the eye to this devastation, and depth to a woman's emotions.

Luke Kennard's poem 'Blue Dog', published in his 2007 collection *The Harbour Beyond the Movie*,[16] evidences the broad trend of contemporary Absurdist poetry attempting to reject the 'female insanity' of earlier Absurdist poetry. In 'Blue Dog', the speaker and a woman discuss a little blue plastic dog, which reminds the woman of being a child (2010, p. 49). Initially, Kennard's opening suggests that the poem will follow the established 'female insanity' dynamic, casting the woman as childish (or preoccupied with childhood); she professes, 'I am in love with the blue dog', while the man nihilistically pronounces that the only detail he remembers from his childhood is 'rows of horror films by the counter in the video store' (2010, p. 49). Paul McDonald, discussing Kennard's oeuvre, suggests that readers are 'meant to see the moral shortcomings' of the characters, and that Kennard is a proponent of 'moral relativism', which is 'consistent with postmodernism's refusal to construct a moral hierarchy' (2017, p. 7). In 'Blue Dog', Kennard's approach to morality and nihilism is ambivalent. At once, the woman rationalises the blue dog as her 'taking joy in the smallest things' (2010, p. 49). She notes that 'people say: *Everyone is searching for something*' and that the blue dog symbolises this search and 'all that it could once evoke' (2010, p. 49). Evidently, the woman's pronouncements of hope and greater meaning are antithetical to the Absurd's and the man's nihilism, and thinking of Rooney's 'Handeyesque' poetry, there is certainly a sense that the woman's aphorisms are essentially meaningless, as she devotes herself to a child's toy.[17] Yet the speaker is no better off, refusing to enjoy the 'smallest things': '"I have learned to group those things together," I say, "and take joy in none of them"', or reacting with childish jealousy: 'The little blue dog sits proudly in the middle of the table. I consider snatching it – and throwing it in a river, or melting it' (2010, p. 49). As such, both the speaker and the woman are childish and hyperbolic, with the woman declaring, 'I won't want to live anymore' (2010, p. 49) if the man destroys the blue dog.

No longer is the woman 'insane', and no longer is the man her longsuffering victim: the woman has her false meanings, and the man has no meaning in his life at all. Rather than recognise this, the speaker deems the woman 'highly strung' and futilely asks the blue dog, 'You think I'm a monster, don't you?' (2010, p. 49), knowing that it cannot answer and reveal the truth. Perhaps this suggests that the speaker might finally be trying to engage with the woman's way of thinking, appealing for the blue dog to enlighten him – but, as Kennard suggests throughout the poem, this is also a pointless endeavour. Kennard does not suggest where these characters might go next, and it seems that they are doomed to repeat their misguided behaviour in perpetuity. This is not to say that all poems – or even Kennard's poem – need to establish a fixed moral binary (for this would simply be reductive), but Kennard's tone is ambivalent.

In thinking of Rooney's and Delville's 'everyman' figure, it seems as though contemporary Absurdist poetics has strived to present the 'everywoman', without necessarily interrogating what this means. There is a featurelessness (and thereby acceptance of a universalising whiteness) to some of the speakers and characters in the poems I have analysed here: they do not describe their positions in society, their appearance or how the world perceives them, beyond their gender. This is most likely a symptom of the poets assuming their reader is white and middle class, and, as I show throughout this book, poets can use this assumption as a means for action. In a less generous reading, this might be considered an attempt to reach for a false 'universality'. In contemporary critical discourse, the 'universal' must be eschewed because it cannot and does not exist; Ben Lerner takes issue with 'universality' in *The Hatred of Poetry* (2016), while Rankine and Loffreda write that 'White writers often begin from a place where transcendence is a given—one already has access to all, one already is permitted to inhabit all, to address all' (in Rankine et al., 2016, p. 16). In attempting to write the 'everyman' or the 'everywoman', contemporary Absurd poetry has, generally, moved on from its 'female insanity' dynamic into one in which the speaker, and the people they talk to, challenge notions of 'female insanity'; but they are mostly white.

Yet, as Rankine and Loffreda write, the solution to this whiteness is not to 'extend the imagination into other identities, that the white writer to be antiracist must write from the point of view of characters of color'; the 'white writer's work could also think about, expose, that racial dynamic' (in Rankine et al., 2016, p. 17). It is not my aim here to suggest how each poet, each poem, might tackle whiteness – this is not the critic's role, after all – but to acknowledge that contemporary British Absurdist poetry has room to tackle whiteness meaningfully. As a poet and critic, this is important to me personally, and this book additionally serves to think through how I might tackle whiteness in my writing. This chapter is not intended to discount or disparage the work of the poets, or claim that they have, in some way, failed. The poems here present contemporary Absurdist poetry battling with its own misogyny and nihilism, shining a light on shortcomings, inequalities, presumptions and flawed thinking, and turning towards something new – a hopeful turn, and one which opens up space to think about race. As Christopher Kempf writes in 'Poetics of Whiteness' (2019),[18] 'reading and writing poems can constitute a form of civic engagement with the capacity to disrupt entrenched thinking, re-route feeling, and, in so doing, imagine into existence a more just society' (p. 123). This is not a straightforward endeavour.

Indeed, in discussing whiteness, it is possible to simply centralise whiteness again and again, without disruption. As Kempf argues, writers must ensure that whiteness is 'resurfaced, dragged, however reluctantly, into the light' if it is to 'remain permanently visible and, therefore, susceptible to critique' (2019, p. 124). He notes that white identity 'intricately [. . .] intersects with – is reinforced by, comes under threat from – lived experiences of gender and class' (2019, p. 137), and, as I aim to show throughout this book, this new aesthetic of the Absurd confidently – if not subtly – engages with issues of class and gender, interrogating them and hoping for something new. When we interrogate our own assumptions about class and gender, we must reluctantly accept, question and change our willingness to engage with stereotypes and to accept a status quo; we must hope for something different, and try to enact that change. If this Absurd is able to do this for gender and class, as I will now show in Chapter 2, it can do the same for whiteness.

Chapter 2

Miscommunication and Failure to Connect in the Absurd

In Chapter 1, I explored how contemporary Absurdist poetry has turned towards gender equality to redress misogyny apparent in earlier Absurdist works. I argued that contemporary avant-garde poetry, including the Absurd, is marked by whiteness. Yet the aesthetic's turn to gender equality and rejection of some of the harmful stereotypes of earlier Absurdist work suggest a chance for contemporary Absurdist poets to develop a more hopeful poetics of change. In this chapter, I want to think about how contemporary Absurdist poetry is preoccupied with the incomprehensibility of life and our failures to connect and communicate with one another. Technology provides the perfect jumping-off point for exploring how systems of creating meaning often fail. I consider 'emotionally non-directive' writing, and how this might unhelpfully trouble the reader–writer relationship, especially concerning hegemonic thinking and race. I include an examination of how white British poet Rachael Allen uses the website 4chan in her *4chan Poems* (2014; 2016) as a means to explore miscommunication through gender and class, and how she might then, too, use this as a space to explore whiteness. I move into an investigation of masculinity and failures to connect in white British poet Crispin Best's *Faber New Poets 14* (2016) and *Hello* (2019), and show how under Best's attempts to destabilise hegemonic masculinity lie an endeavour to subvert the Absurd's nihilism. I hope I will be forgiven for the small range of poets selected for this chapter, but hope through these readings to provide a broader sense of how contemporary Absurdist poetics is engaging with nihilism.

The Trouble with Emotionally Non-Directive Writing

In his essay '"Unlike": Forms of Refusal in Poetry on the Internet' (2011), Riviere writes about post-internet poetry, which, broadly speaking, uses the internet as a basis for inspiration. These texts might repurpose 'found' material online (such as Flarf),[1] or capture the existence of being online through using blogs, social media and internet-inflected language (such as Alt-Lit), or reflect on how, after the internet, we might not ever write or think in the same ways again.[2] For Riviere, post-internet poetry aims to communicate 'constant ambivalence, anxiety about how "serious" someone intends to be', which is 'experienced through the continuous use of qualifiers, non-sequiturs and other non-literary traits' (2011). Riviere notes that 'online discourse opts for deferral every time, and its poetry acts out the same reluctance to commit to anything completely, to demonstrate certainty about one's knowledge or opinions' (2011).

This deferral, ambivalence and uncertainty is for Riviere proof of post-internet poetry's 'sincerity' (2011), since 'uncertainty is the only emotion that does not deceive' (Žižek in Riviere, 2011). Riviere notes: 'We can't ever know what the "right" action is, on the level of a society, so being resolutely uncertain can be understood as a desperate effort to occupy a sincere position' (2011). While Riviere's description of post-internet poetry helpfully characterises an aesthetic, it does not interrogate the problematic apoliticality of some texts. As he notes, post-internet poetry's ambivalence is a 'flat refusal to be emotionally directive, to attempt to manipulate the reader's feelings or attachments, and instead to provide the coordinates of experience without the cues for interpretation' (2011).

Riviere's idea of emotionally non-directive writing seems to mirror a broader sweep, as Caitlin Merrett King writes, towards 'Unsure Theory', in which ambivalence is observed as a 'mobile and aporetic state that, from an individual perspective, embraces the holding of multiple contradictory personal opinions' (2022, p. 1). For Merrett King, ambivalence is 'especially pertinent to the experience of living in the twenty-first century under late stage capitalism and its inherent complications, specifically its impact on mental health', and is not inherently a 'negative' emotion (2022, pp. 2, 7). Merrett King seems to concerningly conflate having unsure feelings towards a piece of art with being 'less classically passionate about politics, feeling the petty and less glamorous emotions of anxiety, passivity, insecurity and ambivalence', and notes that 'Unsure Theory drips towards the desire to repoliticise uncertainty and not knowing' (2022, pp. 3, 8, 9). Certainly, there is space for individuals to claim their own lack of knowledge and need to learn about an infinite amount of subjects – to listen, rather than to speak (or post on social media). Yet ambivalence and emotionally non-directive writing can be troublesome, and do little to disrupt hegemonic ways of thinking and acting.[3]

Miscommunication and Failure to Connect in the Absurd   **47**

There are two infamous instances of poetry which refuses to be 'emotionally directive'. These works, by white American poets Kenneth Goldsmith and Vanessa Place, are labelled as 'Uncreative Writing', which David Kaufmann defines as 'work whose object matter is lifted more or less verbatim from other sources, most often from the Web' (2017, p. 1). In March 2015, at a conference at Brown University, Goldsmith read an altered transcript of Michael Brown's autopsy report, titling it 'The Body of Michael Brown'.[4] Responses to the reading were (and continue to be) damning, with John Keene writing that Goldsmith's practice was 'neither "uncreative" nor apolitical', and in its 'commodifying and reifying action-as-spectacle, it reinscribed the violence of Brown's (and other black people's) tragic death and its aftermath, and the erasure of his humanity, in an effort at ironic, clever entertainment' (2015). Place has also been accused of racism during multiple projects,[5] particularly one in which she reappropriates the novel *Gone with the Wind* by posting excerpts from the book on Twitter (now X; the account is no longer available). The account's profile picture was a photograph of Hattie McDaniel, the actress who played 'Mammy' in the film adaptation, in costume, and Kim Calder notes that 'the account's background photo is a similarly racist caricature taken from the sheet music for "Jemima's Wedding Day," a minstrel song' (2015).

While Calder acknowledges that the materials with which Place is working are undoubtedly racist, she sees Place's work as 'interested in enacting and exploring racism as it operates structurally' (2015). Indeed, she notes that, rather than a 'restatement of the obvious, Place's antagonism explores complicity and interrogates our reception of that complicity, from which none of us are exempt' (2015). Kaufmann follows a similar line of argument, noting that Goldsmith's audience is not 'asked to see a conflict between their structural position and their lived experience', and therefore 'Goldsmith is up to something very different than Place' (2017, p. 72). Jennifer Cooke thinks of Place's oeuvre as belonging, broadly, to an aesthetic in contemporary feminist life-writing, which she names 'The New Audacity',[6] in which 'feminist writers' believe 'it is not just men but women – and sometimes feminists – who need to change in order to address misogyny and discrimination' (2020, p. 4). Cooke notes that these writers 'often demand large-scale and structural change rather than place their hopes in reform, and they are determined to break with conservative thinking wherever they encounter it' (2020, p. 4). As such, it is apparent that Cooke's aesthetic has many similar undercurrents to the ideas of the 'feminist' writing I explored in Chapter 1. Indeed, Kaufmann argues that in Place's *Gone with the Wind* project, the author is suggesting that she is 'openly and guiltily' (2017, p. 87)

48 *Whiteness, Feminism and the Absurd in Contemporary Poetry*

accepting her place in a structurally racist society as a 'perpetrator' of racism, which is ultimately a self-aggrandising move, in which she 'is owning up, not just to tweeting *Gone with the Wind*, but to hundreds of years of racism', and thereby is asking 'to be justly punished for all the transgressions of whiteness'; she has 'personally taken on as her own some of the greatest sins of American history' (2017, p. 88).

For Kaufmann, then, Uncreative Writing (and thereby New Audacity writing, and the Absurd, which shares many qualities with Cooke's aesthetic) can be 'an attempt to turn the privileges of cultural capital into a source of readerly discomfort and offer a critique of the very privilege on which [the] work rests' (2017, p. 39). As such, for Kaufmann, avant-garde poetry 'requires a fair amount of social privilege and cultural capital' in order to 'call forth the small yet privileged audience that will enjoy its own cultural capital and that will be ready to identify with the avant-garde's often aggressive deployment of that capital' (2017, pp. 57, 41); the avant-garde must 'seek to alienate all those who do not have that enjoyment or suffer those identifications' (2017, p. 41). So, I return to a question I posed in the previous chapter: how do writers write about whiteness without reifying whiteness? These examples from Goldsmith and Place – regardless of their different approaches, successful or not – demonstrate how problematic the 'ambivalence' of poetry can be when poets provide 'coordinates of experience' without a clear sense of how the reader might be engaged with them, especially when the reader is assumed to be white and middle class.

In 'A Horizon Line: Flat Style in Contemporary Women's Poetry' (2022), Noreen Masud identifies a style in modern poetry called 'flat style', evidenced in the work of white British poets Rachael Allen, Emily Berry and Sophie Collins (all published by British publisher Faber & Faber). According to Masud, flat style refers to 'writing positioned in relation to confession or revelation, which performs its own indifference to how it is received' and it 'involves causing (gendered) trouble by refusing the labour of responsiveness to its reader' (2022, p. 2), which parallels Attlee's ideas that modern poets are 'fascinated and perturbed by desire for meaning and deconstruct an explanatory approach to poetry' (2015, p. 4). Masud likens flat style to 'a television telling us something we already know in the background as we scroll through Twitter' and the 'atonal flatness of a tweet' (2022, pp. 2, 6). For Masud, flat style reflects a world

> predicated upon the knowledge that there is no answer, or (which amounts to the same thing) that all possible answers are already obvious (because we are savvy and online; because Google exists; because all the

Miscommunication and Failure to Connect in the Absurd   49

questions we could ask have at their root huge systemic answers about which one can do little). (2022, p. 6)

Masud characterises flat style as 'recording of the banal', in which 'feeling is registered but not felt' (2022, pp. 9, 12), which clearly mirrors the characteristics of the Absurd that I identified in Chapter 1. It also recalls Fredric Jameson's postmodern 'waning of affect', which Jameson suggests might lead to 'a liberation from every [. . .] kind feeling' so that feelings become 'free-floating and impersonal' (1991, pp. 15, 16). Considering Riviere's ideas about uncertainty, and Masud's characterisation of flat style as coming up against 'huge systemic answers about which one can do little', the Absurd's nihilism does not seem too far away.

The Absurd appears to be particularly appealing to white women poets (or rather, publishers, especially Faber, who seem keen to publish writing like this by white women). Indeed, Masud acknowledges that all the poets in her article are white, so it is evident that there is something about Masud's 'flat style' and the Absurd that appeals to white women. Masud writes that Berry, Allen and Collins 'write in response to a misogynistic, overexposed context which at once demands too much and too little feeling for what is happening' (2022, p. 18). In this sense, 'flat style' differs significantly from Cooke's New Audacity, in that Cooke's aesthetic, as the name implies, is 'characterised by boldness and a disregard for decorum, protocol, or moral restraints' (2020, pp. 1–2), and thereby has much more in common with the Gurlesque, which I examine in Chapter 4. Yet both flat style and New Audacity seem to be pushing back against ideas of confessionalism to, as Cooke argues, 'confront the imperatives associated with their gender [. . .] the required image of the "good girl", [. . .] to contravene a lifelong training which, in Zambreno's words, normatively impels women "to be nice, to be liked . . . to not show the ugliness"' (2020, p. 85).

Christopher Grobe argues that Robert Lowell's privilege as a white, middle-class, cisgendered, heterosexual man is precisely the source of his ability to write confessional poetry and be celebrated for it, and contends that this 'assurance' is destabilised for women writers, whose poems are deemed 'merely private, merely personal, merely unique' (2017, p. 38). Yet, for the writer of colour, such writing is deemed 'merely public, merely social, and merely representative', as the 'I' of the poem is both the individual 'I' of the writer, and 'the collective "I" of the race' (Henry Louis Gates, Jr. in Grobe, 2017, p. 38). Grobe does not necessarily unpack what happens when the writer of confessional poetry is a woman of colour, but we can see how these assumptions can intersect to destabilise a writer's authority even further. Indeed, Cooke explores

50 *Whiteness, Feminism and the Absurd in Contemporary Poetry*

how, during an interview with New Audacity writer Kris Kraus, Kraus rejected 'the term "confessional" to describe her work, replying instead by quoting Gilles Deleuze: "'Confessional' of what? *Personal* confessions? There's a great line from a book we published by Deleuze: *Life is not personal*"' (2020, p. 113). As Cooke argues:

> If there is no such thing as personal confession, no such thing as a personal life, it is because we are interpolated into social structures which continually speak before us, as well as upon our behalf: one has to have learned what the church deems as sin before one can gain forgiveness for any particular, personal infringement through confession, for instance. (2020, p. 113)

Grobe posits that:

> confessional poetry [is] essentially a genre of identity crisis and, as James Baldwin contends, these kinds of crises could startle only 'white men, who believe the world is theirs and who, albeit unconsciously, expect the world to help them in the achievement of their identity'. (2017, p. 40)

If, then, white women feel themselves to have been pushed out from and limited by confessionalism – since, as Cooke writes, 'confessional' comes 'with all the concomitant implications of sinfulness, secrecy, and a religious doctrine that demands women's subservience to men' (2020, p. 113) – the need for flat style and its indifference to its readership is understandable, but it might also become problematic. If the white woman poet (or speaker) opens up in their poems – audaciously, or flatly – they might 'identify with marginalized others only in order to credential their own feelings of angst and alienation, feelings they harbor in spite of (or, all the more, because of) their extraordinary privilege' (Grobe, 2017, p. 42), or seek absolution for their shortcomings.

What might be happening underneath a poetics which, using Masud's terms, 'performs its own grappling with feelings which cannot – safely, justifiably, forgivably – be expressed, without soliciting an accusation of either excess or paucity' (2022, p. 2)? If flat style is so 'overloaded – with feeling, language and detail – that it turns counter-intuitively into something numb and detached, which seems to shut down further discussion, and create impasse' (2022, p. 2), might it deny the speaker (and the poet) a chance to question and reshape understandings, and chances at communication, by stubbornly denying them? Might it offer absolution or retreat from challenging ideas or the speaker's more shameful thoughts? Might it prevent one from accepting responsibility for shaping systemic reform?

Miscommunication and Failure to Connect in the Absurd   51

It is important, I think, to problematise a straightforward approach between 'experience' and the resulting poem. In an interview with *LA Review of Books*, white British poet Emily Berry explains white American poet Sharon Olds's and her own rejection of the term 'autobiographical poetry':

> An autobiography is meant to be an account of a person's life, and, on the whole, you're not going to get a poem that is a straight description of a person's life – it's usually an essence of that. [. . .] At the same time, some people really want poems – specifically poems written in the first person – to be about someone and something 'real', and they can feel cheated when the poem isn't. [. . .] I'm interested in how Sharon Olds has spoken about her work as being 'apparently personal'. The things of her poems do seem like her 'real life', but she didn't used to own up to that. But even then – I say 'own up' as if I'm accusing her of not admitting something. (Webb and Berry, 2017)

Berry's description suggests a slipperiness in trying to define what is 'autobiographical' or not, and the kind of capital readers place in getting 'real' information about the poet. The description invokes established arguments about confessional poetry, which even M.L. Rosenthal, in coining the term, understood was 'both helpful and too limited' (in Hoffman, 1978, p. 687). As David Yezzi writes in *New Criterion*: 'All poets use their lives for poetry, but not all lives are used similarly' (1998). For Yezzi, the distinction is thus: often, 'the particulars of a poet's life provide the basis for more general speculation, which constitutes the poem's bid for universality'; in the confessional, such 'details can serve to deny universality by delineating the poet as apart and uniquely suffering' (1998). I have already outlined the issues relating to bids for 'universality' in writing, and, as Yezzi notes, confessional poems 'lie like truth' (1998); by relying on 'facts' for a poem's emotional authenticity, the poet slides out of the 'facts', and into an artificial honesty. I do not intend 'artificial honesty' as a criticism per se. In fact, the Absurd revels in artifice, taking elements of 'real life' and imagination, and blurring them until they become indistinct; the result is a sense akin to Freud's *unheimlich*, in which the distinction between imagination and reality is effaced (2003, p. 150).

There is a sense underlying 'confessional' poetry that writing about oneself *inherently* means that the poet's experiences are understandable, because all poets and all readers of poetry look and behave in the same way; it is heavily implied that this is what poetry should be aiming towards. The Absurd sits ambivalently: it wants to communicate, resonantly, the experience of feeling misunderstood, and being unable to

52   *Whiteness, Feminism and the Absurd in Contemporary Poetry*

connect with others. This is ultimately a contradiction in terms, which leads us to Masud's idea of an impasse: emotions and experiences are communicated, but the poet and the poem might not get to the bottom of any problem.

Technology, Class and Whiteness

Feminist theory has long battled with the potentialities of the internet and its lived reality. In 'Neither Cyborg Nor Goddess: The (Im)Possibilities of Cyberfeminism' (2007), Stacy Gillis writes that it is 'arguable that the myth of cyberfeminism – that women are using cyberspace in powerful and transgressive ways and that cyberspace is providing women with a disembodied space in which to move beyond gender – is far removed from online experiences' (p. 168). As Evans notes, 'the Internet has not always been liberating for feminists and women; beyond the proliferation of online pornography, the Internet has been an important site for anti-feminist rhetoric and abuse' (2015, p. 75). Gillis further contends that the 'predominant model of behaviour online [. . .] is a white masculinity' (2007, p. 175). Although Masud cites Allen's work as being indicative of 'flat style' and the 'impasse' that defines it, in this chapter I want to think about how Allen's work demonstrates the potential of the Absurd to grapple with race, class and gender. In particular, I wish to read Allen's *4chan Poems*, published in her pamphlet, *Faber New Poets 9* (2014), and also in Collins's *Currently & Emotion* (2016), an anthology of translations.[7] The *4chan* sequence takes its titles from boards on the 4chan website, an online forum on which, most infamously, users have posted misogynistic, racist and disturbing content.[8] In her introduction to the sequence in *Currently & Emotion*, Collins writes that 'the fact [. . .] that Allen is a female looking in "4chan Poems" is central to the texts' dynamic, especially given their operating from within *4chan*'s overtly misogynistic environment' (2016, p. 202). However, I think this can be pushed further, and that Allen's poems not only wrestle with misogyny but use this to think about white, working-class girlhood and womanhood.

In a 2019 interview with Lewis Johnson for the University of Liverpool's Centre for New and International Writing, Allen discusses her approach to writing about class, noting that 'my experience of my class was without a sense of pride and more the feeling that it was something to escape' (2019).[9] She also admits: 'I feel there's still a level of performance when I'm writing these poems that I'm not necessarily sure is perhaps ethical – perhaps I'm hiding something', but explains: 'I'm not interested that much in conveying the exact details of a life, instead

I use things from my own life alongside all the other things that we bring to poetry – like theatre, visual arts, story' (2019). Allen's own approach to writing about class – and claims to be ambivalent about her approaches to writing about class – might suggest a reluctance to take on 'political' material, and a concern about how blurring 'reality' might, somehow, look away from such topics. Yet I think Allen's assessment of her own approaches is somewhat modest. If, as Charles Whalley writes in an essay about the *4chan Poems* for *The Missing Slate*, 'anonymity on 4chan solicits total confession' and Allen's poems 'revisit the tradition of confessional poetry via the model of the internet's anonymous confessions' (2014), then Allen is using 4chan as a space to think about the power of confession, especially in such a contested space as the internet.

The *4chan Poems* are deeply concerned with girlhood; throughout, the speakers of the poems think about their childhoods and reframe their experiences from their older self's perspective. Allen's poems have a paucity of grammar, and their prose poem form lends the poems to breathless admission, so that it seems that the speakers are absorbed by their memories and imaginings, urging them into reality as they create them. The movement from childhood to adulthood is set against the fleeting nature of posts on 4chan – Whalley notes, 'in a study in 2010, the median lifetime of a thread on the board /b/ was less than 4 minutes' (2014) – and so the internet becomes bound up in how the speakers imagine themselves, understand themselves and communicate their experiences to one another – how they 'confess'. Girlhood, class and race are 'interlocked' (Skeggs, 2002), even when working-class women struggle to articulate this.[10]

I follow Beverley Skeggs's proposition that class is a discursive construction where working-class women undertake a dialogic process in which 'every judgement of themselves [is] a measurement [. . .] made against others' (2002); as Skeggs writes: 'In this process the designated "other" (based on representations and imaginings of the respectable and judgemental middle class) [is] constructed as the standard to/from which they [measure] themselves' (2002).[11] This is an important dynamic in Allen's poetry, in which the speakers 'are never free from the judgements of imaginary and real others that position them, not just as different, but as inferior, as inadequate' (Skeggs, 2002) – as I will show, Allen assumes that her readers are white and middle class, and her poems reflect a sense of understanding that bodies and the home is where 'respectability is displayed but where class is lived out as the most omnipresent form, engendering surveillance and constant assessment' (Skeggs, 2002).

In 'Rapidshares', Allen's speaker recalls how 'Gina G was the pathway to enlightenment and adulthood another of the pathways was my

54 *Whiteness, Feminism and the Absurd in Contemporary Poetry*

pink faux-snakeskin halter neck top that came free with a magazine' (2014, p. 10).[12] The speaker of this poem recognises her body as a physical site onto which ideas about femininity and adulthood can be read, and declares that she feels 'older, I thought thirty' (2014, p. 10). The speaker, as a child, does not recognise the garishness of her new top, or her idea that Gina G's pop music might offer a sense of maturity. There is, of course, a sense that the speaker, now older, is looking back on this memory and offering a 'confession', which acknowledges one's own embarrassing child-self.

Yet, I think there is a greater layering of shame at play here, one which exposes Allen's ideas about class. The speaker wears her new top to a pub and experiences a sense of judgement when someone shouts 'from across the beery carpets "that top looks like something you'd get free from a magazine"' (2014, p. 10). In wearing the top, the speaker has attempted at once to not look like a child, to gain the legitimacy of being older.[13] Allen thereby uses 'age' or 'adulthood' to stand in for class, since, as Skeggs notes, 'the body and bodily dispositions carry the markers of social class', because 'bodies are the physical sites where the relations of class, gender, race, sexuality and age come together and are embodied and practised' (2002). This dressing up to look older might therefore also be an act of wanting to pass as a white middle-class woman, because, as Skeggs notes, 'skills and labour such as dressing-up and making-up are used to display the desire to pass as not working class' (2002). But the speaker's state is inescapable: someone calls out her class play, and critiques her attempts to be read as older, which destabilises the speaker's sense that she can be read as something other than girl and working class. The speaker recalls feeling 'insulted', even though the comment about the top is entirely correct, and continues her class play: 'we puffed out our flat chests for the rest of the evening, skittering on our low heels playing at adulthood' (Allen, 2014, p. 10). Allen therefore demonstrates how the demands of femininity require 'a radical bodily transformation at which virtually every woman is bound to fail', which adds 'shame to her deficiency' (Skeggs, 2002).

Sarah Ahmed writes in *The Cultural Politics of Emotion* (2014) that when a person experiences shame, 'a "bad feeling" is attributed to oneself, rather than to an object or other', and as such, the person is 'consumed by a feeling of badness that cannot simply be given away or attributed to another' (2014, p. 104). Ahmed notes that, in shame, if one tries to expel this 'bad feeling', they must expel themselves in some way (2014, p. 104). It is noteworthy, then, that Allen's speaker does not disavow the top, nor make a disparaging comment about anyone else (especially the person who has insulted her), but rather continues wearing the top and forges on with her class play, suggesting that the 'bad feeling' the speaker wants to expel is her feelings towards her class positioning (or, as she perceives it, her girlhood). While the speaker continues to parade her class play in an act of defiance, Allen suggests at the end of the poem that the older speaker understands that this has ultimately failed. The speaker remembers: 'all around me was *ooh ahh* and *de de da da da* and a tacky smell of sweets that could have been lipgloss or just as easily the encroaching ledge of age' (2014, p. 10). In these final lines, the speaker returns to the gaucherie Gina G's '(Ooh Ahh) Just a Little Bit'[14] and the tackiness of lipgloss, which reinstates her true girlhood and class positioning, and recognises that she will age. This seems like a retrospective comment from the speaker, for the first mention of age ('I thought thirty') is full of hope and the potential of aging – that is, how one might override their class position and be perceived as middle class. This second mention of the 'ledge of age' suggests something far less hopeful, a capitulation, where the (older) speaker understands that age will not enable 'respectability', as Skeggs puts it,[15] for the speaker will always be perceived as – and perceive herself as – working class.

Race as a dynamic of class is more explicit in 'Wallpapers/General', in which people in a shop 'go hell-for-leather arguing for the poppy print or Arabic mezzanine market scene' (2016, p. 203), moving the act of finding a 'wallpaper' for one's computer to a literalised context, in which one physically shops for images for one's home. Immediately, Allen works with ideas of respectability and subjectivity, thinking about how people behave in public spaces. As Collins notes in her essay about the poem for *PracCrit* (2015), the poem 'hinges on the pervasive threat of disturbance', as a 'couple can't decide between the snowdrop pinned back canvas and the pastoral shepherd walker backed on to wood' (Allen, 2016, p. 203) and people are 'man-handling receipts and staff' (Allen, 2016, p. 203). Collins argues: 'The picturesque "Arabic mezzanine market scene", and those featuring a "pastoral shepherd walker", snowdrops and poppies, are all presented as untenable idylls' (2015).

However, I think there are more complex ideas about race and class at play here, especially if I take that Allen assumes that her readers are white and middle class, and her poems reflect a sense of understanding that bodies and the home are where 'respectability is displayed but where class is lived out as the most omnipresent form, engendering surveillance and constant assessment' (Skeggs, 2002). Skeggs notes how working-class women evaluate their own 'buying and creative practices' on the 'basis of the imagined judgements of others'; as such, the women are 'positioned by their furniture and paint' (2002). As Skeggs explains, the pleasure the women should gain from decorating their homes is

56 Whiteness, Feminism and the Absurd in Contemporary Poetry

'always disrupted by the knowledge of a judgemental external other' (2002) – that is, the white middle class. In one of Skeggs's interviews, a participant named Janet states: 'I know you're meant to have real paintings on your wall, but I love these prints' (2002), and so the pictures one places on one's walls become indicative of one's class, and how the middle class might also perceive one's class. To have 'real paintings' is indicative of a middle-class identity, while having 'prints', like the ones in Allen's poem, is indicative of a working-class identity, especially when those prints might be tacky. The dolphin which 'punctures a sunset' (2016, p. 203) is a perfect example of how 'all the boundaries and potentials of the speaker's experience reside in the commodities with which she identifies and which identify her' (Whalley, 2014).

The prints are images of whiteness. The poppy has come to symbolise a resurgence in British nationalism (Edwards, 2018) and, in a more troubling move, has been adopted by xenophobic and racist organisations such as Britain First (Mayne, 2016). As Owen Jones writes, 'All too often, the common image of a working-class Briton is someone who is male, middle-aged, straight, white, lives in a small town and holds socially conservative views' (2020), so the poppy here might stand in for a stereotype of white working-classness. So, too, does the 'Arabic mezzanine market scene' sit uncomfortably as an orientalising and exoticising image (Saïd, 1979; Oshinsky, 2004; Kuehn, 2014) – the 'Arabic' scene is decontextualised, idealised (as Collins suggests) and vague. The image of the 'pastoral shepherd walker' evokes a harkening back to an imagined ideal of a peaceful countryside (Alpers, 1996, p. 89), and also suggests a scene of idealised whiteness, in which, as Paul Cloke and Jo Little write, there is a vision of 'rural life which clearly excludes a host of "others" from a supposed countryside hegemony based on [. . .] a certain conservative Englishness' (1997). The prints thereby become metonyms for stereotypes of whiteness and white working-classness, and, in assuming her reader is (generally) white and middle class, Allen reiterates the 'looked-at-ness' and subjectivity of the white working class. The prints and the precarious equilibrium of the shop suggest a chance for disorder, for norms to be upturned. Allen puts the prints – whiteness and working-classness – upfront, challenging her white, middle-class reader to *really* look at them, in an attempt to make the reader aware of their own assumptions and prejudices, or indeed how the working class more broadly experience real or imagined judgements. As Richard Dyer writes, 'White people need to learn to see themselves as white, to see their particularity. In other words, whiteness needs to be made strange' (2017, p. 10).

The poem splits with a stanza break at the moment the dolphin 'punctures' the sunset, suggesting that Allen is puncturing these assumptions, and sending the poem into new territory. The poem shifts dramatically here, and the speaker remembers when she and her father were also shopping for prints. The speaker suggests they purchase a 'poster with the Ganja leaf on it' which will 'look great by the fluoro fish tank where we keep the chinchilla' (2016, p. 203). Allen subverts the reader's expectations of what a 'respectable' father–daughter relationship should look like, with the speaker suggesting they purchase an illicit poster – something even worse, perhaps, than the aforementioned prints. Collins identifies the speaker as an older version of the 'daughter' (2015), and so there is a sense of the speaker communicating her shame or 'wrongness' of her childhood through the way the pet chinchilla is being kept in a 'fluoro fish tank', which mirrors Skeggs's assertion that 'class becomes internalized as an intimate form of subjectivity, experienced as knowledge of always not being "right"' (2002). Collins asserts that the poem enacts a 'move from a desire for SFW to NSFW images'[16] which signals 'a young girl's development, dropping "the pretence" of innocence' (2015). The speaker instructs her younger self: 'don't drop the pretence' (2016, p. 203), but this is ultimately futile, as the daughter's maturity – the desire for the 'Ganja leaf' poster – and her sexuality become pronounced. In the final lines of the poem, the speaker instructs her younger self to 'say, I would like a spiky dog collar but made of rubber because I like the smell daddy' (2016, p. 203). This is a jarring end to the poem, in which the speaker pronounces her sexuality, and suggests an almost incestuous leaning to this, requesting the dog collar from her father. The use of 'daddy' is at once girlish and sexualised.

The white, working-class woman's body is, as Skeggs notes, 'often represented as out of control' and 'vulgar, pathological, tasteless and sexual' (2002). This is reinforced by the 'couple' in Allen's poem, who are looking at the 'snowdrop pinned back canvas and the pastoral shepherd' (2016, p. 203), which, while not entirely 'respectable', are at least more respectable than the Ganja leaf poster and thereby the speaker. As Lori Jo Marso writes, marriage (or as Skeggs contends, heterosexuality (2002)) is coupled with respectability; 'to be married is to practice legitimate and appropriate sex' (2010, p. 148). As such, the speaker's declaration of her sexuality to her father is taboo and not respectable. 'Wallpapers/General' points to this dynamic of white, working-class womanhood and sexuality, and in doing so returns to the 'looked-at-ness' and prejudices that she highlights to her presumed reader. When the reader looks at working-class women,[17] they do not see someone 'respectable' (Skeggs, 2002). Allen takes this assumption of sexuality and vulgarity, and flaunts her speaker's sexuality in an act that rejects the shame this should induce, directing the assumption back at the (presumed) white, middle-class reader.

58   *Whiteness, Feminism and the Absurd in Contemporary Poetry*

In assuming such a readership, Allen begins the work of making the presumed reader interrogate themselves. Allen does not explicitly refer to the internet in this poem, but the situating of the poem under the umbrella of *4chan Poems* is important. If, as Whalley asserts, this is a positioning that thinks about confession and a platform known for its racist, misogynist posts, then Allen is speaking back to these posts with her own (or her speakers' own) 'confessions' to an audience that will be, largely speaking, white and middle class, about the immutability of class and gender, and also obliquely of race. 'Rapidshares' and 'Wallpapers/General' suggest that, for Allen's speakers, one of the main struggles of connection can be through class and race – attempting to engage with a respectability politics that might allow one to be accepted as white and middle class, and having that opportunity denied. This does not mean that I nor Allen suggest that one should always be trying to escape one's working-classness, but rather that Allen's poems provide a space in which to think about the idea of 'respectability' and how class and race are read. This is not to say that all the poems in the *4chan Poems* sequence deal with whiteness, although there is certainly an interrogation or illumination of class and girlhood in many of them. Allen's poems offer an example of how the Absurd, through its concerns of miscommunication, technology and the inability to connect, can interrogate gender, class and whiteness at once.

Cuteness, Connection and White Masculinity

In his poem 'Dear Racist in the Queue at Tesco', white British poet Kieran Goddard imagines that the speaker confronts a racist person, telling them: 'You are so stupid, I You don't deserve skin' (2013). The speaker imagines elaborate methods to punish the person for being racist, including steaming the racist's 'flesh loose', peeling it 'off your bones', making 'a paper plane from it' and flying it back into the racist's 'stupid skinless face' (2013). This litany of punishments reflects the speaker's anger as they rile against the titular racist, and also suggests a deterioration in their ability to produce 'clever' insults as their anger increases. Goddard ends the poem on its most successful insult, which extrapolates being kicked by a lame horse to it dying of hatred for the titular racist:

> You are a flat rugby ball, being kicked by a lame horse.
> You rode a horse to work once,
> It hated you so much it died in protest.
> It just sat there and died. (2013)

Miscommunication and Failure to Connect in the Absurd **59**

Unlike Allen's poems above, the reader is not invited into the dynamic of the poem, or asked to question their own stance. Goddard does not move the poem to a moment of emotional devastation or resonance for the reader – so the reader learns nothing about the poem's speaker, or themselves. 'Dear Racist in the Queue at Tesco' is, in a sense, too comfortable. The reader naturally aligns themselves with the speaker: he is right; the titular racist is wrong and unintelligent because they are racist. The gaucherie and jokes are aimed at one person, who is ultimately unidentifiable, and so there is nothing of a challenge to the reader or the speaker.

The reader is, in fact, waiting for the delivery of a destabilising demotic, one that will ultimately reveal something uncomfortable about the speaker and society more broadly – a shift that exposes whiteness, the speaker's own racism or the foibles behind his anger – but it does not arrive. The deteriorating insults suggest some destabilisation might be coming, but it is unconsummated. When Goddard's speaker rails against the titular racist, he is, perhaps, creating an imaginary 'other' who needs defending from this racism. Goddard's poem feels unsatisfactory because it does not look at the reader – or itself – honestly.

For Nuar Alsadir, honesty and laughter are closely linked: in certain types of laughter, we find an utterance humorous not because the speaker has been funny but because they have been honest (2022, p. 12). Alsadir writes that we often 'put forward a façade – what Winnicott termed the "False Self"', which is 'built around manners and protocol as opposed to spontaneous expression' and 'flies beneath the radar in order to ensure the survival of the True Self' (2022, pp. 4–5). However, the clown 'gets up before an audience and risks letting whatever is inside seep out' (2022, p. 15). Much in the way that Masud thinks of flat style as registering and neutralising 'the mortification of being caught in necessary postures of unoriginality' through melodrama (2022, p. 13), the speakers in white British poet Crispin Best's pamphlet *Faber New Poets 14* and his debut collection, *Hello*, are clowns who remove the façade and let a version of a 'true self' leak out, especially when that truth is humiliating. However, the 'true selves' Best's speakers reveal are not necessarily honest – they are *performing* honesty.

Technology appears sparsely in *Faber New Poets 14*, and when it is mentioned, it largely ignores social media: there are emails, microwaves, texting and a fax machine (2016, pp. 17, 18). In his debut collection, *Hello* (2019), many of the poems from *Faber New Poets 14* reappear, with slight edits, and yet the sense of remove from social media remains, as though the poems themselves were taking place *on* social media, reimagining the language and form of a meme. I take 'meme' to mean a joke (usually with an image or video) that is imitated with variations

60   *Whiteness, Feminism and the Absurd in Contemporary Poetry*

and spread quickly and widely by social media users; as Alice Marwick states, memes 'encourage a type of iteration, imitation, parody, and satire that can spawn literally thousands of variants' (2013, p. 13). Marwick additionally notes Lior Shifman's comments that memes 'harness what are really "key logics" [. . .] of online culture: sociability, replicability, and participation' (2013, p. 13). Indeed, Best seems to be using the 'sociability' of social media and a paucity of technology in his poems to highlight a distinct lack of connection for his speakers: all their attempts to communicate are thwarted.

In his poem, 'i am a wildman in a white sweater at work for you'[18] (later 'in a white sweater at work for you') the speaker states that he is 'nearer to a fax machine that i have ever been before' (Best, 2016, p. 17) and recalls a series of office stereotypes to explain his feelings:

> so watch me minimise firefox sitting in a swivel chair for you
> bent and straightened beside the water cooler
> eating soup at my desk at my desk
> my doleful finger in so much phone cord
>
> [. . .]
>
> i am most beautiful while printing out emails
> and yes when i think of you i am hard at work (2016, p. 17)

There is undoubtable gaucherie in this poem: the speaker's awkward motions by the water cooler, and the boring lunch he eats. The repetition of 'at my desk' suggests a sort of glitch or sense of recurrence as each day passes by in a similar way. The speaker is able to connect with people through faxes and emails, and the futility of printing out emails exacerbates the feelings of failure in communication. Moreover, he can only contact his love interest through 'six minutes wild texting in a toilet cubicle' (2016, p. 18). Even then, they are physically separate, and his attempts at flirting are graceless; the double entendre of 'i am hard at work' is deliberately cringeworthy. By implementing something so mundane as office work to declare love, Best creates a poem that is seated in the banal and the painfully humorous way the speaker attempts to impress his love interest. Fundamentally, Best's poem is about unrequited love *at work*. Notably, the speaker is alone in the office throughout the poem. Colleagues do not appear or interact with him, adding another layer to the speaker's inability to connect with others, as though they are not really there.

Importantly, the workplace is a key space in which men's 'gender identities are constructed, compared and evaluated by self and others'

Miscommunication and Failure to Connect in the Absurd   61

(Collinson and Hearn, 1996, p. 63), and so I now want to explore how Best's poem might be considering masculinity. Masculinity is not, as Jonathan Rutherford writes, a 'fixed, coherent and singular identity'; it is determined by race and class (1996, p. 22). In her study of 'masculine' humour in the workplace, Barbara Plester explains that 'hegemonic masculinity' is 'a fantasy of masculinity [that] is not embodied by all men', and is 'not assumed to be normal but it is normative' (2015, p. 541). As such, for men to conform to a hegemonic masculinity, they must 'distance themselves from both femininity and homosexuality' by 'displaying overtly heterosexual [. . .] behaviour' (2015, p. 541).

Baker and Levon describe two types of hegemonic white British masculinity: the 'new man', who is a more 'sensitive, caring and anti-sexist type of man', and is a result of a 'more general societal acceptance of broadly feminist principles'; and the 'new lad', who attempts to 'reassert male dominance via the privileging of an imagined traditional and "authentic" masculinity based on sexism, homophobia and avoidance of any traits or behaviours deemed "unmanly"' (2016, p. 108). Crucially, both types of masculinity – or man – are implicitly viewed as white and thereby white masculinity is an unmarked norm (2016, p. 110). This therefore casts the display of anti-racism in Goddard's 'Dear Racist in the Queue at Tesco' in another light: Goddard's speaker is the 'new man', shaped by broadly feminist and anti-racist principles, but his shift into a violent register – threatening the titular racist – causes him to behave in a more normative manner. Still, Goddard's poem does not overtly destabilise this sense of masculinity, showing how either (or both) might be flawed – the poem is at once didactic without being emotionally directive.

In 'i am a wildman in a white sweater at work for you', the speaker's gaucherie and failed attempts at flirting create a sense of 'cuteness', as though the speaker is endearingly awkward. In their article 'Positions of Cute in Post-Internet Poetry', Lucy Burns and Charles Whalley write: 'The cute object, in its demand for care, exerts power over us, we who should be in control, a power that we submit to readily' (2018). Indeed, they note Sianne Ngai's writing on cuteness and explain that 'the experience of cuteness is matched by the immediate suspicion that "we judge things cute all too easily;" it is a trick to undercut our judgement with such an easy emotional response, or so it can feel' (2018). As such, the gauche admissions of emotion in Best's poem feels simultaneously genuine and suspicious – as Sofia Leiby writes, in poetry, 'what is sincere is not opposite to what is ironic' (2011). Best undermines ideas of authority and authenticity in his poetry by creating 'cute' speakers who on the surface helplessly fail to navigate interpersonal relationships, and reject a normative masculinity.

62 *Whiteness, Feminism and the Absurd in Contemporary Poetry*

Yet the speaker's cute awkwardness is undermined, and a dark *peripeteia* is constructed when he asks, 'what right now are the different ways i can hurt myself' and pointedly mentions: 'we are on the fifth floor with an unstopped window | yes ma'am the projector's plenty heavy at that height' (Best, 2016, p. 17). The speaker's suicidal thoughts might be genuine, or a reflection of the helplessness he feels in discussing unrequited love. Regardless, Best's *peripeteia* surprises the reader by refiguring the speaker as someone who might be capable of causing themselves harm through explicitly violent (if not hyperbolic) measures. The speaker's perceived 'cuteness' and gaucherie are undermined, and revealed to be a performance. Interestingly, this stanza is changed significantly in the version published in *Hello*: the speaker still declares his intention to hurt himself, but the mention of the unstopped window and projector is removed. In both versions of the poem, the speaker states: 'the strings that control these blinds might take my weight at the neck' (2016, p. 18; 2019, p. 87) so the threat of violence is still apparent, and the speaker's *peripeteia* still serves as a moment where the 'cuteness' is pulled back.

This suggests that when the speaker's 'new man' masculinity fails, he – like Goddard's speaker – turns to a more normative, violent masculinity, even if he (and Goddard's speaker) render this gauchely. Indeed, Best's speaker might only be gesturing, but the threat remains. Sally Robinson explains how the 'logic through which the bodily substitutes for the political, and the individual for the social and institutional' suggests that the '"marking" of whiteness and masculinity has already been functioning as a strategy through which white men negotiate the widespread critique of their power and privilege' (2000, p. 6). As such, the 'display of wounds and of male suffering is central to elaborations of a crisis in white masculinity' (2000, p. 13). In Best's poem, then, the speaker threatens violence against himself – wanting to make the 'wound' visible – when his attempts at non-normative masculinity fail to allow him to connect to his love interest or any of his colleagues. Best's speaker lives in a world devoid of contact and connection, and so he must make this wound apparent, thereby demonstrating how masculinity (which is undeniably a white masculinity) – both normative and non-normative – cannot hold answers, because the workplace, as Mac an Ghaill, Rutherford and Plester note, requires an already shifting sense of masculinity, one that might be very different from the kind needed with a love interest (which will also shift based on the love interest). But suicide is not, as Camus writes in *The Myth of Sisyphus* (1955), a 'revolt' against the Absurd – it is, rather, 'acceptance at its extreme'. Best is holding a mirror up to these kinds of nihilistic thought, critiquing them and suggesting that – as Camus does – we must acknowledge the absurdity of life to work past it.

Miscommunication and Failure to Connect in the Absurd   **63**

Best's poetry returns to dynamics of masculinities, highlighting their gaucherie and threat, which in turn highlights their ridiculousness. Yet there is a sense of whiteness being latent throughout: it is central to the formation of these masculinities, but not yet articulated or prodded as in Allen's work. In 'they are building a building' (renamed 'is it still brunch if i am alone' in *Hello*), the speaker dreams that he 'found out that my dad I was a wheelie bin' (2016, p. 5):

> and i hugged the wheelie bin
> and my mum said
> 'not that wheelie bin'
> but i stayed hugging it (2016, p. 5)

At first, Best calls masculinity into question, since the speaker does not know his father, and believes that his father is an inanimate object – one that is, pointedly, full of rubbish. The speaker therefore does not have a model of masculine behaviour to re-enact, and is marked by his father's absence, and longs for connection. Best then transposes this need for connection into another situation of unrequited love; the speaker asks the poem's addressee: 'when i asked if things are serious I with your new boyfriend I did you say you are just dating I or gestating' (2016, p. 5). The joke ('just dating I or gestating') indicates the speaker's awkwardness in speaking to the woman, and his failure in being able to connect with her in the way he wants. A few lines before this, the speaker declares, in a bathetic demotic: 'there are things i have I been confused about II there are things about which I i have been confused' (2016, p. 5). This is a tricky moment in the poem: do we take the speaker's 'confusion' as genuine, or a ploy in which to catch the addressee out, and ask her an uncomfortable question about her boyfriend? Is the speaker genuinely confused, or only pretending to be? Might he be expressing a greater sense of existential dread *through* his relationship to masculinity and unrequited love?

Throughout the poem, the speaker pronounces a series of things he 'wants' for the addressee: 'i wish for you butterflies in the airport' (2016, p. 6); 'i wish for you birds I to find an uninflated balloon in your pocket' (2016, p. 7). The bizarre 'cuteness' of the things the speaker wishes for the woman push the poem further into gaucherie, moving the poem from romantic longing (a clear emotional gesture) into the bizarre and unreadable. Here, the speaker is amazed by simple occurrences in the everyday world, and communicates his feelings by imagining all the things that astound him in almost childlike wonder. Yet the speaker also appeals – in an admittedly gauche manner – to normative masculinity by using his physical strength: 'i have crushed cans I while

64 *Whiteness, Feminism and the Absurd in Contemporary Poetry*

thinking of you' (2016, p. 6). He also undermines these appeals again: 'i have also cradled I a croissant I like a baby I so' (2016, p. 6). As Rutherford suggests, to become 'an acceptable masculine man means adopting values of male superiority', but these ideals are no longer reassuring, and there 'is increasingly a note of hysteria about them' (1996, p. 24). Best's speaker constantly destabilises his masculinity, moving from normative masculine behaviours to non-normative behaviours, which are self-consciously bizarre.

The speaker also reflects on life more existentially, noting 'i have been thinking I about the time the universe I was the size of a cantaloupe' (2016, p. 5) and repeatedly exclaiming 'oh my'. The repetition of 'oh my' suggests wonder or amazement at the world, as though it is too impressive to comprehend, and as he continues to 'wish' for his love interest, he tries to connect to and understand the world. It is my contention that this relates quite clearly to the Absurd's fascination with existential dread. Love is unrequited and masculinity indecipherable in Best's poems because, while both might be ways for people to find meaning in the world, love and an 'acceptable' form of masculinity might be unobtainable. The reader understands that the world is completely beyond our comprehension. This is a central concept in the Absurd, and reflects Jean-Francois Lyotard's ideas of the postmodern condition and technological advances in contemporary society, which, Lyotard writes, have a 'considerable impact' on how 'knowledge' is exchanged (1984, p. 4); here, I interpret 'knowledge' in terms of communication, to mean how we relate to one another and understand ourselves. For Lyotard, the 'grand narrative' has lost its credibility (1984, p. 37), and in the Theatre of the Absurd, these grand narratives are 'the decline of religious belief' which deprives humankind 'of certainties' (Esslin, 2023, p. 339). In Best's poems, these grand narratives are love and masculinity.

In 'fao: barack obama', the speaker addresses forty-fourth US President Barack Obama. Appealing to Obama involves a complex layering of authority and destabilisation of that authority, because, as David W. Wise writes, 'as the first African American nominee of a major political party and then as president, Obama came into the office with pressures and expectations unique to that fact' (2019). While Obama held an official and important title at the time of 'fao: barack obama's' publication, his position itself has been constantly undermined and his policies criticised. While I do not have space here to legitimate or debunk these claims, criticisms aimed at Obama have related to him being positioned as a 'Magical Negro', who, as David Ehrenstein explains in the *Los Angeles Times*, is 'there to assuage white "guilt" [. . .] over the role of slavery and racial segregation in American history, while replacing stereotypes of a dangerous, highly sexualized black man with a benign figure for whom interracial sexual congress holds no interest' (2007). Obama has also been criticised for engaging in respectability politics (Harpalani, 2020), a term which refers to, as Frederick C. Harris writes, what began as 'a philosophy promulgated by black elites to "uplift the race" by correcting the "bad" traits of the black poor'[19] and grew, 'in the age of Obama' into a 'governing philosophy that centers on managing the behavior of black people left behind in a society touted as being full of opportunity' (2014, p. 33). Under respectability politics, 'the virtues of self-care and self-correction are framed as strategies to lift the black poor out of their condition by preparing them for the market economy' (Harris, 2014, p. 33). As Pitcan, Marwick and boyd write, emphasis on 'individual uplift' ignores structural inequalities, which cannot be changed by class status (2018, p. 164).

So, what is Best doing by appealing to Barack Obama in his poem? In his review of Best's pamphlet, Daniel Roy Connelly writes that, in the poem, 'the powerful appeal to political authority is undermined by the mundanity of the ensuing details' which exposes 'the absurdities of our time and our times' (2016, p. 42), but Connelly does not suggest, truly, what this means or what Best is trying to say. Perhaps British reviewing culture's overall reticence to discuss race in poetry is exemplified by the fact that several reviews of Best's pamphlet and *Hello* (Connelly, 2016; Malone, 2016; O'Brien, 2016; Rogers, 2020) focus on 'fao: barack obama' but do not explore why Best is appealing to Barack Obama. It may follow that appealing to Obama helps the speaker to assuage his 'white guilt' in the way Harris describes, but there is little to evidence this in the text. The appeal to Obama may suggest that Best is making an appeal to someone who has authority, but does not hold much threat – because they are 'respectable'. Perhaps it is that Obama embodies a masculinity that this speaker aspires to – authoritative, 'respectable', unthreatening – but this masculinity is ultimately out of reach.

The speaker expresses his existential dread to Barack Obama, asking 'what should i do | with my only life', explaining that 'at every turn | people find things quite unbelievable' (2016, p. 8). At the moment the speaker discusses existential concerns, they undermine the serious sentiment and appeal to authority (however complex) with an apparently gauche and underwhelming one, such as: 'caring about a person | is like asking a bagel | how to live' (2016, p. 8). What might seem like 'distraction', as Connelly puts it, is, I contend, a layered consideration of masculinity and systems of meaning. If we consider that Best's speaker is a 'new man', attempting to be in touch with his emotions, we can see that

66 *Whiteness, Feminism and the Absurd in Contemporary Poetry*

this system of identification falters – caring becomes futile. Throughout the poem, Best makes repeated comparisons between food and emotion: 'inviting a person to care about you is like I telling them "take a seat" I and pointing at a month-old pretzel'; 'caring about a person is like I praying to a doughnut in the darkness'; 'a custard pie in the face I of certain death' (2016, pp. 8, 9). The food – sugary, doughy – is inanimate, insubstantial and cannot communicate, and no longer a source of pleasure or comfort because it cannot communicate. Religion cannot offer solace either, because systems of belief have lost meaning: praying is a futile action because the speaker is praying to something that cannot listen and react or provide a sense of comfort.

The poem is undoubtedly nihilistic. Death is 'certain'; the speaker can only 'laugh' at the 'sheer I machinery of feelings', as though he cannot feel anything anymore (2016, p. 9). Everyday objects and experiences lose their significance and meaning, and ultimately leave the speakers and characters unable to connect with one another, with anything. This too, extends once again to masculinity, which is questioned and made ridiculous. The speaker opines:

> barack i cannot wait to have
> a son and tell him
> 'you're almost like a son to me'
> and then powerwalk away (2016, p. 8)

Here, Best creates a joke a comedian might tell mid-set as a digression from the main joke: it is underdeveloped, and likely to produce a kind of disbelieving laughter from the audience, which may explain why this stanza no longer appears in the version published in *Hello*. However, considering how this echoes the absent father in 'they are building a building', Best makes another attempt to destabilise received ideas about masculinity. This speaker re-enacts the abandonment in 'they are building a building', which undermines the father–son relationship twofold: not only is the son abandoned, but he is also just 'almost' like a son, so the emotional bond is not developed either. As such, the speaker cannot count on biological relationships, or emotional ones, to bring any meaning to the world.

In this sense, Best is also trying to show that appealing to Barack Obama is ultimately a futile act, too. World leaders cannot solve our problems, no matter their politics or promise, and so appealing to Barack Obama is as pointless as praying to a doughnut or bagel. 'fao: barack obama' was written in the shadow of the 2016 presidential election, where the potential (and eventual) election of Donald Trump signalled a swing towards right-wing politics (Müller, 2017; Wendling, 2018). So, then, Best's appeal to Obama is a kind of lament – for what might have been, but ultimately could not be, and what might be coming in the future. Yet it is impossible to notice that the most pertinent threat to the speaker is his own existential dread. In Britain, the speaker is relatively safe from Trump's presidency (although perhaps not the creep of right-wing politics), but, as a white man, he is far safer than those for whom Trump's policies have proven to have high-stakes consequences, including (intersectionally): women, transgender people, people of colour, immigrants and the working class (Oppenheimer et al., 2018; Clayton et al., 2019; Baker and Timm, 2021).[20] This is not to say that the speaker should not feel existential dread, or should not be concerned about politics and the impact that policies have on people in circumstances different from his own. Yet the existential dread the speaker experiences creates a sense of inertia; Best ends the poem with a final, nihilistic demotic: 'again and again the grass fills this useless space | between the ground and the air || and again' (2016, p. 9), which suggests a repetitive, looping, futile manner to the world.

Best is, however, ridiculing this sense of futility, and the privilege one needs to take such a pessimistic view. In an interview with Megan Nolan for *i-D*, Best comments: 'I feel like part of why the poems work is because people assume rightly or wrongly that it's all some kind of pose – some sort of high wire act of lowbrow' (2016). Here, Best suggests, archly, that he has tricked the reader into believing he is the naïve, cute and distracted speakers of his poems; he is cleverer than this, he states: 'I know what I'm doing [. . .] I'm confident enough that if it's twee, then that's what I was aiming for' (2016). Conversely, Connelly refers to Best as a 'manchild' in his review of the pamphlet (2016, p. 42), while Sean O'Brien characterises Best as 'bouncing Tiggerishly into view' and being 'full of beans' (2016) in his review for the *Guardian*. These infantilising comments suggest that Best's speakers' 'cuteness' has worked: the exuberance and gaucherie of the poems is memorable, while the darkness – and deeper meanings – fade into the background.

Perhaps Best's childlike speakers expose how respectability politics is forced onto people of colour, while white men are allowed to fall into gaucherie and despair. Best's speakers' vacillation between modes of masculinity only serve to highlight its ridiculousness, especially when considering the critical attention the *Faber New Poets 14* pamphlet received. As Nina Power writes, the male '"genius" typically possesses feminine characteristics – imagination, intuition, emotion, madness' but is not of course 'an actual woman: the great artist is a feminine male, but not a feminine female or a masculine female. Women can be mad, but not aesthetically inspired, or they can be sane, and provide comfort for the true creators, who are a little bit womanish, but not too much' (in Cooke, 2020, p. 84).

Perhaps, then, the speakers of Best's poems are at once bouncing through the world *and* fearing it, and that dichotomy is essential to understanding the politics of the poems: the distractions can only last so long. Once the speaker has catalogued all the wonders of the world – big or small – and has been distracted by them while other, terrible things are looming, he realises that there is little to put faith in, because he has put his faith in the wrong things. Best does not suggest where his speakers or readers might go with this revelation, and it appears that several readers and reviewers have missed this dynamic in his work, or are reticent to think about it – which raises questions about who the poems are for, and what they are for. Have Best's poems failed to be emotionally directive? In the interview with Nolan, Best admits that he does not see his writing as a means to 'connect with people' but that he wants to 'be useful to the world' (2016). Neither of these comments is unpacked, so it is not possible to take them truly at face value, but perhaps the usefulness Best is striving for is not yet developed in *Faber New Poets 14* or *Hello*; it is almost there, almost addressing an assumed (white, middle-class) reader-ship about its privilege and ignorance. The Absurd – as Allen's poetry shows – can be emotionally directive, political, if it is willing to firmly look at whiteness, to challenge its readers. But poets must also be aware of the overly emotionally directive poem: for there is nothing a reader hates more than being told what to think or do.

Chapter 3

The Apocalypse in the Absurd

In Chapter 2, I discussed how the Absurd is preoccupied with our failures to connect and communicate with one another, and how two white British poets have begun to use this concern to explore whiteness, class and gender. I examined ideas of 'emotionally non-directive' writing and how this is shaped by modern technology, as are contemporary poets' responses to questions about race, class and gender. In this chapter, I return to technology – specifically, cyborgs, androids and robots – to see how this features in contemporary Absurdist poetry's fascination with the apocalypse. In reading Samuel Beckett's *Endgame* (2006), Tom Stoppard's *Rosencrantz and Guildenstern are Dead* (1999) and Never Angeline Nørth's *Sara or the Existence of Fire* (2014), I demonstrate that death, repetition and 'ongoingness' are key elements of Absurdist apocalypses. Through reading Bennett's interpretation of Camus's 'The Myth of Sisyphus' (1955), I argue that contemporary Absurdist poetry suggests that we must learn to work with the Absurd and the apocalypse, rather than trying individually to make meaning of the world. Reading poems by Franny Choi, Morgan Parker, Jane Yeh and Jennifer L. Knox, I then show how Absurdist apocalyptic situations are symptomatic of feminist concerns of anxiety (Ahmed, 2014), and gender and racial inequality. I examine how the cyborg can speak to these inequalities and symbolise hopeful change; I also explore how the cyborg, robot and android can be representative of 'dangerous possibilities' (Haraway, 2016), and how poets invite their readers to consider their own attitudes to the apocalypse.

The Absurd, Death and the Apocalypse

According to Cornwell, the Absurd and nihilism are inextricably connected, with the Absurd being 'born of nihilism, out of existentialism, fuelled by the certainty of death (anxiety, dread and death being the scourge of the existentialist)' (2006, p. 5). Ideas of existentialism, of

70 *Whiteness, Feminism and the Absurd in Contemporary Poetry*

free-agency and choice, feature heavily in the Absurd. Eugene Ionesco suggests that 'cut off from his religious, metaphysical and transcendental roots, man is lost; all his actions become senseless, absurd, useless' (in Cornwell, 2006, p. 3). In this layering of anxiety, fear of death, loss of religion and loss of meaning, nihilism becomes apparent. Indeed, this is ostensible in Daniil Kharms's *Elizaveta Bam* (1927), in which the titular character locks herself in her room and is illogically detained for the murder of one of her arresting officers, Pyotr Nikolayevich, who is later killed by another character, 'Daddy', Elizaveta's father. The play ends with a repetition of the first scene, but this time, Elizaveta hands herself over to her arresters. The play is therefore indicative of the Theatre of the Absurd's use of looping time, repetitive storylines and futility in the face of power and bureaucracy.

These dynamics of looping situations and meaninglessness are no more evident than in Samuel Beckett's *Endgame*, first performed in 1957, and Tom Stoppard's *Rosencrantz and Guildenstern are Dead*, first performed in 1967, both plays widely considered as being indicative of the label 'Absurd'.[1] Beckett's *Endgame* is a tragicomic one-act play about a blind, elderly man named Hamm, his parents, Nagg and Nell, who live in barrels and do not have legs, and Clov, his companion. The characters live in an abandoned hut in a post-apocalyptic world ('Outside of here it's death', says Hamm (2006, p. 96)). Throughout, the characters make reference to the 'end' of something: 'It must be nearly finished', says Clov (2006, p. 93); 'It's time it ended' and 'Will this never finish?' says Hamm (2006, pp. 93, 103); 'It's always the same thing', says Nell (2006, p. 101). But the characters are caught in circular, repetitive actions and conversations: Clov threatens to leave Hamm, who is cruel to him, but cannot; Hamm keeps on returning to a story about taking in Clov as a child and berating his father; Nagg and Nell reminisce about their engagement and stories they have told one another time and time again. As such, time does not move in *Endgame*, and the characters are stuck in a purgatory where they cannot enact change, and fear whatever awaits them outside their home (almost certainly death). Nell dies during the play and is screwed into her barrel by Clov under Hamm's instruction – so there is truly no escape. Yet, as I noted in Chapter 2, death (or suicide) is, according to Camus, not an escape from the Absurd but a logical continuation of it (1955) – so, then, when characters express a fear of death, they are expressing a fear of the Absurd, and are placed in a logical bind: to truly be 'free', Camus writes, we must accept 'there is no future' (1955). This is a nihilist proposition, certainly, which points to apocalypse.

Rosencrantz and Guildenstern are Dead uses Shakespeare's *Hamlet* as its backdrop, following Rosencrantz and Guildenstern, who are old –

The Apocalypse in the Absurd   71

and now considered deceitful – friends of Hamlet. Prince Hamlet is banished to England by his uncle, Claudius, now King of Denmark, who has murdered Hamlet's father to obtain the throne. On a boat to England, Hamlet discovers a letter from Claudius, carried by Rosencrantz and Guildenstern, which commands that Hamlet be put to death upon his arrival in England. Hamlet rewrites the letter to order that Rosencrantz and Guildenstern be put to death instead, and then escapes back to Denmark. While ostensibly more plot-driven than *Endgame*, *Rosencrantz and Guildenstern are Dead* is characterised by circular conversations peppered with non-sequiturs, miscommunications and repetition. The title of the play acts ironically: the audience knows the titular characters will die before they do, so as the play opens, it seems as though Rosencrantz and Guildenstern are already dead (Cowart, 1994, p. 34) – it is fait accompli, and the audience is just watching it happen.

Once again, throughout the play, the pair contemplate death and the meaning of life. Guildenstern opines: 'The only beginning is birth and the only end is death – if you can't count on that, what can you count on?' and tells Rosencrantz that 'There's a logic at work – it's all done for you, don't worry. Enjoy it. Relax' (1999, p. 31), which is, seemingly, quite antithetical to the Absurd's nihilism. Later on, though, Guildenstern's belief takes on a more pessimistic bent: 'Wheels have been set in motion, and they have their own pace, to which we are . . . condemned'; he believes: 'If we happened, just happened to discover, or suspect, that our spontaneity was part of their order, we'd know that we were lost' (1999, p. 51).

According to Camus, before 'encountering the absurd, the everyday man lives with aims, a concern for the future', but after the absurd, 'the idea that "I am," my way of acting as if everything has a meaning' becomes impossible (1955). In other words, accepting the Absurd means accepting that there is no logic or meaning to the world, and encountering the Absurd means understanding that an apocalypse is nigh, either literally or in the sense that an individual cannot continue to live with such existential dread. As such, during the course of the play, the audience watches Rosencrantz and Guildenstern become aware of the absurdity (or Absurdity) of the world, and how death cannot offer respite or meaning either. As they face their death, Guildenstern notes that 'Death is not anything. [. . .] It's the absence of presence, nothing more', while Rosencrantz ponders, 'That's it, then, is it?' (1999, p. 117).

Through Camus's writing and Beckett and Stoppard's plays, we can see that the Absurd is preoccupied with death, with nihilism, with the end of the world. For Camus, death does not provide the answer, and the world, once the Absurd has been encountered, is meaningless.

72 Whiteness, Feminism and the Absurd in Contemporary Poetry

Yet Bennett's interpretation of Camus's thought offers another reading. Bennett argues that 'rebellion [from the Absurd] finds its justification in human solidarity in that suffering [. . .] is a collective experience in rebellion, for one must realize that he or she, in suffering, suffers like the rest of humanity' (2015, p. 42).[2] As such, this suffering, caused by the Absurd, rather than alienating the individual from others, in fact binds them together. The answer is not to *deny* the Absurd by trying to individually create meaning in one's life, but to rebel against it by *accepting* the Absurd into one's life and understanding that the Absurd causes suffering for all.

Indeed, as I wish to demonstrate in this chapter, contemporary British and US Absurdist poetry has turned towards the apocalypse to symbolise a shift towards eschewing neoliberal discourses about individual self-improvement and self-optimisation, as Fredrika Thelandersson writes, towards a concern for 'the wellbeing of the greater good' (2022, p. 17). The turn towards accepting the Absurd and striving for a better future must be set during apocalypses because, as Catherine Keller writes: 'We the denizens of Western postmodernity of many possible classes, races, or genders, cannot extricate ourselves from apocalypse' because 'we are in apocalypse: we are in it as a script that we enact habitually when we find ourselves at an edge' (1996, p. 13). In other words, for Keller, 'the apocalypse is both a state of affairs and an interpretation of that state of affairs' (1996, p. 13). The apocalypse and the Absurd are inextricably linked: both represent our current political climate, environmental concerns and an unwillingness to accept things as they are. Keller notes that the apocalypse 'provides a kind of kaleidoscope for cultural self-consideration' (1996: xiii), while Matt Wray writes that 'the onset of apocalyptic fantasies [. . .] signals a kind of resistance to mainstream culture and politics, offering a means of voicing protest against existing or emergent social orders' (1997, p. 194).

In her poetry collection *Sara or the Existence of Fire* (2014), white American poet Never Angeline Nørth ostensibly takes a nihilistic approach to the apocalypse, stating in an interview with Paul Cunningham for *Fanzine* that the collection's protagonist, Sara, 'is cynically resigning herself to the idea that she exists only to do the things she is already doing. Set up a life, realize she is still trapped, still miserable, and then burn it down' (2015). Nørth does note that Sara eventually 'moves to a place that's already burning' (2015), which suggests that Sara might, at times, accept the Absurd into her life. In her interview with Cunningham, Nørth notes that the collection is inspired by: 'being disgusted by your body (admittedly, in some pretty specific ways)', as this is 'pretty much criteria number one for being trans, and I think I

The Apocalypse in the Absurd   73

was channelling this in some more general ways throughout the book' (2014); as such, the collection can be read as a meditation on disgust and existential dread.

In the collection, Nørth makes several references to fire, or things being on fire (in fact, too many to count) and death. Fire is a character too: in 'Pets', the reader is told that 'Sara's first pet was a giant fire' (2014, p. 6). The fire is symbolic of Sara's desire for destruction: she feeds it 'things she didn't want, things she found around the house' (2014, p. 6). Indeed, Sara's house is often the site of devastation: Sara frequently burns it down or leaves at short notice. In 'Flies', Nørth creates nightmarish scenes, utilising plague-like imagery to destroy Sara's home, which becomes infested with flies 'pouring through the windows in numbers like she's never seen before' (2014, p. 34). Sara's dog, her one true, stable companion, dies, 'suffocated after one of the large flies muscled its way into his mouth' (2014, p. 34). Horrifyingly, Sara cannot 'even see his body after he died because of the flies on her eyeballs, pushing up under the insides of her eyelids' (2014, p. 34). The plague-like descending of the flies is unexplained and excessive, and the flies are attracted – as in real life – to what is dying, or decomposing. Nørth suggests that Sara's world is in fact Hell: the flies certainly recall Beelzebub, Lord of the Flies (Matthew 12:24, 27; Mark 3:22; Luke 11:15, 18); Sara cannot escape from the cycles of destruction; there is fire everywhere; and she cannot stop the annihilation of herself or her dog. Perhaps Sara is already dead.

There is a clear mirroring of *Endgame* and *Rosencrantz and Guildenstern Are Dead* here – ambiguity over the apocalypse or death, and characters futilely struggling against it. However, at the end of the poem, Sara capitulates: 'She gave up and let herself hang there, upright and limp in what used to be her kitchen but now was just flies' (2014, p. 34). At this moment, Sara accepts the inevitability of the Absurd. So, she does not 'die', for death does not offer a solution, but accepts the perpetual nature of her torture, which, Nørth explains in her interview with Cunningham, is a key theme in the collection (2015).[3] I do not necessarily take, then, that Sara's existence is inevitably nihilistic when she chooses to accept the Absurd. Certainly, hers is an existence of repetition and destruction, but Sara benefits (even if marginally) when she capitulates, rather than trying to resist. In 'Wreaths', the poem directly after 'Flies', Sara ages at an incredibly slow rate, hanging a wreath on her front door daily 'every day for 100 years' (2014, p. 35). After a thousand years, Sarah burns 'down her house' and drifts down a river (2014, p. 35), seemingly escaping her torture. But not quite: while she is drifting, she thinks only about wreaths (2014, p. 35). As in *Endgame* and *Rosencrantz and Guildenstern Are Dead*, death is not a certainty,

74 *Whiteness, Feminism and the Absurd in Contemporary Poetry*

and does not create meaning. Nørth hints that Sara might finally die at the end of 'Wreaths', but her torture begins again in the next poem, 'Hair Dream', in which Sara has a nightmare about her 'childhood bedroom' (2014, p. 36), setting her back to the beginning of her life.

In 'Ending', which mirrors *Endgame* most ostensibly, Sara wonders 'What happens if nothing ends?' (2014, p. 63) and becomes overwhelmed by the world and what she cannot explain; as she does so, punctuation becomes scarce, and so systems of meaning and language break down also. However, like Sara and her dog have before, the speaker regenerates and appears in the next poem, and 'Ending' resists its title. The apocalypses Nørth imagines for Sara do not seem to offer satisfactory solutions to gender dysphoria or bodily disgust (Sara is constantly reborn into her body), nor to Sara's feelings of alienation from her family. In 'Bones', Sara imagines killing her family during Thanksgiving, an act which demonstrates Sara's need for annihilation, and how she wants to feel destruction and death inside her body in an attempt to understand herself, even in a damaging way. But this revenge fantasy does not offer hope or change, and Nørth thereby reinforces Camus's ideas about death and the incomprehensibility of the world: trying to resist the Absurd in an individualistic way is futile; one needs to work with it, and accept that others suffer too. Killing her family members does not alleviate Sara's suffering, because she has not acknowledged the ubiquitous absurdity of the world. Of course, it is not Nørth's responsibility (nor Sara's) to solve issues about transgender rights and acceptance in a world positioned against her – this cannot be an individual responsibility. Nørth's poems offer the possibility that individual suffering is meaningless, but acknowledging collective suffering and accepting the Absurd into one's life may offer a way out.

The Internet, Cyborgs and the Apocalypse

The internet sits ambivalently in feminist theory and criticism: Evans notes the positive consequences of technology for feminism, including 'space for virtual forums' and 'introducing feminist debates and campaigns to a wider audience' (2015, p. 3). She also recognises the ramifications of the internet, stating that women are 'increasingly aware of the insidious ways in which technology makes the sexual objectification of women's bodies impossible to ignore' and that the internet 'has been an important site for anti-feminist rhetoric and abuse' (2015, pp. 66, 75).

Perhaps one of the most memorable controversies in British contemporary poetry centres around Oliver Thring's 2016 *Sunday Times* article, in which he discussed Chinese-British poet Sarah Howe's T.S. Eliot Prize-winning poetry collection, *Loop of Jade* (2015). On Twitter (now X), Thring was criticised for his dismissive approach to Howe's poetry and for describing Howe as 'sixth-formy' in her 'intelligence' (Evans-Bush, 2016). When people – particularly women – began to criticise Thring and his article by directly tweeting him or 'mentioning' him in a tweet, he responded: 'This gentle interview with a leading young poet has led various deranged poetesses to call me thick, sexist etc.' (2016). By calling women 'deranged poetesses', Thring corroborated views that he was being sexist, delegitimising women's experiences and emotional reactions as 'unreasonable' or 'crazy' (Thelandersson, 2022, p. 19). To satirise and undermine Thring, a globally trending hashtag, '#derangedpoetess', was created.

It is therefore apparent that the internet, particularly social media, does not always provide a 'safe space', but it does, when needed, provide women with a chance to 'speak out' against the kind of misogynistic vitriol that is common on social media. Once women began to challenge or ridicule Thring, several men jumped to his defence. Twitter user @anukasan1977 responded to poets Sandeep Parmar and Amy Key: '@SandeepKParmar @msamykey She won a top literary prize for the political platitudes she represents. Reductive yet accurate.#derangedpoetess' (23 January 2016). One of the main arguments of Thring's supporters was that Howe's win suggested a bias towards to people of colour; in an anonymous letter to *Private Eye*, a contributor wrote that Howe's win was due to 'extra-poetic reasons': 'As a successful and very "presentable" young woman with a dual Anglo-Chinese heritage, Howe can be seen as a more acceptable ambassador for poetry than the distinguished grumpy old men she saw off' (21 January 2016). The negative reaction to Howe's win was a layered attack of misogyny and racism. As such, the internet is an ambivalent space: at once used for community and connection, and also a space in which gendered and racial attacks are conducted, even within the supposedly progressive locus of the arts and literature.

Contemporary Absurdist poets have responded to these ideas about gender and race through depicting apocalypses centred around cyborgs, androids and robots,[4] which have come to stand in for a range of contemporary anxieties. As Keller writes, apocalypse 'rages out of the bitter heart of systemic suffering' and 'anxiety' (1996, p. 85). We are, as Sarah Dunant and Roy Porter claim, living in an age of anxiety, and this is likely caused by 'unprecedented expansion of everything from technology through communication to shopping' (in Ahmed, 2014, pp. 71, 72). With this unprecedented expansion comes 'increased demands of choice (in itself something of an anxiety)', and an 'expanding potential for feeling out of control' (Ahmed, 2014, p. 72). This, according to Ahmed, creates a 'loss of certainty about the future' (2014, p. 72). Capitalist growth, expansion and development in technology are at the centre of this anxiety, which is, as Thelandersson writes, 'the dominant affect that holds contemporary capitalism together, and [. . .] functions to control and maintain the unequal status quo' (2022, p. 189).

Evans notes that the cyborg was originally meant to symbolise a 'post-gender world', and that the internet, it was thought, would create a 'shift in our conceptualisation of gendered identities' (2015, p. 17). Yet, as Meiya Sparks Lin writes, many cyborgs are written or visualised as female and Asian, and become a 'pleasure/horror object for white American consumption' (2022, p. 6). Donna Haraway posits that a cyborg represents 'transgressed boundaries, potent fusions, and dangerous possibilities' (2016, p. 14), and while I think the cyborg continues to stand in for these things (and will return to these ideas later), I want to follow Sparks Lin's assertion that Haraway's cyborg 'fails to take into account racialized cyborgs whose identity is not a choice but a trope' (2022, p. 22), and to think about how the cyborg comes to represent the politics of race, gender and technology.

Korean-American poet Franny Choi's collection *Soft Science* (2019) explores the relationship between race, gender and technology through a series of speakers who are cyborgs. These cyborgs are coded as Asian, as they so often are in popular culture, a positioning that embodies Techno-Orientalism, as Sparks Lin writes, in which 'hypertechnological imaginings of Asia, often manifested as speculative representations of a future in which technology is the method with which Asia secures both cultural and economic domination' (2022, p. 9). The coding is also racially gendered, in that portraying Asian women as robots or cyborgs intensifies racist and misogynistic stereotypes in which Asian woman are 'fetishized as naturally hypersexual and submissive', and paradoxically 'at once distinctly hyperfeminized and deprived of womanhood' (Sparks Lin, 2022, p. 10). In Choi's 'The Price of Rain', the cyborg's sexuality is considered a public knowledge and right, and the cyborg feels caught in this expectation of sex, believing it to have social value. 'no man has taken anything | I didn't give him' (2019, p. 23), the cyborg realises, noting: 'I thought, | if I lay my legs on the altar, I thought something | would come back to me' (2019, p. 23). The cyborg's admission, 'my wet was in | the common domain', demonstrates how submission and sex for the Asian woman and the Asian cyborg alike are bound together – and, also, that technology (signalled by 'domain') is a key part of this.

The speaker's repetition of 'I thought' mimics a glitch, and, elsewhere, this glitching language comes to the forefront of Choi's poetics as a way to explore race and gender. In 'Turing Test_Problem Solving',

The Apocalypse in the Absurd   **77**

a cyborg is repeatedly told '*if you don't like it here why don't you go somewhere else*' (2019, p. 53), a demotic that chillingly recalls a racist cry for immigrants and anyone who is not white to 'go home'. This line of questioning causes the speaker to break down into self-hatred: 'my stupid | stupid need / my country / my cunt / i hate it why won't / it work / why won't / | my country / my country / my country / my country' (2019, p. 54). Here, the speaker's relationship to gender and race become entangled, so that 'cunt' and 'country' come to symbolise herself. As 'my country' repeats line after line, it becomes apparent that these are at once *everything* to the speaker and also mean nothing, for she will never truly be a woman or have a 'home' in the eyes of those who perceive her.[5]

Choi also uses the voice of Kyoko, a robot from the 2014 film *Ex Machina* (directed by Alex Garland). In the film, Nathan Bateman, the CEO of a search engine company, creates robots with women's appearances: Kyoko, his servant (who apparently is mute) and appears to be Japanese,[6] and Ava, who looks white and is confined to a separate apartment. The race and gender politics here are evident: Bateman designs his robots to look like those who have less power in a patriarchal society, especially one that privileges whiteness. It is no accident that Kyoko is the servant, designed to be a 'less intelligent' type of robot, and cannot communicate with Ava or others – Bateman retracts her ability to communicate by ensuring that she cannot speak the same language as everyone else in his house. Moreover, as both robots have the appearance of women, Bateman feels he is able to exert power over them, and so his visitor, Caleb, feels that he must rescue them. *Ex Machina* foregrounds ideas of gender stereotypes – that the 'women' robots are helpless and find a saviour in Caleb – only to subvert them into another trope, by having Ava and Kyoko kill Bateman (and, by extension, Caleb) in order to escape and live life in the real world. Caleb is convinced of Ava's need to be rescued because she is sexualised – she is attractive, and flirts with him – and thereby convinces him of her 'humanity'. While Ava seems human, or 'sophisticated', she appears to be so because of her supposed sexuality, her whiteness and her ability to speak English.

In an early poem, 'AI v.2.1', published before *Soft Science* and then excluded from its publication,[7] Choi uses Kyoko's voice to explicitly link technology, race and sex:

whats a mouth for	what hand	whats a tongue:	slug machine
who chases	whose mouth flaps	saliva spit	whose fists
pliers plowing	screw drivers	seeking: warm	skin-like
eyes saying yes	but not saying		whats a mouth for
clitless soft, trigger	whose weapon	whose knife	fish flesh (2015)

The repeated questioning suggests a cyborg trying to understand the world quickly, a series of progressively sexualised and violent images flitting before her eyes. The opening questions suggest that the speaker is attempting to understand her body – what *use* does it have? – and progressively begins to comprehend that her mouth is useless – it 'flaps' and spits saliva (if it truly can), producing nothing of meaning; she sees herself as a 'slug machine' – in other words, disgusting. This self-view is borne from the way the world perceives her, the way she has been taught to perceive herself: she is 'clitless' – *her* pleasure does not matter – and her eyes must say 'yes', even if she does not consent. Alongside this, the mentions of a knife, 'screw drivers', 'pliers plowing' (the puns of 'screwing' and 'ploughing' are hard to ignore) and 'weapon' mix the violent with the sexual, until the two cannot be separated. The glitching images rush past the speaker as time stands still: the words and images are repeated and refigured throughout the poem, as though Choi is resisting a linear narrative, or a progression towards meaningful understanding of the world. This non-linearity and looping time recall an Absurdist apocalypse.

Sparks Lin argues that hauntology is central to this glitching and looping sense of time in *Soft Science*. Jacques Derrida describes hauntology as 'a question of repetition' (2006, p. 11), which in fact figures as 'repetition *and* first time, but also repetition *and* last time, since the singularity of any *first time*, makes of it also a *last time*. Each time it is the event itself, a first time is a last time' (2006, p. 10). As such, a haunting in this sense is cyclical – always anticipated, and always a first and last, for a spectre 'begins by coming back' (2006, p. 10). The looping atemporality of *Endgame, Rosencrantz and Guildenstern Are Dead* and *Sara or the Existence of Fire* mirrors this idea, and it is this cycle and inevitability that characterises an Absurdist apocalypse. For Sparks Lin, hauntology in *Soft Science* is bound into Techno-Orientalism, because Euro-American fears of a 'hyper-technological East Asia are directly informed by similar fears of a "historical" East Asia which is backwards, traditional, and barbaric' (2022, p. 39). As such, 'the digital [. . .] becomes anticipatory: reflective of both fears and dreams that have not yet occurred' (2022, p. 21).

In the chapter 'Lost Futures' from *Ghosts of My Life* (2014), Mark Fisher highlights Franco 'Bifo' Berardi's idea of 'the slow cancellation of the future' (2014, p. 30); Berardi explains that we might understand this not as 'the direction of time' but as 'the psychological perception, which emerged in the cultural situation of progressive modernity' and 'cultural expectations [which] were shaped in the conceptual frameworks of an ever progressing development' (in Fisher, 2014, p. 30). For Fisher, this charge in technological advancement has resulted in 'a deflation of expectations' (2014, p. 31), which very closely mirrors the waning

The Apocalypse in the Absurd   79

of affect and loss of grand narratives that preoccupies the Absurd. In this idea of a cancellation of the future, Fisher identifies two types of hauntology: 'that which is (in actuality is) *no longer*, but which *remains* effective as a virtuality (the traumatic "compulsion to repeat," a fatal pattern)'; and 'that which (in actuality) has *not yet* happened, but which is already effective in the virtual (an attractor, an anticipation shaping current behavior)' (2014, p. 37). In thinking about my earlier examples of death, repetition and Absurdity, we can see hauntology as having a similar presence in the Absurd: the apocalypse is both what is 'no longer' – the compulsion to repeat, the 'fatal pattern', repetition being a key element of the Absurd – and what has 'not yet happened' – what might also offer possibilities of accepting the Absurd into one's life (and therefore moving through apocalypse in a less nihilistic sense). As such, the cyborg comes to stand in for these ideas and apocalypse: in one sense, the cyborg begets fears of a world frighteningly transformed by technology; in another, this technological advancement – the cyborg – might offer at least some solutions to issues of gender and race.

In 'A Brief History of Cyborgs', Choi uses anaphora and repetition of 'once' to establish and disrupt linear time, and thrust the reader into an apocalyptic situation. As the speaker tells the story of Alan Turing, inventor of the Turing Test (which asks, '*Can machines think?*'),[8] the speaker also intersperses their own memories of being at Disneyland, watching 'a robot dance the Macarena' (Choi, 2019, p. 14). The speaker is a cyborg and the 'daughter' of Turing, and tells an atemporal story of creation and development where language is a 'technology' the speaker must learn, while she must somehow reconcile herself to the Absurd by bringing together the softness and hardness alluded to in the collection's title. In Choi's version of the creation story, Turing first 'made a machine girl and wedded her to the internet', and the internet 'filled her until she spoke swastika and garbage', gesturing to the 'trolls [who] rubbed their soft hands on | their soft thighs' (2019, p. 14). Here, softness and hardness come together, but unhappily, because the softness has malintent – there is a predatory undertone to the trolls' gesture – and what they teach the speaker about hardness is the worst of humanity. Trying to make these two halves meet proves difficult: when Turing calls the speaker 'hard', she softens, and when she softens, she claims: 'I broke sentences to prove him wrong and what and what did I prove | then did I' (2019, p. 15). As in 'AI v.2.1' and 'Turing Test_Problem Solving', the repetition and glitching language suggests a system of meaning that cannot work. It does not serve the speaker to be wholly soft or wholly hard, although the world begs her to be one of these things. Eventually, Turing 'grew afraid and took his daughter back', and tries to fix the

80 *Whiteness, Feminism and the Absurd in Contemporary Poetry*

speaker, only to find that she has outgrown him, and has 'both hard and soft parts' (2019, p. 15).

The poem's ending: 'Can machines think I come here let me show you I ask me again' (2019, p. 15) might initially appear to be a threat, but in fact enacts a blurring of softness and hardness. 'Come here let me show you' might be read as antagonistic, but it is a moment of openness and vulnerability, as the speaker opens her 'glittering jaw' (2019, p. 15), letting the reader (or listener) look inside. This can be read as a genuine invitation, based on how the movement echoes a line in the poem 'In the Morning I Scroll My Way Back into America', where softness becomes 'proof' of a 'promise to rot' (2019, p. 57). 'If tenderness is any sort of currency II maybe I don't want what it can buy' the speaker says, recalling, in a viciously self-critical recitation, various moments in which she has 'asked to be unstitched' and 'asked' for the 'sharpness' she has received (2019, p. 57). Still, she does not learn, and arrives at 'the square early and naked again' (2019, p. 57). The poem ends with the speaker opening her mouth, unstitching herself, making herself vulnerable once more. As such, the final lines of 'A Brief History of Cyborgs' suggest that the speaker has learned to bring these two halves together, vulnerably opening her mouth, while 'ask me again' is undoubtedly antagonistic, and the speaker's jaw snaps shut.

I contend, then, that this merging of softness and hardness acts in a way to accept the Absurd and the apocalypse. In Choi's poems, there is not a key to unlock the meaning of the world, or to understand its language. It is only by blurring softness and hardness that her speakers accept the Absurd and continue moving through its repetitions into a world which no longer casts the cyborg as racistly submissive and vulnerable. The answer is, as Choi states in her interview with Todd, to 'move past horror as our primary affective response to tech. (Maybe even move past the next one, too, which I think is a kind of fetishistic desire)' (Todd and Choi, 2019); in other words, 'we have to figure out a way to think past either terrifying destruction or terrifying addiction' (2019). For Choi, there might be multiple apocalypses, and so working through this position is crucial to 'survival' (in Todd and Choi, 2019).[9]

'Dangerous' Possibilities

I now wish to return to Donna Haraway's contention that the cyborg represents 'transgressed boundaries, potent fusions, and dangerous possibilities' (2016, p. 14), to think about how the cyborg and the apocalypse are read and represented differently in the work of three poets:

The Apocalypse in the Absurd   81

Morgan Parker, Jane Yeh and Jennifer L. Knox. If, as Haraway posits, the cyborg is 'oppositional' (2016, p. 9) to the status quo, then the cyborg will always be perceived simultaneously as a positive symbol of change ('utopian', as Haraway puts it (2016, p. 9)) *and* a threat to present circumstances – for the cyborg will 'mark the world that marked them as other' (2016, p. 55). The Absurdist apocalypse holds both these potentialities, and these are clearly communicated through perception of race – in that dominant whiteness can be perceived to be 'threatened' by the cyborg while such an apocalypse represents positive change.

Black American poet Morgan Parker's 2017 poetry collection, *There are More Beautiful Things than Beyoncé*, is concerned with, as Parker puts it, 'black female sexuality', the 'way that it's been bought, sold, and distributed' (Hairston and Parker, 2017). In the poem 'Hottentot Venus', Parker takes on the voice of Sarah Bartmaan, a Khoesan woman exhibited as a 'freak show' attraction in early nineteenth-century Europe (van der Schyff, 2011, p. 147). As van der Schyff writes, Bartmaan's body has come to symbolise the period's 'pseudoscientific obsession with race and its associated discourse of Eugenics', and the 'first time that the "freak show" cast the black female body in the trope of "deviant" hypersexuality' (2011, p. 156) – Bartmaan's genitalia and buttocks were a source of racist fascination (hooks, 2014). In Parker's poem, the speaker claims that she wishes 'my pussy could live | in a different shape' and 'get some goddamn respect', understanding that she – and other Black women – are 'technically nothing | human' and 'will never be | a woman' (2017, p. 6). As in Choi's poems, racist notions of hypersexuality deny the speaker her womanhood, and she becomes a sexualised object.

In her collection, Parker uses Beyoncé as a Black 'everywoman', so that, Parker claims, her name is a 'kind of stand-in for everything that we see and are and how folks see us' (Hairston and Parker, 2017). For Parker, using Beyoncé allows her to 'get at the fact that black women are so different and can be looked at in so many different kinds of ways' (2017). Parker concedes that when she initially began writing these poems, Beyoncé's cultural position was far different, and since the release of Beyoncé's 2016 music video 'Formation' and her 2016 visual album *Lemonade*, her oeuvre has taken an ostensibly political turn, so Parker's poems are now read with Beyoncé's much more evident politics at hand (Andrews and Parker, 2018, p. 157). Hanna Andrews notes that Beyoncé represents 'the complexity of being a female pop artist ensconced in commercialism and a symbol for what agency within that system might look like' (2018, p. 156), which emphasises that Beyoncé's public politics are often ambivalent and subject to criticism.[10] For the purposes of this chapter, I am most interested in Parker's poem 'RoboBeyoncé', in which

82 *Whiteness, Feminism and the Absurd in Contemporary Poetry*

Parker creates a cyborg version of the popstar, and which most clearly meets Francis' definition of Afro-surreal: that which recentres 'blackness at the core of surrealism' (2013, p. 100).

RoboBeyoncé represents 'dangerous' possibilities to a racist, patriarchal society, for she rejects stereotypes about Black women and portends an apocalypse. RoboBeyoncé recognises how she is perceived as a Black cyborg: 'It's mostly about machine tits', she quips; she is 'artificially [. . .] interested' in men (2017, p. 23), acknowledging that she has been built for men's pleasure, and to

> [. . .] outlast some terribly
> feminine sickness
> that is delivered
> to the blood through kale
> salad and pity and men
> with straight-haired girlfriends (2017, p. 23)

RoboBeyoncé's sarcasm is palpable, and Parker shows how the Black cyborg can at once eschew the trappings of whiteness (symbolised here through a gauche penchant for superfoods) and suffer under white supremacy – the 'straight-haired' white girlfriend is always preferable to the Black woman. Yet, the speaker suggests that the joke is ultimately on everyone else, for they might not be able to recognise her as a cyborg and therefore fail to assess her threat correctly ('Tell me apart from other girls', she dares the addressee (2017, p. 24)). Her idea of 'outlasting' a 'sickness' portends an apocalypse, which becomes clearer throughout the poem, as the speaker states: 'The future's a skirt of | expectation to mourn' and 'The future's a girlish helmet | with circuits that need doctors' (2017, pp. 23, 23–24). In these visions of the future, there is an expectation to grieve the loss of human life, but the speaker will not partake in this sorrow. The speaker's visions of the future imagine a new type of Black femininity, suggested by the skirt and 'girlish helmet', one in which women more closely resemble cyborgs, with 'circuits' and 'wires | unbuttoned to you' (2017, p. 23). These new cyborg women can simultaneously be hard and soft: 'Exterior shell, interior disco' (2017, p. 23).

Parker ends the poem with a threat: the elliptical line, 'In the future our bodies can't' (2017, p. 24), suggests a future in which the cyborg's body might not be an object of sexual desire, free of racist and hypersexualised stereotypes. But the thought is incomplete because the speaker cannot yet fully imagine this post-apocalyptic future; she is still subject to the 'quiet, calculated shame' (2017, p. 24) she has been conditioned to feel. We might characterise Parker's poem as having 'ugly feelings', as Ngai puts it: emotions which are 'explicitly *amoral* and *non*cathartic,

The Apocalypse in the Absurd   83

offering no satisfactions of virtue, however oblique, nor any therapeutic or purifying release' (2005, p. 6). Parker's poem – and, indeed, all of the poems quoted in this chapter, and of the contemporary Absurd – are not epiphanic, because this is antithetical to the Absurd and to accepting the Absurd into one's life. Yet the Absurd can resist epiphany at the same time it hopes for and points us towards a better future.

The poet Jane Yeh was born and studied in the US, and later moved to England to study at Manchester Metropolitan University; she continues to reside and publish her work in Britain. Androids and robots feature frequently in her 2012 collection, *The Ninjas*, and in 'After the Attack of the Crystalline Entity',[11] Yeh's speaker is an android. In the world of the poem, there are 'escape pods everywhere' (2012, p. 9) and scene-setting that is deliberately stereotypically and gauchely futuristic: 'There was a shoe on the pavement, a metal hand, | Unreplicated litter, some kind of space-mat' (2012, p. 9). After introducing the world, the android presents itself by saying, 'Only half of me still exists' (2012, p. 9), a phrasing that sinisterly suggests that humans have been eradicated (since an android has the appearance of a human, and humans would have created it, only its robot half remains). The android does not reveal what has caused the apocalypse; it only offers the results and oblique references to the source:

> I can see outside if I bother to look.
> Outside it looks like the inside of everyone's houses
> Dumped inside out. Outside, the air
>
> Leaks bad particles into people's blood. (2012, p. 9)

The android reveals its ambivalence towards the apocalypse: it cannot be bothered to look at the world outside, and, in the absence of human life, the android does not seem devastated but enjoys the solitude: 'Inside the lab, I can talk to myself | Without anyone noticing' (2012, p. 9). Additionally, the android creates cruel 'experiments' to pass the time: 'Fireball and rat in a glass tube, | First one to reach home wins', and then reveals: 'Behind home plate is a catcher made of stakes' (2012, p. 9). The android's elliptical, declarative, end-stopped and capitalised lines suggest these phrases are being generated, imitated, rather than felt and spoken. As such, this android appears to be the most transgressive. It *enjoys* suffering and feels almost nothing towards the apocalypse – nihilism or hope.

However, the android reveals the experiment it is conducting on itself: 'how many days does it take ‖ To give up waiting for anyone to come home?' (2012, p. 9). This shifts the reader's understanding of the android as a being capable of emotion; the very concept of 'home' conveys emotional depth, as does the android's hope that 'anyone' will come back. The android is bereft. In this poem, then, Yeh enacts a sleight of hand, tricking the reader into believing the android is a cruel, callous and inhumane outsider, and then demonstrating its ability to feel, its need for connection. The apocalypse has the potential here to upend social order, and reveal the reader's prejudices, hopefully pushing them towards a nuanced way of thinking about 'difference'. Yeh is, as Coates acknowledges, reluctant to discuss the motivations behind her writing, and her poems 'discuss social marginality without explicit narratives of marginalised people' (2019), but this idea of Otherness, the threat it supposedly poses and undermining that threat, is a key element of her poetics. That the android is like a human after all of course does not mean that Yeh is suggesting that prejudice is acceptable if a being acts cruelly. Rather, she poses these binary visions of 'humanity' and lack thereof as a way of demonstrating that ideas of 'good' and 'bad' and 'belonging' and 'other' are deeply flawed. Why does the android only gain the reader's sympathy once they realise it is lonely?

In 'On Being an Android', the android speaker reflects on their experiences of dating: 'My first crush was a Roomba I mistook for a person. | Second crush: a person, but don't even go there' and opines: 'Everyone says looks don't matter, as long as you've got personality' (2012, p. 14). By repeating platitudes, the android conveys its assimilation into human culture. Indeed, both its 'crushes' are human – it does not feel attracted to the Roomba because it is a machine too; it is attracted to it because it thinks the Roomba is human. Yet the android's love is forever unrequited and complicated, because although it feels human, it is eternally locked out of human experience because it is never perceived as human. In the final stanza of the poem, the speaker hints at an impending apocalypse: 'It's easy to predict the future when there's a timer in your neck'; 'the lightning in my head means a brainstorm is coming' (2012, p. 14); it is apparent that the android is the catalyst for the end of the world. Yeh ends the poem by stating that 'nobody wants to touch' the android's 'artificial skin' (2012, p. 14), demonstrating the revulsion the android knows it engenders. The android is, in Freudian terms, *unheimlich*: that which 'arouses dread and horror' (2003, p. 219). In 'The Robots', Yeh uses third-person narration (a recurring technique in her work) so that the robots are consistently referred to as 'they', highlighting the difference between humans and robots, and creating an oppositional 'us and them' mentality. By removing the reader from the robots' point of view, Yeh makes the robots (and the apocalypse they threaten) seem even more frightening. When the poem's speaker reveals that 'the rest of

The Apocalypse in the Absurd   **85**

us will be snuffed out like vermin' (2012, p. 18), they seem to be disclosing the robots' intention to destroy the human race.

What sort of apocalypse might Yeh's androids and robots bring, then? Unlike Choi's and Parker's work, Yeh's work is less ostensibly bound up in racial and gender politics – although this does not mean that it does not have a politics at all. The androids and robots are always *almost* human, but never quite accepted – and so their isolation (pre- or post-apocalypse) propagates Absurdist repetition, waiting and futility. Yeh's poems, unlike Choi's and Parker's, imagine that the apocalypse is already here, has already happened. What comes next? How do these speakers accept the apocalypse and the Absurd into their lives? The apocalypses in Yeh's work suggest that there is potential to undermine and conquer systems of oppression, prejudice and exclusion. For those who benefit from the status quo, the possibility of an apocalypse seems dangerous, terrifying. For those who suffer under oppression and prejudice, who might want to imagine a better future (even if the Absurd governs us), the apocalypse is hopeful. If we look out the window, who knows what we might imagine and create.

The promise of an apocalypse pervades white American poet Jennifer L. Knox's collection, *Days of Shame and Failure* (2015), in which speakers imagine how 'we'll slip out of this world | our swan songs clogging the ears of all | the wordless species going first' (2015, p. 85). This demotic suggests a human self-centredness, a selfishness that cannot change even as the world ends, and, as Ailbhe Darcy writes in her review of Knox's collection for *Critical Flame*, 'sparks off questions of individual adaptability, change, and inevitability that, because they are writ large upon our civilization, are urgent' (2016). Knox's poems are ambivalent – sometimes emotionally directive, often not – as they blur irony with sincerity. For Darcy, 'sufficient irony pre-emptively absolves the poet of sentimentality, so that the sentiment can in fact ring true' (2016), but as I have shown in the previous chapter, such refusal to be emotionally directive can cause trouble, especially concerning whiteness, and – as I will demonstrate in the next chapter – Knox's work contains a complex and often unconsummated interrogation of whiteness.

For now, I am most interested in Knox's poem 'Our Robots', which depicts an apocalypse in which humans become obsessed with robots. Everyday technology is defamilarised, so that a television is a 'TV robot', a radiator is a 'warm radio robot', a camera is a 'photograph robot' and a gun is a 'gunpowder robot' (2015, p. 83). Thereby technology's control becomes evident: it changes language to make itself central, or humans have allowed it to become so important that they have changed their language to accommodate it. This insidious apocalypse becomes

86 *Whiteness, Feminism and the Absurd in Contemporary Poetry*

more threatening as the speaker notes that 'when the movie robot was invented, we couldn't pull | ourselves away' and 'some starved in the seats. We died | in front of the TV' (2015, p. 83). As humans become obsessed with the robots, they become distracted and fail to look after themselves; therefore, they die. Knox's constant repetition of 'died' and 'robots' becomes comedic as the reader imagines humans dying in bizarre situations: each time 'died' is mentioned, the scenario becomes more ridiculous.

As such, Knox re-enacts the distraction and diverts her reader's attention away from the threat of the apocalypse into its comedic potential. Knox's robots and apocalypse invoke carnival laughter, described by Mikhail Bakhtin as 'a festive laughter', which is not 'an individual reaction to some isolated "comic" event', but is 'the laughter of all the people' and 'universal in its scope; it is directed at all and everyone', so that the 'entire world is seen in its droll aspect, in its gay relativity' (1984, p. 11). But carnival laughter is also ambivalent: 'it is gay, triumphant, and at the same time mocking, deriding' (1984, pp. 11–12). As such, carnival laughter acts as a Menippean satire, (momentarily) eradicating inequalities, allowing everyone to laugh at the same subject.[12] Knox's apocalypse, in which humans die at the hands of robots, has been happening for centuries: the speaker notes that people have 'died screwing around | like punks with gunpowder robots, died carving stars | in stone with chisel robots, wheel robots, fire robots' (2015, p. 83); in other words, all our attempts to find new technology, to do things better and faster, have led, and will always lead, to our demise. We have been stuck in this Absurdist, repetitive and looping behaviour since the beginning of civilisation.

The speaker is not entirely unconcerned about this impending apocalypse, and seems to want to find meaning from it. The poem begins with the speaker comparing two famous robots from films: 'Hal, the robot in *2001*' who 'wants to kill the astronaut' and 'Gerty, the robot in the movie *Moon*' who 'wants to save the astronaut' (2015, p. 83). The speaker wonders if 'Gerty is a nicer robot because we are nicer | now (too late?) and robots have our faces' (2015, p. 83), at once acknowledging that the human race is most likely doomed and also that humans have been instrumental in their own demise: they have 'taught' robots, dedicated their lives to robots and are now obsolete. Knox also revels in the irony of the speaker believing humans are 'nicer | now', and provides absolutely no evidence to suggest that this is true. The speaker acknowledges: 'That's how people get smarter: dumbly, | without knowing it, until years after the smart's set in | and we're dumb in whole new ways' (2015, p. 83); the poem ends with an image of a cave painting of a buffalo hunt, setting the human race back to the beginning again, to make the same mistakes. As such, in Knox's vision of the Absurd, the human race is doomed because it cannot accept the absurdity of life; we are always trying to improve things, obsessed with growth and development.

Knox's apocalypse does not – as Choi's, Parker's and Yeh's – clearly state that there may be a new possibility after an apocalypse. Knox might be implying that the end of the human race is perhaps a good thing: but it seems that this comes more clearly from a nihilistic bent, in which the end of the human race means at least we are not doing any further damage. There is little suggestion of a better future here. It is noteworthy that Knox does not inhabit the voice of the cyborg, android or robot in the way Choi, Parker and Yeh do, as though Knox's nihilistic approach might be locking her out of truly disrupting the status quo and taking on the voice of a being willing to disrupt order. Carnival laughter may mute inequalities, but it can only do this briefly, so it does not offer a solution alone.

Knox is, perhaps, subtly criticising the speaker's (and, broadly speaking, humankind's) inaction, their apathy as the world ends – their acknowledgement of what has caused their demise, but their detached reporting of events, as if nothing can change. I do think this reading is possible, for Knox is not always generous towards her speakers: they are flawed and often coded as imprudent and, as I will demonstrate in the next chapter, white and working class, so that the presumed white, middle-class reader can simultaneously ridicule them and ridicule themselves, while also acknowledging a sense of superiority. Yet there is a sense that for readers of Knox's work, denial is still possible and still a source of humour. How might she confront this complacency? In the next chapter, I demonstrate how Knox's poetics has a complex relationship to social change, and can at once be directive and uncertain, and how, at times, her humour demonstrates her poetry's potential to destabilise and challenge whiteness.

PART II

Chapter 4

Authority, 'White Trash' and Culture in Jennifer L. Knox's *A Gringo Like Me*

In this chapter, I hope to take a similar stance to Jill Magi in her exploration of Gertrude Stein's poetry for Rankine, Loffreda and King Cap's *The Racial Imaginary* (2016), in which she notes that criticism which explores whiteness is not asking for 'didactic literature' but is encouraging a kind of reading that 'sees race and privilege, even and especially when the one we are reading is white, and even and especially when the one we are reading is considered experimental' (p. 168). Indeed, white American poet Jennifer L. Knox's poetry fits well into this category: her approach to race is unfixed and at times unclear, but, as I will contend throughout this chapter, the poems in *A Gringo Like Me* (2007) can attempt to resist whiteness and destabilise it, even if its execution is unstable itself. I analyse how Knox employs a self-effacing humour to destabilise the reader–poet relationship and deflate elitist, classist approaches to poetry through direct engagement with 'high' and 'low' culture in her poems. In doing so, I explore how Knox uses popular culture to ridicule systems that extol privileged, male writers and reductive narratives for women. Knox's poetry also, at times, attempts to grapple with assumptions of cultural capital and privilege.

Deflating 'High' and 'Low' Culture

In an interview with Josephine Yu for *Emry's Journal* (2019), Jennifer L. Knox mentions one of her most well-known poems, 'Chicken Bucket', published in *A Gringo Like Me*. The poem's speaker is a fourteen-year-old white girl, Cassie, who lives in a trailer, smokes marijuana, has sex with her teacher and a strange man in his van, and is impregnated by her mother's boyfriend. In the poem, Cassie is 'white trash'[1] and, according to Knox, 'has no idea how stupid she is in so many directions, which is

92 *Whiteness, Feminism and the Absurd in Contemporary Poetry*

exactly the way I was when I was [fourteen]' (2019). Knox states that the poem is autobiographical, and that perhaps she was 'punching down' at herself in the poem: 'I used to give my speakers a really hard time [. . .] I would never write ['Chicken Bucket'] now; it's punching down, which is a term Chris Rock coined. Good funny is when you go after those above you, i.e. punching up' (2019). However, neither Yu nor Knox interrogate this further, and it is not clear to what extent autobiography might mitigate the 'punching down' or, indeed, to what extent Knox is thinking about how 'punching down' meets ideas of class, gender and race in her work.

In Chapter 3, I suggested that Knox's poetics has a complex and ambivalent relationship to irony and sincerity, and that this affects how readers engage with her ostensible nihilism: is it truly nihilism, or is she holding a mirror up to a privileged audience (white, middle class) which should recognise this and change its behaviour? And where does this leave readers who are not white and/or middle class? Indeed, in 'Chicken Bucket', Cassie might be the subject of the joke, but she can punch down too, falsely claiming: *'Some Mexicans jumped me!'* (2007, p. 46) when someone steals the chicken bucket her mother has asked her to buy. In Cassie's world, being Mexican is worse than being 'white trash', which sets up a complex system of privilege: if Cassie is, by Knox's own admission, 'stupid', then what does this make the Mexican population, who are used in a moment that allows Cassie to gain some authority? If Knox is 'punching down' when she features Cassie in a poem, then what happens when Cassie 'punches down' further? In Knox's poem, Cassie knows she might be stupid, but – Cassie seems to say – at least she is not Mexican.

In his formative essay for *The American Poetry Review*, 'A Mystifying Silence—Big and Black' (2007), Major Jackson writes:

> We are less willing to be repulsive and repugnant in our poems, so caught up in our quest for linguistic and emotional beauty and earnestness—so earnest are we in the vision of poetry as the province of communal good that we fail to create 'speakers' in our poems who are contemptible and dishonorable. Add to this our knee-jerk desire to hide our faults or the less admirable parts of our own lives in our poetry. There's a little racist, sexist, classist, ageist, homophobe in all of us. So, we expose ourselves in more acceptable and overly mined areas of embarrassment and shame, even then, seeking the redemptive glow of self-reflection and the post-epiphanic splendor of personal triumph and enlightenment. (2007, p.19)

In 'Chicken Bucket', Cassie is a conduit for some 'contemptible and dishonorable' views – either from the reader or from Cassie herself or, perhaps,

Knox. Cassie makes knee-jerk racist comments about Mexican people, and as Jackson contends, this is somewhat refreshing: at least Knox is not trying to make Cassie seem like an angelic victim, and exposes thinking other poets might want to hide. Yet it is Cassie, a poor, 'white trash' child who says these things. The poem is a complex portrait of class and prejudice, with regard to how the reader responds to Cassie – might the poem seek to expose the reader's prejudice against a poor, working-class girl? – and how Cassie might garner sympathy even as she is cast as unintelligent and racist, or how this might absolve a reader of similar thinking, as Cassie has these thoughts because she is 'white trash'. Can one 'punch down' at whiteness, or can one only 'punch up'? 'Chicken Bucket' shows the reader that whiteness always allows some privilege, even when class affects cultural capital.

In his review of Matthew Dickman's collection *Mayakovsky's Revolver* for *The New Criterion*, William Logan takes issue with Dickman's 'hyperactive lines, unrelenting trivia, and a devil-may-care manner' and deems the poems 'sweetly unserious' (2013) for this, damning them with faint praise. He particularly takes issue with Dickman's depiction of everyday life, which involves the speaker of one poem watching 'reruns of *The Donna Reed Show* | or the Marx Brothers' or 'movies about people who are funny | all the time'; the speaker admits: 'I keep watching the same rap | video on YouTube' (Dickman in Logan, 2013). Logan writes, in response, that 'Dickman has charm to spare, and a teasing cheekiness that's hard to dislike—yet you wonder if life should be as dull as this' (2013). He continues: 'When I've read too much of such vacant mental stock-taking, I remember what Coleridge did one afternoon when he was bored—he wrote "This Lime-Tree Bower My Prison"' (2013). Logan makes the age-old argument that canonical poetry is somehow superior to modern poetry because its concerns are with nature, and evidently favours poetry as an elite form of art: mentioning television and YouTube seems almost vulgar, not fitting for poetry. Logan sneers at Dickman's boredom, as though he is not creative enough with it, but is impressed by the resulting output from Coleridge. However, Logan fails to understand that it is highly likely that if Coleridge had been bored in the twenty-first century, he would have watched the same rap video on YouTube repeatedly, too. Dickman's poem attempts to capture twenty-first-century boredom by indicating exactly what it is like to be bored with the internet at your fingertips, while Coleridge captures what it was like to be bored before the internet was invented. Logan dismisses Dickman's poems as 'dull' and 'vacant mental stock-taking', refusing to accept that modern technology – and modern everyday life – has a place in poetry.

94 *Whiteness, Feminism and the Absurd in Contemporary Poetry*

Yet culture and class are ostensibly inseparable, and culture is indicative of class, as Pierre Bourdieu notes:

> A work of art has a meaning and interest only for someone who possesses the cultural competence, that is, the code, into which it is encoded. The conscious or unconscious implementation of explicit or implicit schemes of perception and appreciation which constitutes pictorial or musical culture is the hidden condition for recognizing the styles characteristic of a period, a school or an author, and, more generally, for the familiarity with the internal logic of works that aesthetic enjoyment presupposes. (2010, p. xxv)

However, as Wayne Holloway-Smith explains, someone who is 'bereft of "the specific code" of sensibility becomes displaced in an incoherent accumulation of properties in the artist's work' (2014, p. 27). In this way, the individual who has 'not inherited the skills or language' can only respond by 'gut reaction', and this response is always considered to be worth less than 'the considered educated response' (2014, p. 27). Therefore, Holloway-Smith argues that 'the moral positioning of "taste" as marker of individual worth' becomes the 'means by which one group of people, possessing this faculty, can be distinguished' (2014, p. 28). In short, possessing the right language to talk about esteemed art is desirable; anything less is unwelcome. As art house cinema is considered culturally superior to 'trash' or 'daytime' television, poetry is typically considered to be 'high' culture, and even Knox's poetry, which draws heavily from 'low' culture, is still thought to be superior – a dynamic that Knox ridicules throughout her oeuvre.

Poetry is, generally, viewed as too challenging for the everyday person to understand and enjoy. In *The Hatred of Poetry*, Ben Lerner notes that poets who publish their work 'observe no contradiction in the fact that they are attempting to secure and preserve their personhood in a magazine that no one they know will see' (2016, p. 22). As J.T. Welsch writes, poetry's 'relatively low economic value becomes part of its heightened cultural value' (2020, p. 9). Indeed, poets – and society in general – glorify the poet as a figure, rather than the reality of being a poet; Lerner argues this at length in his book. Nor is this merely a twenty-first-century preoccupation. It is precisely what Frank O'Hara pertains to in his 'Personism: A Manifesto', in which he argues against the privileging of 'high' art in poetry, opining: 'Nobody should experience anything they don't need to, if they don't need poetry bully for them, I like the movies too' (in Cook, 2004, p. 368). O'Hara places poetry, film and popular culture side by side; for O'Hara, the film is just as important as the poem, and the poem is no better than the film. Indeed, this marrying of 'everyday' and poetry has been a common preoccupation for writers: in their 'Advertisement' for *Lyrical Ballads*, Wordsworth and Coleridge discuss how their poems were written 'chiefly with a view to ascertain how far the language of conversation in the middle and lower classes of society is adapted to the purposes of poetic pleasure' (Gamer and Porter, 2008, p. 47); the New York School, according to Lehman, 'embraced popular culture but not at the expense of the high end of the cultural scale; to them it was not an either/or proposition' (1999, p. 330). In the New York School, 'you could enjoy both, you could derive inspiration from both' (Lehman, 1999, p. 330); this is part of the legacy of the New York poets and now a key part of Absurdist poetics, and so Logan's comments hark back to privileging a kind of poetry which is undeniably exclusionary and elitist.

Knox's *A Gringo Like Me* pushes this dynamic between poetry and popular culture further, mocking gendered expectations of poetry, exploring the role of humour in poetry and, indeed, who and what belongs in poetry. Knox's poems advocate a levelling of 'high' and 'low' culture, and class and culture are at the heart of her poetics. As Gael Sweeney writes, there are actually three distinctions of culture:

> High culture like the opera, ballet, and literature is authorized and supported by the elite, while popular forms such as Hollywood cinema (as opposed to art or foreign films), television, and pop music is ranked as middlebrow. But even lower would be the White Trash forms, such as the tabloids and cable TV (as opposed to PBS for the elite and network television for the middle class). (1997, p. 260)

Knox engages with these 'low' and 'white trash' forms of art and foregrounds them, confrontationally including them where they might not be thought to belong. Sweeney's distinctions are important, indicating that in 'low' culture, 'white trash' is its own category, even 'lower'. Knox takes somewhat obsolete ideas of shunning new technology and popular culture in poetry – as evidenced in Logan's review of Dickman – and deliberately emphasises its presence in a kind of antagonistic gesture towards typical, backwards-looking views of what poetry should be. Poetry that attempts to belong to 'high' culture – by offering 'universal' platitudes and often clumsily reaching for profundity – ultimately fails because the reader cannot connect with the poem, because the 'universal' does not exist; indeed, Claudia Rankine, Beth Loffreda and Lerner argue against 'universality' in writing, specifically poetry, in *The Racial Imaginary* (2016) and *The Hatred of Poetry* (2016), respectively.

As Kaufmann notes, it is common practice for the '(white, male) poet' to be considered the 'universal (lyric) subject', and for the '(white, male) reader' to be considered the 'universal (lyric) audience' (2017, p. 93). Kaufmann cautions against 'fine old-fashioned liberal demands for inclusion and mutual recognition' and advocates for recognising the 'dignity of diverse experience' (2017, p. 93) in poetry – that is, for poetry not to reach for 'universality'. As Rankine and Loffreda write: 'If we continue to think of the "universal" as better-than, as the pinnacle, we will always discount writing that doesn't look universal because it accounts for race or some other demeaned category'; consequently, 'the universal is a fantasy' (in Rankine et al., 2016, p. 22). When we consider (as I have argued throughout this book) that the imagined reader of an Absurdist poem is largely white and middle class, Knox's poetry, which references popular culture (and therefore low culture) and 'white trash' culture, may well appear more emotionally resonant to a white readership because it uses specific and widespread habits to reflect 'everyday' life in the West. Knox employs low culture, such as television and music videos, to create high culture (poetry) and thereby ridicules the very idea of having a divide between high and low culture, undermining the narrative of there being one great tradition or type of poetry. Yet, recalling Kaufmann's claim that avant-garde poetry 'requires a fair amount of social privilege and cultural capital' (2017, p. 57), even if *all* readers are not white, it is likely that they possess a good deal of cultural capital to be reading a book of poems.

In what Knox calls 'self-effacing humour', she recognises that her instinct is to become the target of laughter but that she 'must reclaim authority at some point in the poem' (2016). As such, even the poet is subject to ridicule; Knox makes the speaker or herself the target of the laughter in the first instance. As she notes in her interview with Yu: 'My joke is: writing poetry to be funny is like becoming a nun to get laid. It's absolutely the wrong way to go about it. For many poets— especially those in positions of power—funny undermines your authority' (2019), and yet undermining the poet's authority is a distinct feature of Knox's work; as Darcy notes in her review of Knox's later collection *Days of Shame and Failure* (2015), this pits the serious and the funny against one another, as though gravity cannot come from humour. Indeed, Knox's poetics is very much of Gabriel Gudding's definition of Menippean satire, which he describes as a kind of satire in which 'you can't tell what's not being satirized, as if the very way a society thinks or is as a culture is being satirized' (in Loden and Silem Mohammad 2007); Gudding notes that there is simultaneously 'a sense of the author loving some aspect of the society s/he's dissing' (in Loden and Silem

Mohammad, 2007). What does this tension between 'loving' and 'dissing' mean for whiteness, then? David Lehman has written extensively about the avant-garde's apoliticalness and its own championing of an 'aesthetics over morality' poetics, but, as I will argue in this chapter, the two are not binary opposites. Absurdist poetics like Knox's might have a more complex understanding of its relationship to politics, recognising that politics affects everything we do and everything we are.

Throughout *A Gringo Like Me*, Knox highlights the act of writing, artifice (or artifice perceived through the act of writing) and making the reader aware of this pretence, and subsequently foregrounds the speaker (or herself) as a poet. Knox's approach is evidently of Susan Sontag's influential understanding of camp: a 'mode of aestheticism' that is defined by its 'love of the unnatural: of artifice and exaggeration' and of 'the "off", of things-being-what-they-are not' (2018, pp. 4, 1, 9). Camp 'discloses innocence, but also, when it can, corrupts it', is imbued with 'the spirit of extravagance' and, crucially, 'turns its back on the good-bad axis of ordinary aesthetic judgement' (2018, pp. 15, 16, 22). In camp, a writer can be 'serious about the frivolous, frivolous about the serious' (2018, p. 26). In 'The Laws of Probability in Levittown',[2] Knox opens with an address from the speaker, who is also a poet, and claims: 'I've been smoking so much pot lately, | I figure out what my poems are going to do | before I write them', which means when they 'finally sit down in front of the typewriter . . . well . . . you know . . .' (2007, p. 17). The speaker punctures any grandiose ideas about 'the writer' as a figure, and the writing process. For this speaker-poet, smoking pot is the process, and the process is actually detrimental to writing.[3]

The speaker of this poem, then, seemingly gets high with little consequence; smoking is part of his daily routine, and the only consequence of this might be not writing a poem, which is – the joke appears to be – no real consequence at all. This is, subtly, a way for Knox to ridicule the reader's perception of canonical poets. It is well acknowledged that many canonical writers were opium users (Milligan, 2003, p. xxxiii; Crawford, 2018) – Sharon Ruston notes that Elizabeth Barrett Browning, Lord Byron, Samuel Taylor Coleridge, Wilkie Collins, George Crabbe, Charles Dickens, John Keats, Percy Bysshe Shelley and Walter Scott were all known to take the drug (2014) – so there seems to be an indirect observation on considering drugs as being in the service of genius in opposition to drugs being in the service of muddled thinking. Knox therefore highlights the hypocrisy of considering an opium-using poet 'canonical' and a marijuana-smoking poet a 'failure'. Her comparison suggests that the two are closer than we would perhaps like to admit.

98 Whiteness, Feminism and the Absurd in Contemporary Poetry

In the next stanzas, she continues this nuanced deflation, as the speaker admits that he has 'moved back in with my parents' and has become 'really good at watching TV' (2007, p. 17). The speaker is outwardly somewhat a 'failure'. The writer, then, is no longer to be revered, but appears as a flawed being. Knox foregrounds high and low culture, and places them in opposition: the speaker cannot write, but he enjoys watching TV and believes that it is something for which he can develop an ability. Importantly, the speaker does not feel shame in not writing and enjoying television instead. The speaker sees both as achievements, and noticeably takes pleasure and merit from being 'right' about 'the killer'. The speaker's admission of watching television and enjoying it allows the reader to feel exempt from the guilt of their own television-watching habits. There may be a latent shame here, but if so, it speaks to the reader, to show that watching television and smoking marijuana should not be a source of shame – but that the speaker and Knox still understand those feelings.

In this way, Knox appeals to the reader: in order to understand and write poetry, we must accept what it is like to be alive in Western society in the twenty-first century, and be honest about it. Of course, this kind of approach is met with criticism, as in Logan's review of Dickman's collection, or, as Marlisa Santos argues: 'as "hip" or "relevant" as poetry tries to be in contemporary life, it may always be a bit more divorced from everyday life than other art forms' (2013, p. ix). Knox is deliberately writing against these kinds of dismissive statements, and she acknowledges that poetry must reflect what modern life is like – technology, drugs and all. However, there is a noticeable neglection, here. Whiteness allows Knox's speaker more impunity, and so his drug-taking can be carried out with licence.[4] The poem's irony and humour take place in – and are caused by – a world which allows white people to be lazy, take drugs and fail with freedom. There is, then, a happy-go-lucky naivety in Knox's speaker, and this reflects a world that will always protect whiteness, seeing whiteness as 'default'.

Knox's speaker is meant to be regressive, sneered at. He uses stereotypical, surface labels for the women he watches on television, such as 'the housewife' (2007, p. 17), and his gender politics are backwards, as he gleefully recalls a joke about Jamie Lee Curtis: 'Remember whenever Jamie Lee Curtis would come | on TV and we'd yell *Hermaphrodite!* all happy?' (2007, p. 17). Here, Knox uses a real-life rumour about Jamie Lee Curtis being intersex to create an uncomfortable joke. The joke here works as a *peripeteia*, further destabilising the reader's understanding of the speaker-poet as an enlightened individual; the speaker uses queerness as a punchline. The speaker turns his attention to Jamie Lee Curtis' father instead, describing him as an 'American treasure' (2007, p. 17). The speaker claims to have a 'list of examples why' and claims that his 'shit's backed up' (2007, p. 17), suggesting that there is an ongoing dialogue with someone outside the poem with whom the speaker is seriously analysing 'low' culture – another moment where the reader might feel some sense of superiority over the speaker.

The speaker reveals more of his TV-watching habits later in the poem, comparing 'Robert Frost talking about his backyard | on *Large American Voices* and Farrah Fawcett on *True Hollyweird*' (2007, p. 17). The speaker chooses Farrah 'because I knew what was going to happen and I was right' (2007, p. 17). Superficially, the speaker prioritises the woman's narrative, rather than the man's. However, the speaker chooses the woman's narrative because he knows what is 'going to happen', because mainstream narratives about women are predictable. The speaker also suggests that he knows what is going to happen in '*Inevitable Justice*' and '*True Hollyweird*' because these narratives of 'trash TV' are predictable: the housewife as the clueless victim or bystander to the husband's crimes; Jamie Lee Curtis as a woman vilified by the media for not fulfilling arbitrary standards of femininity; her father considered superior; and Farrah Fawcett as a 1980s 'sex-symbol' and cultural icon who quickly rose to fame due to her beauty. The speaker takes pleasure in knowing what will happen to these women and knowing that he can rely on these gender narratives. Yet what the poem does not explicitly acknowledge is that *everyone* in the poem – the poets, the celebrities – are white. It is worth noting that the stereotypes afforded to Black women in the media would be far different, as I demonstrated in Chapter 3; I will return to this later in the chapter, when thinking about sexuality.

Knox undermines and ridicules these narratives for white women subtly through the titles of the TV programmes, all of which are fictional. Clearly, '*Inevitable Justice*' points to the predictability of crime-based TV programmes (and therefore of the narratives of such TV programmes). '*True Hollyweird*' highlights the strangeness of being interested (or even obsessed with) the lives of celebrities; it is a comment on the peculiar construction of Hollywood as a place where dreams come true. Finally, '*Large American Voices*' turns the satire back towards poetry, showing how white, male voices dominate the American literary canon. As Marsha Meskimmon has noted: 'Female subjectivity and women's agency [. . .] are not relics of a now-discredited social system, but important emergent conceptual structures' (2003, pp. 7–8). She writes that 'the authoritative "I" who authored texts, the intellectual subjects capable of rational thought and the genius who created high art' have long been considered 'masculine, heterosexual, white, Euro-ethnic, middle-class and able-bodied – the normative subject of western epistemology and ontology' (2003, p. 71). Knox's treatment and ridicule of Frost ostensibly makes 'The Laws of Probability in Levittown' a challenge to white, male-dominated poetics. Frost is, of course, one of the most famous American poets, and Knox calls his voice 'large'. 'Large' here means 'dominating' rather than 'important': in this fictional world, there is a TV programme about 'Robert Frost talking about his backyard', and Knox suggests that people will engage with anything about white, male literary 'greats', even things that do not relate to their writing; their voices are prioritised because this is 'high' culture, not 'trash TV', and the juxtaposition furthers the inequality. Knox, then, is ridiculing these gender specific narratives, and also ridiculing her speaker for engaging with them (even if the speaker passively consumes them). The speaker is 'right' about the narratives, but in being right undermines his own intelligence, as he is not equipped to tackle the narratives and so participates with them instead. Knox is, of course, ridiculing systems that extol male writers, and that provide predictable, narrow stories for and about women.

Knox's consideration of race in this poem is latent and ambivalent. Indeed, there is a sense that the figures in this poem are the product of a sense of 'universal' whiteness. The poem is, ultimately, an interrogation of white masculinity versus white femininity, where whiteness is an unconsidered default. Knox's speakers seem resigned to inaction, and a self-effacement impossible for anyone without such cultural capital. One might argue that this simply perpetuates privilege, yet Knox is offering a critique of this inaction. If her speakers are doomed to repeat their destructive habits, if they refuse to change their behaviour, then the (white, middle-class) reader is being invited to see their own reflections in the speakers, and perhaps to learn from them. Indeed, Knox depicts these speakers as fools, and there is a sense she is 'punching down' as she does this, pointing at those who are easy targets of critique. Knox assumes the reader is white – but she does acknowledge, at least, the inaction and privilege that comes with whiteness. Equally, as Kaufmann writes, it is all too easy to slip into 'narcissism here, to a self-aggrandising self-effacement or self-hatred' as if the 'realities of class division and the unequal distribution of cultural capital were our own personal fault as either readers or poets' and could be 'eliminated if we were somehow better people' (2017, p. 65). Indeed, reading or writing poetry does not inherently make people 'better', but there is space within poems – and within poetry reading, reviewing and criticism – to critique the structural privileging of whiteness.

'White-Trashing' Culture

Contemporary Absurdist poetry has much in common with Gurlesque poetry. Arielle Greenberg defines the Gurlesque – not always concretely – as poetry that 'incorporates and rejects confession, lyricism, fragmentation, humor, and beauty', employs a 'tone that [is] tender and emotionally vulnerable but also tough' and contains 'a frank attitude towards sexuality and a deep, lush interest in the corporeal' (2003). Greenberg writes that Gurlesque poems 'own their sexuality, wear it proudly, are thoroughly enmeshed in the visceral experiences of gender'; they 'are non-linear but highly conversational, lush and campy, full of pop culture detritus, and ultimately very powerful' (2003). She comments that the Gurlesque aims to include the 'fundamental parts of the human experience [. . .] that are often written out because they are part of the woman's sphere, normally considered trivial or shameful' (2003).

In a discussion recorded online for the Poetry Foundation, 'Be Gay, Do Crimes: On the Gurlesque, Lana Del Rey, and Teen Girl Theory' (2020), Ben Fama, Rachel Rabbit White and Sandra Simonds explore the troubled legacy of the Gurlesque. Simonds opines that Greenberg and Glenum's definition of the Gurlesque is 'very heteronormative and white' and argues that many of the poets included in Greenberg and Glenum's anthology 'were middle class white women and really that was the imaginative horizon' (2020). She deems the Gurlesque 'a nostalgic move backwards to a, more than likely, very stable kind of gated-community-childhood (that's a metaphor) with maybe a few minor horrors thrown in' (2020). Ultimately, Simonds argues that 'the current political climate, fascism and white supremacy calls for an aesthetic that though rooted perhaps in some Gurlesque practices, is able to more broadly encompass the political immediateness and despair of the moment' (2020), citing Anne Boyer's work as an affirmative exemplar.

This criticism has been levelled at the aesthetic on several occasions (King, 2010; Bloomberg-Rissman, 2010; Andes, 2020). Indeed, Greenberg herself acknowledges in a reflection for *The Volta* (2013) that the aesthetic was 'too heterosexual, too biologically determined, too white, too middle-class, too suburban in its focus' (2013). She writes of plans for a new edition of the anthology, noting: 'Lara and I were trying to present the evidence of an aesthetic in progress, an aesthetic defined by very particular historical, cultural and stylistic parameters' and 'the goal was not to show a wide range of voices: it was to try to pinpoint a very particular vantage point from which art was being made' (2013). This tension – between wanting to mark and name a particular aesthetic, and understanding that the process of doing this might be flawed – reveals one of the tensions in this book, too. How does one account for an aesthetic with a limited 'membership'? How does one put that aesthetic into conversation with a wider sphere of poetry, acknowledging the aesthetic's flaws as it investigates it? Indeed, Morgan Myers writes on the rain taxi website: 'the characteristically hyperbolic rhetoric of the avant-garde [. . .] buzzes through Greenberg's introduction, which promises that the Gurlesque is "just the apocalypse . . . just the second coming of a baby girl messiah"', and notes that 'Glenum and Greenberg [. . .] devote the majority of their essays to establishing a historical pedigree for the Gurlesque' that somewhat generously includes "90s riot grrls, to 20th-century poets like Alice Notley, Sylvia Plath, and Gertrude Stein, to 19th-century burlesque theater, and finally to proposed ur-Gurlesque figures like Emily Dickinson or Shakespeare's Ophelia' (2010). It is impossible to ignore that there is not much linking the poets they mention, other than they are white, and women.

This type of approach, as Cathy Park Hong (2014) writes for *Arcade*, is the avant-garde's 'delusion of whiteness':

American avant-garde poetry has been an overwhelmingly white enterprise, ignoring major swaths of innovators—namely poets from past African American literary movements—whose prodigious writings have vitalized the margins, challenged institutions, and introduced radical languages and forms that avant-gardists have usurped without proper acknowledgment. Even today, its most vocal practitioners cling to moldering Eurocentric practices. Even today, avant-garde's most vocal, self-aggrandizing stars continue to be white.

Such claims of innovation are ultimately contradictory, as Rachel Greenwald Smith writes in her article 'Fuck the Avant-Garde' (2019), because the term 'avant-garde' is a movement intended to critique 'art as an institution'; the institutionalisation of the avant-garde 'gives us not only the thoroughgoing commodification of the avant-garde, but also the systematic exclusion of nonwhite experimentalists from its very definition'. In her reflection for *Volta*, Greenberg does not write about why the Gurlesque might be flawed, nor does she offer incisive criticism into the aesthetic (or 'theory', as she names it). Earlier, in an interview with Amy King (who has elsewhere criticised the Gurlesque), Greenberg claims: 'I think it's crucial that we white poets write about whiteness, too', but undermines this by stating 'but I'd say we've got a long way to go in figuring out how to write about money and class in poetry' (2010). As Reed states, this is an 'untenable position' (2014, p. 3) which does not reflect the intersections of class and race. In the interview with King,

Greenberg does not reflect on the omissions of the Gurlesque, and, to date, a new edition of the anthology has not been released, and so the criticisms and new commentary Greenberg promises in her reflection for *Volta* have not come to light.

Yet, for all its flaws, the Gurlesque is a helpful tool to read Knox's work against. Lara Glenum comments that the Gurlesque is a 'camp performance' (2010, p. 14), and I wish to show here, using Nada Gordon's poem 'She Sure Likes the Cream', how both the Gurlesque and Knox's poetry undermine ideas about sexuality. In Gordon's poem, sexuality is expressed, celebrated and also ridiculed. The speaker's assertiveness in her sexuality, demonstrated by her request for the reader to 'Come pet my kitty' (in Glenum, 2010, p. 16), is an unabashed expression of desire, but this quickly unravels with the repetition of 'kitty':

> Come pet my kitty sweet kitty
> Yes, those with Empathy you like kitties
> you're nice you care Kitties are nice electric ferret
> DOES YOUR SWEET KITTY LOOK AT YOU LIKE THIS
> WHEN ASKED TO OBEY? My Little Kitty (in Glenum, 2010, p. 16)

The speaker's repetition of 'kitty' (which the reader simultaneously associates both with kittens and a euphemism for the speaker's genitalia) enforces ideas of girlishness and cuteness – as Burns and Whalley write: 'Ngai reminds us that the cute object is always one that can be squeezed and fondled—and it crucially encourages and appeals to us [. . .] to touch and manipulate it' (2018). As a result, Gordon's speaker becomes less assertive and more submissive in her girlish sexuality. The speaker then subverts expectations by reasserting her voice through the upper-case lines and demanding her listener (or reader) 'obey'. Her cuteness is then reinstated through the final 'My little kitty', which diminishes both the 'kitty' and the speaker's assertiveness once more, thereby destabilising its initial allure. That girlish cuteness and sexuality go together is mocked, but not so much that the speaker's expression of her sexuality is completely undermined.

In 'Reticence in the Afterglow of a Powerfully Frisky Fit', Knox's speaker is 'lounging on the sofa | fondling a battery-operated Shih Tzu', 'rattling a bright orange bottle | of expired antibiotics' and 'surrounded by fat men | in neoprene wetsuits' (2007, p. 20). The whole situation is so bizarre that it can hardly be real, as if it were a scene from a nightmare or dream. It is camp: self-consciously overly stylised; everything is deliberately exaggerated, pushing the reader to the point of ridiculousness. Knox exaggerates the speaker's sexuality to the point of lurid, consumer-sexual gestures, and mimics and augments ideas about feminine sexuality and pornography – 'I'm primping in peanut butter | pasties and a candycane g-string' (2007, p. 20) – until the sexuality is hyperbolic and technicoloured. This is, as Jo Pickering writes, the hyperfeminine: a 'highmaintenance look', which might involve 'fake tan, hair extensions, false lashes, dyed hair, lots of make-up and, often, very flamboyant, colourful and/or revealing outfits' (2014, p. 197). The hyperfeminine is 'at once childlike and X-rated' and arguably '[raises] status in some way, to acquire a form of feminine capital through exercising control over the body' (Pickering, 2014, p. 197). However, Pickering writes, drawing on Skeggs, that these 'attempts to "do femininity" are read as a class drag act, an unconvincing and inadvertently parodic attempt to pass' (2014, p. 197). As such, Pickering writes that women's bodies are 'sites of rigorous control in this sense, whilst simultaneously declaring a kind of sexual abandon' (2014, p. 197). Knox's speaker uses food and inanimate objects to express her sexuality, which is not reciprocated by men, who are instead trying to 'tip over a vending machine' (2007, p. 20), absorbed in a consumerism that is somewhat uncomfortably signalled by their fatness.[5] The 'battery-operated Shih Tzu' and 'expired antibiotics' (2007, p. 20) undercut and deflate typical ideas of luxury and intemperance.

The speaker's outburst, 'GIVE ME BACK MY WIG YOU SHITS!' (2007, p. 20) completely disrupts any sense of allure or desire she has created.[6] At once, it reveals the speaker's underlying 'trashiness' and also undermines stereotypical images of femininity: the wig suddenly reveals an abject falsity to her femininity. Whereas Gordon's speaker's outburst and cuteness are both expressions of sexuality and attempts to be alluring, Knox's speaker is not 'cute', does not pretend to be 'cute', and through her utterance deflates the sense of desire she has performed by revealing herself to be brash, profane and outspoken, almost the epitome of camp. It suggests that stereotypes of (hyper)femininity are constraints which cannot last. Like the Gurlesque, Knox's poetry takes sexuality as a point of ridicule, but she also deploys this to make comments about class in the United States.

According to Gael Sweeney, 'white trash' culture is 'an aesthetic of the flashy, the inappropriate, the garish', and privileges 'details, brightness, presentation; it fills a lack, covering every empty space with stuff and effect, powerless to anything but collect junk and show it off' (1997, pp. 249, 250). In Knox's poem, the speaker's unstable hyperfemininity and lurid sexuality work in conjunction with 'white trashness', because 'white trashness' is held in the body. As Laura Kipnis writes: 'Improper bodies have political implications, and are particularly valenced in relation to issues of class' (Kipnis and Reeder, 1997, p. 114). As such, 'white trash' bodies might 'defy social norms and proprieties of size, smell, dress, manners or gender conventions' or display 'lack of proper decorum about matters of sex and elimination; or defy bourgeois sensibilities by being too uncontained and indecorous' (1997, p. 114). In this way, Knox's speaker displays her 'white trashness' by being so luridly sexualised and mentioning so much 'stuff'; her destabilised hyperfemininity and 'white trashness' not only threaten but obliterate perceived racial and sexual conventions. Through this, Knox pulls the reader into an uncomfortable position in which they must confront their own perceptions. Returning to Kaufmann's ideas about the avant-garde and cultural capital (2017, p. 57), it is my contention that Knox's poetry at least understands that privilege and capital, and wants to ridicule it, destabilising the idea of poetry as something to be revered and to afford privilege and capital, and placing class, race and poetry into a complex conversation.

Wray and Newitz write that '["white trash"] designates a set of stereotypes and myths related to the social behaviors, intelligence, prejudices and gender roles of poor whites [in America]' (1997, p. 7). Indeed, 'by behaving in a manner considered indecorous by [. . .] whites' those considered 'white trash' disrupt 'implicit understanding of what it means to be white' (Hartigan in Wray and Newitz, 1997, p. 46). In this way, 'Reticence in the Afterglow of a Powerfully Frisky Fit' destabilises ideas of whiteness, class and decorum. By acting indecorously, the speaker suggests that she is 'white trash', which is at odds with the reader knowing that this character exists in a poem, is the speaker of the poem and is not straightforwardly the target of the joke. The distinctions between 'high' and 'low' have been eliminated.

In Knox's poem, the gap between being truly rich and feigning being rich suggests there is a class discrepancy – the speaker is pretending to live an opulent lifestyle. Holloway-Smith notes that 'the "bourgeoisie" have drawn moral boundaries, encompassing valuations of worth amongst types of people through examinations of behaviours, practices of employment and tastes' (2014, p. 44). According to Holloway-Smith, the bourgeoisie, or middle class, creates this divide in order to differentiate themselves from lower classes (2014, p. 44). He argues that cultural competence is strongly alluded to by the tastes which persons possess (2014, p. 45); for Bourdieu, tastes are 'first and foremost distastes, disgust provoked by horror or visceral intolerance [. . .] of the taste of others' (1986, p. 56). Therefore, what is deemed indecorous – garishness, popular culture detritus – can be deemed aspirational in other contexts, as Knox explores in 'Reticence in the Afterglow of a Powerfully Frisky Fit', and is determined by both race and class.

To examine this, I wish to now look at Chris Brown and Tyga's music video for their song 'Ayo' (2015), which epitomises the conspicuous consumption on display in Knox's poem. As the music video opens, Tyga has bought a new toilet, designed as a throne featuring Egyptian iconography. Tyga creates a video on his phone, where a gold pharaoh appears on the screen and blocks of gold fall over the toilet. The video ends with the words: 'I'm shittin' on you'. At the same time, Chris Brown asks two men operating a small excavator to place a large pile of money into the swimming pool. Brown takes a photo of himself with a fan made of money. A tiger wanders through the mansion. Brown spends the majority of the video lounging in the pool on an inflatable gold cushion, surrounded by the money. Both men wear incredibly garish, mismatched outfits and several gold chains. The video is filled with copious amounts of gold and leopard print and multiple sports cars. When women appear, they are in underwear, or partaking in sports (early in the video, two women fence as Brown and Tyga play chess; later on, women pose behind the performers in polo equipment, on top of horses). Typically, these are sports played by white, wealthy middle or upper classes. In the video, then, Tyga and Brown use traditional, established images of wealth to legitimise their own wealth: they must prove that they are authentically wealthy. Moreover, the men who work for Brown and Tyga are white. Tyga and Brown, both people of colour, appear to be converting the 'rich white male' narrative and flaunting their own success in the face of dominant whiteness.

However, all the luxury – beginning with the money pool and throne toilet – indicates a lack of taste. The level of garishness and the lack of humility in showing wealth notably has bearing upon 'white trash' culture, as Sweeney shows: 'White Trash lives in a trailer, but aspires to a deluxe double-wide with purple shag carpeting, red crushed velvet sofas, and gold foil wallpaper' (in Wray and Newitz, 1997, p. 250).[7] In the video for 'Ayo', Brown and Tyga undermine the social code of respectability, whiteness and wealth with their conspicuous consumption. There is, then, a clear link between Knox's speaker's lurid and technicolour opulence and music videos like 'Ayo'. Knox – like Brown and Tyga – uses stereotypical images of luxury and then undermines them: rather than having a tiger wandering around her mansion, Knox has a toy shih tzu. Knox's poem highlights these images of hedonistic extravagance and reimagines them as even more gauche, lower-class, trashy versions. She breaks the fetishisation of class by recreating how, in many cases, being supremely wealthy often creates a lack of taste. In thinking of the garishness of 'Ayo', Brown and Tyga flaunt their wealth while also revealing that money can buy *things*, but it cannot buy *taste*.

The speaker of Knox's poem copies and exaggerates an opulent lifestyle to the point of preposterousness. What the speaker means by 'Oriental pleasure' (2007, p. 20) is unclear, and she seems to have created this term to sound lavish, to impress, whereas it actually falls into disrepute via the overtly racist connotations. She admits elsewhere: 'I'm making your socks say I profane things to Puerto Ricans' (2007, p. 20). Here might be more 'punching up' then – another case of Knox using a white speaker's racism to highlight their stupidity; equally, it might be 'punching down', if the speaker is also 'white trash' (they are stupid because of their class). But taking Jackson's claims about poetry needing to show less 'acceptable and overly mined areas of embarrassment and shame', Knox may be doing something slightly more subversive than an initial reading suggests. If Knox's presumed writer is white and middle class, and she expects the reader to laugh at her 'white trash' speaker, then the reader's laughter is undercut when the speaker says something racist, perhaps reminding the reader that their own classism is no better than racism. It is, ultimately, a risky manoeuvre, one which courts several readings, all of which may be true, all of which do not seem firmly settled.

Elsewhere in *A Gringo Like Me*, Knox offers a more generous satire, as seen in 'Hot Ass Poem':

> Hey check out the ass on that guy he's got a really hot ass I'd like to see his ass naked with his hot naked ass Hey check out her hot ass that chick's got a hot ass she's a red hot ass chick I want to touch it Hey check out the ass on that old man that's one hot old man ass look at his ass his ass his old man ass [. . .] (2007, p. 23)

Here, Knox repeats 'ass' (or 'hot ass') so frequently that it becomes ridiculous. Initially, Knox's use of 'ass' and the subject of the poem is humorous, but as the poem continues and repeats itself, it becomes more pointed. In her discussion of the 'white-trashing' of pornography, Constance Penley describes John Stagliano's creation, 'Buttman', who 'goes around the world (and Southern California) seeking the perfect shot of a woman's perfect ass . . . Licking ass, caressing ass, ogling ass' (1997, p. 106). It is important to note that the fetishisation of the 'ass' is grounded in racist depictions of Black women. In her influential essay 'Selling Hot Pussy: Representations of Black Female Sexuality in the Cultural Marketplace' (2014), bell hooks writes: 'In the sexual iconography of the traditional black pornographic imagination, the protruding butt is seen as an indication of heightened sexuality', and Black 'butts' are coded as 'unruly and outrageous' while the body of a Black woman gains 'attention only when it is synonymous with accessibility, availability, when it is sexually deviant' (pp. 63, 65). As Diane Railton and Paul Watson write, 'in mapping *availability* onto black women's bodies and *unavailability* on to the bodies of white women', Black women are presented as 'fascinating curiosities for the entertainment of a white audience' (2011, p. 92). As such, white women are often coded as 'precisely above and beyond the base needs and desires of the "primitive" body' (2011, p. 92).

Knox's deflation in 'Hot Ass Poem' acts to examine the very fetishisation of the 'ass' in isolation. With every repetition of 'ass', the reader begins to question this fetishisation, addressing their unexamined, reflexive statements and reactions until they seem ridiculous. 'Hot Ass Poem' is about destabilising ideas of sex (and thereby their underlying racism). In this poem, everyone has a 'hot ass', which deflates the 'unavailability' of white women in contrast to the 'availability' of Black women: in 'Hot Ass Poem', everyone is available, even dogs and bikes. This, then, diminishes the racist stereotype of the Black 'ass' and highlights the ridiculousness of this fetishisation, to shame racist notions of bodies and sexiness. Here, Knox recognises the kinds of culture that are valued in society: while poetry is viewed as a high art form, sex – and pornography like Stagliano's – is more regularly consumed. Ultimately, this is further self-effacement to destabilise the poet–reader relationship, an attempt to create a levelling humour, a subversion of what is considered high culture and a dominant whiteness that determines how we view sex and bodies.

Destabilising Authority

The collection's titular poem, 'A Gringo Like Me', is written in the style of a western screenplay, and borrows its title from Ennio Morricone and Peter Tevis' song of the same name, which was used on the soundtrack of the 1963 spaghetti western *Duello nel Texas* (*Gunfight at Red Sands*). The western film is notoriously reliant on racist stereotypes, which depict Native American people as bloodthirsty, violent, unintelligent and likely to abduct white women (Price, 1973, p. 153; Berny, 2020, p. 1). Even when depictions are positive, they rely on the equally racist stereotype of the more positive 'noble Indian' figure (Berny, 2020, p. 1). Indeed, the racism, absurdity and imprecision of the genre (Dyer, 2017, pp. 32–3), and the song – which proclaims: 'There's just one kind of man that you can trust, | That's a dead man, or a gringo like me' – is the basis of Knox's poem.

Notably, Knox eschews the racist depictions of Native Americans. Instead, the screenplay becomes the vehicle of a satire of distinctions between 'high' and 'low', and of the genre more broadly. Knox uses gauche stereotypes and clichés of the western to introduce the reader to the world of the poem: there is tumbleweed, an empty street, high noon. In 'A Gringo Like Me' the hero, Red Farben, behaves in a stereotypically hyperbolic manner, entering 'on tiptoe with shush finger pressed to pursed lips' (2007, p. 29); this is compounded by the bathos and deflation in the joke of his name. 'Farben' is the German word for 'colour', so the hero's name is 'Red Colour'. This name also points to the red western genre, the Soviet Union's answer to the American western, and the ostern, the East German response to West German 'westerns' (Lavrentiev, 2013). As Sergey Lavrentiev writes, 'in the Soviet Union, the western was considered a reactionary genre which praised the white colonialists' extermination of [. . .] Indians' (2013), while Rossiyskaya Gazeta and Vadim Davydenko note that the red western 'depicts the Indians with sympathy, as an oppressed people that are fighting for their rights' (2014). Conspicuously, Knox's brief mention of special effects ('prairie wind') also points to the falsity of western film sets, and especially those of red western and ostern films – not filmed in the US but made to look like the US.

Knox exposes the absurdity of the genre by utilising further gauche and cartoonish stereotypes:

(Enter left **CARNE BROTHERS** leaping / snapping fingers / yee-haaing / flicking lighters in fifty-gallon cowboy hats / mirrored contact lenses.)

CARNE BROTHERS
(In unison – metallic spaceman voice.)
Sheeeeriff Faaaaaarbeeeeeen, preeeepaaaaare to deeefeeeeend yoooour-seeeeeelf!

Music: Swells.

(Enter right **GIRLS**, spinning in fringed, sequined leotards with miniature ponies strapped to tap shoes.) (2007, p. 29)

At first, when the Carne Brothers enter, their actions place them directly within the western's logic, as they act as stereotypical cowboys, yee-haaing and wearing cowboy hats. However, their 'mirrored contact lenses' undermine this logic quickly and offer a surprise to the reader, who has until now believed that the world logic is predictable. Knox undermines the archetypal logic of the poem's world by interrupting with another layer of cliché. Dyer writes that the western genre is 'carried by signs of pastness' and an imprecise and a 'geographical location' (2017, p. 33), but

110 *Whiteness, Feminism and the Absurd in Contemporary Poetry*

Knox refigures the western with slightly more modern, but still outdated, references: the Carne Brothers appear to be robots or 'metallic spacemen', whose speech is a gauche formula of low-budget science fiction. Just as the reader has begun to re-comprehend the world logic, which now consists of overlapping clichés, Knox challenges the limits of plausibility. Knox does not explain who the 'girls' are, and now the reader must understand that, in the world of the poem, horses can be small enough to be tied to tap shoes.

The characters begin to sing their dialogue, and the Harlem Globetrotters' Theme is played as the characters 'invent the game of basketball with severed heads' (Knox, 2007, p. 29). The poem's logic is disrupted by anachronisms, grotesque images and a change in genre, and the chaos of the screenplay creates a dark humour through confusion. As Ira Berkow writes for *The New York Times*, the Harlem Globetrotters are controversial: some see the group, especially the teams from the 1960s and 1970s, as performing 'dimwitted stereotypes, trying to do nothing more than give whitey a chance to laugh' (2005). Berkow notes that others, such as American civil rights activist Jesse Jackson, took another view: 'They did not show blacks as stupid. On the contrary, they were shown as superior' (Jackson in Berkow, 2005). Berkow opines that when Mannie Jackson, a 'onetime Globetrotter turned successful businessman' bought the team in 1993 and revived it, he 'eliminated some of the "racially stereotyped gags"' (2005); the team was inducted into the Basketball Hall of Fame in 2002.

In Knox's poem, it is not clear who the severed heads belong to, nor how they came to be severed. However, there is a gesture towards the violence of performing racist stereotypes – in much the way the 'ass' in isolation is fetishised – to entertain white people. The western follows a similar trope: ostensibly fun, but dark and terrible in reality. Knox's new conception of the genre – borrowing from western, red western, ostern and sci-fi – still nods towards these racist tropes, the severed heads a reminder of the danger and horror of this; while the basketball game looks fun, it can only exist because people had to die. While the Carne Brothers and dancers create a cacophony, this strange, unsettling scene unfolds. The poem shares its title with the collection, and so it is worth revisiting its meaning: 'gringo' is intended as an insult, and as a marker of a kind of white ignorance. The poem, then, seems to enact this ignorance by creating a distracting chaos as racial stereotypes are ignored – we might have moved on from 'Cowboys and Indians', but white people still make everything about themselves.

The surreal and bizarre scene continues to develop:

BOYS, GIRLS, WHORES
(Form shape of optometrist seen from above: when dancers open legs in unison, optometrist changes to an eye chart. Close legs: optometrist. Open legs: eye chart.) (2007, p. 30)

Knox's inclusion of an optometrist and eye chart at this stage of the poem appears to be an exceptional non sequitur, but the Harlem Globetrotter's Theme is 'Sweet Georgia Brown', a song about men who 'all sigh, and want to die | For sweet Georgia brown!'. Perhaps the severed heads come from men who have sacrificed themselves for this cause. It is worth highlighting that the women in the poem are described as 'whores' or 'girls', and that there are evident sexual connotations to the dancers' legs opening and closing in unison. Knox is gesturing towards conflicting ideas of women's sexuality: women are either a 'Georgia' – 'sweet', 'a girl', the kind of woman 'no gal made has got a shade | On', who wear shiny outfits with ponies on them – or a 'whore', opening and closing their legs.

Knox's switching between eye chart and optometrist suggests an ultimate moment of honesty: Knox here admits that she is attempting to look at something (race, gender, status quo in genre or poetry) clearly, to tackle it, but keeps on getting distracted by the camp, popular culture, and all the other distractions her speakers and characters suffer from. She is no better, no more enlightened. The poem cannot resolve this conflict, and its content is too chaotic to prove a direct an attack on whiteness, but the zany scenes and deflation of gauche stereotypes throughout the poem speak to these ideas: in ridiculing the very idea of a western and all its madcap and racist tropes, Knox seems to be thinking through a great tradition and exposing all its flaws.

If the reader remembers the Carne Brothers' mirrored contact lenses, and considers that the above image creates a kind of kaleidoscope, then the images are subtly linked and referred to throughout the poem: Knox is creating a shifting and complex logic which reveals the utter ludicrousness of the western, and thereby the structures of race and gender it relies upon. Knox uses the tropes of the western film to undermine its popularity and legacy, while allowing the reader to feel as though they understand the poem's logic. She then undercuts the reader's knowledge, creating a chaotic world with subtle references, so that the reader always feels one step behind. It is never clear who is in charge in this poem, but one thing is clear: the Gringo is to be ridiculed.

In a discussion of Knox's poetry, particularly 'Chicken Bucket', Rachel Loden notes: 'There is a way, I think, where the denigration can be so wholesale, mean, and scathing that one gets a sense that that wand of ire could easily be turned on (a) anyone in the audience, and (b) the poet herself' (in Loden and Silem Mohammed, 2007). For Loden, this is 'redemptive' because it suggests that 'we are all damned together, we are all fools together, even the least of us' (in Loden and Silem Mohammed, 2007). Indeed, we might all be damned together (i.e. heading towards an apocalypse), but Loden's comments gesture towards a resigned return to an accepting apoliticalness, an acceptance of things as they are, rather than looking forward to what they might be. What if, instead, Knox's wand of ire is meant to cause the white, privileged reader to evaluate their own prejudices, and become more active? Knox's speakers are, as I have shown, often doomed to repeat destructive behaviours, and, as a poet, Knox does not offer straightforward, tangible solutions. Yet her opinion of this is complex, often latent: indeed, she is damning inaction, condemning foolish behaviour. Her conception of what might challenge this is unclear, but Knox is willing to try to look at whiteness and interrogate it, even if she does not manage to push it completely off the pedestal.

Chapter 5

Sadness in Caroline Bird's *The Hat-Stand Union* and *In These Days of Prohibition*

In Chapter 4, I explored how Jennifer L. Knox's *A Gringo Like Me* (2007) employs self-effacing humour to destabilise the reader–poet relationship and deflate elitist approaches to poetry through direct engagement with 'high' and 'low' culture in her poems. In doing so, I demonstrated how Knox uses popular culture to ridicule systems that extol privileged, male writers and reductive narratives for women. Knox's poetry attempts – sometimes unclearly – to grapple with assumptions of cultural capital, privilege and whiteness. In this chapter, I turn my focus to the 'Sad Girl' internet movement. While this movement is wrought with worrying fetishisations of whiteness and inertia, in some guises it demonstrates how sadness can be a site for movement and change, which in turn can be used to understand white British poet Caroline Bird's collections *The Hat-Stand Union* (2013) and *In These Days of Prohibition* (2017). I argue, drawing on Dave Coates, Louis MacNeice and Samuel Beckett's *Waiting for Godot*, that Bird's poems act like parables, in which Bird warns her (presumed white, middle-class) reader against their own ennui and inaction.

Sad Girls

i-D declared 2015 the year of the 'Sad Girl', a movement heralded by Lana del Rey's debut album *Born to Die* (released in 2012) and a penchant for 'PDS' – public displays of sadness (Newell-Hanson, 2015). As Hannah Williams writes: 'Instagram began to take hold, and YouTube continued to cement its place in media. With new technology came the opportunity to share your most intimate moments in a way that wasn't possible before' (2017). On the internet, women and girls were declaring themselves 'sad', and revelling in it, turning away from, as Thelandersson writes, a '(post)feminist can-do spirit' (2022, p. 11). Can-Do Girls, are, as Anita Harris describes, a 'unique category of girls who are self-assured, living lives inflected but by no means driven by feminism . . . assuming they can have (or at least buy) it all' (in Mooney, 2018, p. 176). The Sad Girl flew in the face of such neoliberal consumption and self-optimisation, using internet platforms such as Instagram and Tumblr to express sadness and demonstrate that 'the privileged can-do girl does not fully address the effects of sexism and patriarchy' (Mooney, 2018, p. 178). As Thelandersson writes, some examples of content circulated by Sad Girls are 'pictures of pills in bright pink colors; animated texts that read things like "having a threesome with anxiety and depression"; glittering words that spell out "100% Sad"' (2022, p. 162).[1]

The Sad Girl movement is the subject of great debate, engendering passionate arguments about its cultural appropriation, stasis and 'clicktivism', which Emma Maguire describes as enabling 'a lazy form of "armchair" activism whereby the expression of support for a social cause replaces taking action to make material changes for that cause, fostering political passivity' (2018, p. 141). Sad Girl postings are exemplified in the work of Audrey Wollen, the self-dubbed creator of Sad Girl Theory (Tunnicliffe and Wollen, 2015), and Melissa Broder, creator of the @sosadtoday Twitter (now X) account. Wollen proposes that the 'sadness of girls should be witnessed and re-historicized as an act of resistance, of political protest' rather than an 'act of passivity', because it 'isn't quiet, weak, shameful, or dumb: It is active, autonomous, and articulate. It's a way of fighting back' (Tunnicliffe and Wollen, 2015). Wollen claims that a 'limited spectrum of activism excludes a whole history of girls who have used their sorrow and their self-destruction to disrupt systems of domination. Girls' sadness [. . .] is a way of reclaiming agency over their bodies, identities and lives' (Watson and Wollen, 2015). Wollen previously posted Sad Girl content on her Instagram account (@tragicqueen), including 'taking selfies with books during her regular visits to hospital' (Fournier, 2018, p. 650) and juxtaposing 'images and characters from *Sailor Moon* with such texts as Judith Butler's *Gender Trouble*, Simone de Beauvoir's *The Second Sex*, and Shulamith Firestone's *The Dialectic of Sex*' (Fournier, 2018, p. 659). In early 2016, Wollen announced that she would be taking a break from her account due to 'the climate of online feminism' and how '"sad girl theory" is often understood at its most reductive, instead of as a proposal to open up more spacious discussions abt [*sic*] what activism could look like' (Wollen in Thelandersson, 2022, p. 172).

As Fournier writes, Wollen's work advances a 'Consumerism 101 view' in which 'one's identity is based on the things one consumes' (2018,

p. 653), even if those objects are feminist or theoretical. For Fournier, then, Sad Girl Theory is 'suffused with irony and implicit (ambivalent, complicit) capitalist critique' (2018, p. 653). The movement as a whole is fraught with worrying fetishisations of mental illness and what Thelandersson describes as a '"profitable vulnerability" that serves to show acceptance and tolerance of weakness while keeping a distance/remaining unthreatening', which ultimately becomes a sellable brand (2022, p. 12): many of the most popular Sad Girl accounts become monetised, sell merchandise and create minor celebrities of their creators.

For Williams, the Sad Girl movement is 'undone by the very platforms it thrives on' (2017). Williams describes Melissa Broder's Twitter (now X) account, 'so sad today' (@sosadtoday), as 'an infinite scroll into the depths of sadness, stripped of complexity and context' (2017). Some of Broder's posts are genuinely amusing and emotionally resonant, such as 'i came, i saw, i hid in the bathroom' (2017a),[2] 'you say potato i say inevitable death' (2017b) and 'she died as she lived: kind of ready for it but not really' (2017c); these posts create their humour by utilising everyday examples of introverted behaviour. There is a gauche 'honesty' to these self-deprecating admissions of sadness and loneliness, and a sense that the speaker is ridiculing herself. However, other posts from the account such as 'crying internally' (2018) and 'i feel bad for all of us' (2021) lack emotional resonance because they do not provide any context for the sadness. This is not to say that all sadness and depression require a context or 'reason', but in this form, the expression of sadness becomes a meaningless statement rather than an effective communication of sadness, because the reader cannot connect in any way with the speaker or online persona. As Williams argues, this sadness, 'repeated over and over again [. . .] becomes empty, no longer an outlet but a parody of sincere emotion, a stereotype and fetishization of female sadness' (2017). Popularity and acceptance via social media are gained by being sad and sharing Sad Girl content, so that it becomes a desirable self-projection and is therefore replicated, ultimately becoming as ubiquitous as self-help aphorisms.

Broder's initial intentions for her 'so sad today' account seem to have focused on needing a form of expression for her mental health (Bromwich and Broder, 2016) rather than consciously creating an internet movement. Initially, the account was a means for her to share her sadness anonymously (Bromwich and Broder, 2016) and to create 'commonality' through the posts about sadness. Broder's Twitter (now X) account is not the same as writing a confessional diary, as social media platforms provide audiences for writing and thoughts in a way that a private diary does not: the posts are meant to be seen. Broder has expressed that she

116   *Whiteness, Feminism and the Absurd in Contemporary Poetry*

is pleased that her account has helped people to address their mental health issues (Bromwich and Broder 2016) but, as Williams notes, the Sad Girl movement 'hinges on the idea that women should be inherently sad, never moving forward or growing' (2017). For all Broder's account is said to have helped people, the account is still live, and Broder is still posting content about sadness – there is no sense of improvement or change in the posts. Depression and serious mental health issues do not have cures, so I am not proposing that Broder's posts suggest that she is 'cured' of her depression. However, many of the posts are actually humorous and 'relatable' snippets of gauche, introverted behaviour and sadness, rather than a discussion of mental health and depression.

Indeed, Broder's posts on the 'so sad today' account mimic much of Wollen's work, turning the Sad Girl movement into a series of commodifiable and 'cool' objects, as in this post from 21 October 2022: 'charcuterie board: vibrator, twizzlers, empty pack of cigarettes belonging to a dead man, crystal that didn't heal me, therapy copay' (2022a); in the discourse of the Sad Girl, going to therapy is a 'cool' activity that legitimates one's status as a Sad Girl – but therapy never seems to help (and neither do crystals). In several examples of the Sad Girl movement, there is a distinct lack of movement: perpetual sadness is the goal, or, as Broder puts it: 'i was born to give up' (2022b).[3]

For Thelandersson, there are two types of Sad Girl, broadly speaking: Tumblr Sad Girls and Instagram Sad Girls. Tumblr Sad Girls are engaged in 'impasse', which allows 'sufferers to rest in "bad" feelings without having to immediately work to get rid of them', their wilful stasis a 'protest of the neoliberal demands of becoming a laboring and "happy" subject' and an attempt to make 'depression central to what it means to be human', thereby making it unexceptional (2022, pp. 167, 168). But the Tumblr Sad Girls do not make overtly political statements, do not attempt to challenge structures of power that create the material conditions of their sadness and idealise their sadness as 'romantic, mystical, and inspirational' (2022, p. 169).[4] Broder's 'so sad today' account is clearly akin to this. Instagram Sad Girls, on the other hand, use a self-effacing humour in which the open 'display of one's diagnoses and medications becomes an act of defiance against normative discourses' (2022, p. 179), and the humour is, according to Thelandersson, intended to create a community and space to communicate; crucially, the 'display of vulnerability here is not of the kind common in confidence culture[5] – where difficulties are shared after they have been successfully overcome' (2022, p. 179). According to Thelandersson, the most pertinent difference is that Instagram Sad Girls are, broadly speaking, often more 'explicitly political' and thereby followers 'learn to associate also critical, anti-capitalist, thought into the experience of mental illness, and connections can possibly be made between personal suffering and larger, structural issues' (2022, p. 183).[6]

I return again, then, to Kaufman's definitions of feminist and feminine humour, which clearly map onto these categories of Sad Girl. Of course, the Sad Girl – especially the politically engaged Sad Girl – has roots in feminist theory, for as Nancy A. Walker writes, 'how it feels to be a member of a subordinate group in a culture that prides itself on equality, what it is like to try to meet standards for behaviour that are based on stereotypes rather than on human beings' is a crucial element of feminist humour, since women have used humour to 'frequently protest their condition' (1988, p. x). The Sad Girl movement is perhaps so controversial because it uses dark humour to make light of – and commonality in the experience of – mental illness.

Yet the Sad Girl movement has a problem with whiteness: white, thin girls are the default image of an acceptable sadness (Thelandersson, 2022, p. 11); Fournier skewers Wollen's work as a 'savvy move at self-branding in light of the influence that framing one's work as theory [. . .] for young women with class mobility who have been exposed to theory in art school' (2018, p. 655). Indeed, as Heather Mooney demonstrates, the Sad Girl movement has been co-opted by white women, appropriated from the 'Sad Girls Y Qué' who offer an alternative to 'solidarity and intersectional protest to colonization, machismo, white feminism, and the devaluation of youth and femininity' (2018, p. 182). Drawing on Ahmed's (2004) work, 'Affective Economies', Mooney notes that in the white Sad Girl movement, the 'performativity of white affect through the commodification and consumption of "the Other"' reifies legacies of whiteness' (2018, p. 184). This does not mean that all Sad Girls are white: activism-based online groups, such as the Sad Girls Club and the Asian Sad Girls Club, have welcomed multiple racial identities and engaged with systemic racism, providing support and community for their followers (Thelandersson, 2022, p. 186; Maguire, 2018, p. 142).

The Sad Girl movement – particularly its relationship to stasis and movement, and whiteness – sheds light on how humour in contemporary Absurdist poetry functions, namely in the work of Caroline Bird, a prolific and highly decorated poet whose work focuses (at times obliquely) on mental illness and addiction. It is important to note that Bird's poetry does not simply take the Sad Girl movement and employ it under a new guise. Bird's work, including poems in her earlier collections, *Trouble Came to the Turnip* (2006) and *Watering Can* (2009), predates the ubiquity of the Sad Girl movement. Yet the Sad Girl movement is a useful example for thinking about white women's sadness and inaction, and thereby how sadness might have the capacity to engender action and be

118 *Whiteness, Feminism and the Absurd in Contemporary Poetry*

politicised. In this chapter, I wish to look at two of Bird's collections, *The Hat-Stand Union* and *In These Days of Prohibition*, which can be read as companion texts, to demonstrate how Bird's poetry interacts with the idea of sadness, how this can perpetuate and challenge notions of white sadness and how her work interacts with ideas of stasis and movement.

In the poem 'Mystery Tears' (from *The Hat-Stand Union*), sadness becomes an omnipresent trend and people purchase 'Mystery Tears', a drug that causes its users to cry. The speaker recalls how they 'first became popular on the young German art scene' and how 'thin boys would tap a few drops into their eyes' and 'paint their girlfriends' legs akimbo and faces cramped | with wisdom, in the style of the Weimar Republic' (2013, p. 17). Here, the deadpan voice delivers a dark joke that undercuts the sadness, and then reaffirms the actual despondency of the episode by highlighting the artificial sadness of everyone buying synthetic tears. The Mystery Tears are a means of producing artificial sadness, a performative sorrow not too far removed from Broder's Sad Girl despondency. The sadness in this poem is framed as artistic and performative, and the sufferers are like the white Sad Girl: privileged and reaching for an image that is 'sexy' (2013, p. 17).[7] Bird refers to real suffering by recalling the Weimar Republic,[8] and then further highlights the disparity between real suffering and performative sadness by noting that the Mystery Tears are different from Hollywood tears, because they *act* more like real tears by having a 'staggered release system' (2013, p. 17) and catching the user by surprise, as real emotions can: 'One minute, | you're sitting at the dinner table eating a perfectly nice steak | then you're crying until you're sick in a plant pot' (2013, p. 17). By framing Hollywood tears as less authentic, Bird highlights the inauthenticity of the Mystery Tears too: they are, after all, just another means of performing sadness.

Rather than a direct invective against privilege, Bird's poem becomes a nuanced consideration of addiction and its totalising and devastating effects. The speaker recalls how her partner 'sadly became addicted to Mystery Tears' (2013, p. 17), a phrasing which, in the bathos of 'sadly', seems to set up a joke. The reader is then wrongfooted as the speaker explains: 'A thousand pounds went in a week | and everything I did provoked despair'; the partner buys Mystery Tears named '*Not Enough*' – a suggestion that behind her drug-induced sadness, there is a real sadness too. But the speaker's partner declares: '"It's so romantic," [. . .] "and yet I feel nothing"' (2013, p. 17). Therefore, the sadness becomes completely performative as there is no way for the partner to *feel* her sadness, and thereby no way to change things. On the other hand, the speaker becomes genuinely sad, and affected by her sadness and her partner's addiction. The real sadness is so total that it has a physical effect: their flat 'shook and dampened' (2013, p. 17), as though it is crying, too. The speaker asserts that she 'never I touched' the Mystery Tears to indicate that her sadness is real and worsening, while the partner grows 'calmer and calmer' (2013, p. 17). The final line of the poem is separated into its own stanza, enacting the growing space between the speaker and her partner. Indeed, the poem suggests that the situation will only worsen; as the partner grows calmer, the speaker becomes genuinely unhappier. The silence surrounding the final line of the poem emphasises that genuine sadness has crept insidiously into the speaker's life.

Static Quests

In his review of Caroline Bird's *The Hat-Stand Union* (2012), Dave Coates states that Bird's poetry includes 'examples of something often attempted but rarely well-executed in contemporary poetry: parable. By parable I mean a semi-narrative piece that uses a central metaphor or repetend to explore an idea' (2013). In the Introduction, I explained the difference between the Absurd and a central metaphor – as in Pascale Petit's collection *Mama Amazonica*. So, while I do not entirely follow Coates's definition of a poetry parable, I do want to follow his assertion that Bird's poetry – and the Absurd more broadly – might be better understood through its relationship to the parable.

In his influential *Varieties of Parable*, first published in 1965 and firmly influenced by Esslin's *Theatre of the Absurd*, Louis MacNeice discusses 'one very valuable kind of parable', the 'kind which on the surface may not look like a parable at all', and turns to Esslin's *Theatre of the Absurd* to discuss how playwrights are 'doing what poets have done so often', asking 'the age-old unanswerable questions' (2008, pp. 3, 14). This leads Beckett – who for MacNeice offers the perfect example of the Absurd and the parable's relationship – to ask an 'underlying, paradoxical riddle' in his work: 'When is unbelief *not* unbelief?' (MacNeice, 2008, p. 118). For MacNeice, religion (loss or otherwise) is a key part of the Absurd, and 'a religious theme, when it gets to literature, requires some sort of parable form' (2008, p. 119). MacNeice argues that the 'parable takes the guise of a quest, and either *Waiting for Godot* or *Endgame* could be described, if paradoxically, as a static quest' (2008, p. 119). Esslin suggests that Beckett is working 'at a level where neither characters nor plot exist' and that 'characters presuppose that human nature, the diversity of personality and individuality, is real and matters; plot can exist only on the assumption that events in time are significant' (2023, p. 52).

120   *Whiteness, Feminism and the Absurd in Contemporary Poetry*

Biblical parables, while dense with the meaning necessary in establishing a universal order in which everything is significant, are also potentially opaque, strange and open to multiple interpretations. If we take Luke 11: 5–8 as an example:

> And he said unto them, Which of you shall have a friend, and shall go unto him at midnight, and say unto him, Friend, lend me three loaves; For a friend of mine in his journey is come to me, and I have nothing to set before him? And he from within shall answer and say, Trouble me not: the door is now shut, and my children are with me in bed; I cannot rise and give thee. I say unto you, Though he will not rise and give him, because he is his friend, yet because of his importunity he will rise and give him as many as he needeth. (Luke 11: 5–8)

Superficially, the parable does not contain much meaning. As a story, it is unremarkable: a man visits his neighbour late at night and asks for three loaves of bread because he has another friend visiting. Due to the man's persistence, not their friendship, his reluctant friend eventually acquiesces and gives him the loaves. The construction of the parable causes its obliquity. The initial question is posed as though it is rhetorical, or even bizarre, but it is also a pertinent statement regarding faith and the need for persistence in prayer and belief. The characters act bizarrely: the man, speaking from inside, clearly can help his friend but refuses (and we are not given a reason for his refusal). It is also unclear why the first man's visiting friend needs three loaves of bread, but the parable resists logical answers. The parable teaches a specific lesson, and the reader must spend time with it to truly understand its significance. Esslin's comments about the Absurd apply here: the characters and plot are not important in this parable; the importance lies in how the characters and plot relate to faith. Crucially, the biblical parables are tethered to the Abrahamic tradition, and are therefore antithetical to the nihilism for which the Absurd is well known.

Let us return to the idea of a 'static quest', a futile waiting game as seen in *Waiting for Godot*.[9] In this Beckett play, two men named Vladimir and Estragon wait for a man named Godot, claiming that they will remain under a bare tree 'Until he comes' (2006, p. 16). The characters are confused about how much time has passed, asking each other in Act 1, 'What did we do yesterday?' and 'But what Saturday? And is it Saturday? Is it not rather Sunday? [*Pause.*] Or Monday? [*Pause.*] Or Friday?' (2006, pp. 16, 16–17), and grow increasingly frustrated as they wait and pass the time by talking and telling stories. They meet Pozzo and Lucky; Pozzo is trying to sell Lucky, a seemingly mute man whom he controls via rope and clipped, barking orders, and makes carry his heavy luggage. During a strange encounter with the men, Vladmir announces his intentions to leave ('Let's go!' (2006, p. 29)) while Estragon, sensing Pozzo might be charitable with them, states: 'We're in no hurry' (2006, p. 29). This interaction is refigured throughout the play in which the men, including Pozzo, attempt to leave and fail (or manage with great effort in Pozzo's case, although this is not without consequence) or change things, but continue waiting for Godot.

Vladimir and Estragon seemingly (and passively) accept their torturous wait (which feels very much akin to purgatory (Robinson, 1979)), while Pozzo waits to rebel against his. At first, it seems as though Pozzo is very much in control of Lucky, but in Act 1, it becomes apparent that this might not be the case – Pozzo is being tortured by Lucky (Gurnow, 2014). As Pozzo groans, clutching his head (as though possessed, or going insane), he says: 'I can't bear it . . . any longer . . . the way he goes on . . . you've no idea' (2006, p. 34). Vladimir chastises Pozzo for wanting to sell Lucky, telling him: 'After having sucked all the good out of him you chuck him away like a . . . like a banana skin' (2006, p. 33), but then, upon hearing of Pozzo's torture, admonishes Lucky: 'How dare you! It's abominable! Such a good master! Crucify him like that! After so many years!' (2006, p. 34). Pozzo's plea for Vladimir and Estragon to 'Forget all I said' (2006, p. 34) as he emerges from his tortured state resets the dynamic, and solidifies his claim that 'I might just as well have been in [Lucky's] shoes and he in mine. If change had not willed otherwise' (2006, p. 32). At the end of the first Act, a boy approaches Vladimir and Estragon with a message: Mr Godot has told the boy to tell them that he 'won't come this evening but surely tomorrow' (2006, p. 49).

In the second Act, stage directions suggest that the action takes place the 'next day' (2006, p. 53), yet the tree under which the characters sit has multiple leaves, suggesting more time has passed. Vladimir and Estragon carry on in much the same way as before – wondering how much time has passed, passing the hours talking – yet claim that they are 'happy', and now that they are happy, the only thing to do is 'Wait for Godot' (2006, p. 56). When Pozzo, now blind, returns, with Lucky on a much shorter rope, Vladimir mistakes them for Godot: 'We are no longer alone, waiting for the night, waiting for Godot, waiting for . . . waiting. All evening we have struggled, unassisted. Now it's over' (2006, p. 72). He claims to know the answer to a true existential question ('What are we doing here, *that* is the question' (2006, p. 74)), claiming that they are 'blessed' to 'know the answer': 'Yes, in this immense confusion one thing alone is clear. We are waiting for Godot to come' (2006, p. 74). This does not prevent Vladimir from claiming that they are 'bored' (2006, p. 75). Pozzo does not recognise the men and alleges that he did not meet the men the day before – again, time is slippery and the world logic of Beckett's play is oblique. Yet it is apparent that Godot will never turn up: the boy returns at the end of the play to repeat his message. Vladimir and Estragon claim they will 'hang ourselves tomorrow' if Godot does not come (2006, p. 88) – an act that would not provide an escape from the Absurd, as Camus writes – or, if he does arrive, they will be 'saved' (2006, p. 88).

Despite Beckett's insistence that the Godot is not God, and the play is not about 'Godot but waiting, the act of waiting as an essential and characteristic aspect of the human condition' (in MacNeice, 2008, p. 117), there are evident parallels here to the parable in Luke 11: 5–8: the persistence in faith, even as all events suggest otherwise. Indeed, Vladmir's moralising to both Pozzo and Lucky might also be read as parable-like, instructing the two men to care for one another, and remember their duty to one another. Yet, as in *Endgame*, the characters fail to move – to change things and escape their boredom – because they do not know how to accept the Absurd into their lives; they try to pin meaning on Godot's appearance, try to escape through suicide, try to leave and fail. We might also read *Waiting for Godot* as a warning against petty distractions. What might Vladimir and Estragon have done with their lives if they were not waiting for Godot?

In Bird's 'How the Wild Horse Stopped Me' (from *The Hat-Stand Union*), a horse accosts the speaker while she is trying to call her 'date', and asks her to complete a survey. The horse begins with a self-referential series of questions: 'And your ideal survey . . . would it have A) Big questions B) Small | questions. C) Stupid questions. D) Impossible questions?' (2013, p. 38), and when the speaker refuses to answer, says, 'I'll put you down for E) I just want silence in my head' (2013, p. 38). The question and potential answers become seemingly more oblique, with no real connection to the idea of a 'survey'; the horse asks the speaker to: 'Write your favourite colour on this scrap of paper then drop it in the fish bowl', and then to 'pick one from the bowl' (2013, p. 38), ignoring the speaker when she points out her scrap of paper is the only one available for selection. The survey is therefore futile: it is a pointless distraction.

Yet the speaker's resistance dwindles as the poem continues; she becomes distracted herself and acquiesces:

'Do you ever go down to the river?

A)   Not since mother/ father/ sister/ brother/ everyone went mental.
B)   Not since I fell in love.

Sadness in Caroline Bird   123

C)   Not since I pretended to move on.
D)   My face is wet with river water. I have a watermark across my chin.'

'B. No. C. No. C. No. C.' (2013, p. 38)

The horse's survey, in fact, seems designed for the speaker, to ask her specific questions – in the style of a magazine personality quiz – intended to distract her and evoke gauche memories of a sorrowful visit to a river to wallow in her melancholy. Indeed, the speaker's indecision over her answer at once reflects her inability to 'move on', as the question puts it, from whatever has caused her pain and to recognise that she has become absorbed in the trivial game of the survey. The speaker becomes embroiled in the horse's questionnaire, and so involved that she cannot focus on anything else. The speaker tells us: 'Three months had passed and I hadn't called you. | You had found somebody else, or starved to death by the phone' (2013, p. 39). Here, Bird deflates the horror of the speaker having lost three months of her life by creating a melodramatic response. The speaker's pain is emphasised at first, particularly with the idea that the date has found someone else to love: the speaker's loneliness becomes apparent, as she has been held captive for three months and no one has attempted to find her. Bird undercuts this when the speaker histrionically imagines her date having starved to death while sitting by the phone. It is an image of extreme dedication, and sheds further light on the speaker's ability to be (self-)absorbed.

At the end of the poem, the speaker confronts the horse, and the realisation that her life has been ruined: '"Do you realise what I've sacrificed for your pointless survey?" I shouted. | "What survey? I'm a horse"' (2013, p. 39). In the realisation that the survey is not real comes a sense of horror – of having wasted time for nothing – and a sense that the world is very cruel, that the speaker's life has become worse as a result of her inability to stay focused rather than as the result of some terrible action or an outside source.

As the situation worsens, and when it is revealed to be truly terrible, the poem ends and ostensibly offers no resolution or implied sense of improvement. What might the speaker of Bird's poem have done (presumably, had a nice time with her date, at least) if she had not allowed herself to become distracted by a horse who was and was not conducting a survey? The Absurd is well known for its stance of futility, but I think Bird (and maybe even Beckett) might be gesturing towards the possibility that people *can* change their circumstances – they are not so powerless. They just need to not become distracted.

In her exploration of a 'New Feminist Absurd' in theatre, Klein writes that the new aesthetic differs from earlier Absurdist theatre in that it considers 'women's anger' in a context of 'what has been lost', including 'the promise of collective feminist solidarity, the dream of "having it all" or at least some form of work-life balance' and 'hope for reproductive rights and bodily autonomy, and freedom from gender-based discrimination, harassment, and assault' which, she notes, is quite a different range of losses to those Esslin named in the wake of the Second World War (2022, pp. 30, 29). This stance is, for Klein, intersectional because women's anger today responds to the privileges white women have received in exchange for silencing their anger, and the consequences women of colour, especially Black women, have experienced, despite having always had reasons to be angry and having been offered very little in return for diminishing their anger (2022, p. 30). So, while the plays might be about the 'crashing down of American neoliberal and feminist "mythic ideals"', Klein sees the plays as ultimately 'nihilistic', stemming from 'feminism's rage-inducing failures' which leads to 'the same exhilarating emptiness as the writers in Esslin's foundational study' (2022, pp. 31, 33, 29). In Klein's reading of these plays, then, anger is futile. While systems of oppression come crashing down, all that is left is an emptiness. This puts Klein's definition of a feminist theatre in opposition to Kaufman's idea of a feminist humour, which is an ultimately more hopeful endeavour – one that moves away from nihilism.

In thinking about challenging stasis, Thelandersson (2022, p. 190) points towards the Institute for Precarious Consciousness, which advocates for a 'transformation of emotions', in which 'unnameable emotions' or a 'general sense of feeling like shit' must be 'transformed into a sense of injustice, a type of anger which is less resentful and more focused' and which moves to 'a reactivation of resistance' (2014). With this, the Institute promotes 'recognising the reality, and the systemic nature, of our experiences' (2014); for this to happen, they argue, we must 'affirm that our pain is really pain, that what we see and feel is real, and that our problems are not only personal' (2014). While the Institute acknowledges anger as part of this process, they note that the anger stems from a sadness (i.e. 'feeling like shit'), and must become active (i.e. hopeful) and promote a collective sense of change.

As I have discussed elsewhere in this book, poetry does not necessarily depict these outcomes explicitly, because a poem is not the same as, say, a piece of legislation. But poems can obliquely point to a solution because they communicate to and with readers' emotions, using these as a site for change. Poetry is not passive; at its most powerful, it might be

Sadness in Caroline Bird   125

able to influence its readers to reflect on their own behaviour, values and judgements. I will return to this in more detail later in the chapter, but now I wish to think about how Caroline Bird uses sadness to subtly put forward a politics and poetics of moving out of inaction. Importantly, Bird does not create a dynamic in which empathy or compassion is used to demonstrate how the pain of an 'Other' can be overcome 'only when the Western subject feels moved enough to give' or act, in Ahmed's terms (2014, p. 22). Indeed, what 'action' looks like is unclear in Bird's poems, but, crucially, she does not direct the reader back to an empathy which 'may also reinforce the very patterns of economic and political subordination responsible for such suffering' (Spelman in Ahmed, 2014, p. 22).

As with much of the Absurdist poetry I have explored thus far, 'Genesis' (from *The Hat-Stand Union*) presumes its reader is educated, middle class and white; the poem uses this presumption to question complacency and lack of conviction.[10] In each stanza, Bird introduces a group of people who have lost faith in a system of belief and have become embroiled in their own joyless lives. The people 'from the London suburbs don't believe in God', perform a liberal politics in which they engage with racism from a distance by reading 'books about slavery on American soil' and outwardly participate in socialist politics by concurring 'that the homeless get a raw deal' and advocating that 'the kids in state schools should get bikes, | free bikes or free books or something' (2013, p. 24). The people 'from West End theatres don't believe in Heaven' and argue that the 'afterlife is something cavemen invented to make sense of death' (2013, p. 24). There is not much meaning to these people's lives: they 'drive cars that are too big for us and everyone gets divorced' (2013, p. 24), which quite clearly suggests that capitalism (i.e. buying *things*) does not bring happiness, and people cannot connect to one another. The people in 'Oxford drinking establishments don't believe in ghosts' and suppose they could 'think' their 'way out of a genocide situation' (2013, p. 24) – the joke here being, presumably, that there are genocides underway, and not one of these intellectuals has 'thought' their way out of it, let alone done something useful to prevent it.

Bird also highlights the presumed reader's own snobbery about systems of belief – moving from God, to fate, to heaven, to karma, to elves. What might initially appear as a sneering conflation of Christianity or Buddhist tradition with belief in fantasy actually shows how belief in anything – and creating a community out of a wide range of experiences – is likely to bring more happiness than the arbitrary groupings these people have chosen for themselves based on their class positioning, work and education. The people are shown to sit in their unhappiness, counting 'to ten before we explode and observe the red axes | in the big glass cabinets

126 *Whiteness, Feminism and the Absurd in Contemporary Poetry*

that say "break in case of emergency"', and then suppressing their own need for change by keeping their 'chins up | without the help of buttercups' (2013, p. 25), an image that certainly recalls the British 'stiff upper lip' (Guiberteau, 2020).[11] Sadness, Bird seems to be pointing out, might be the very thing that could cause change if these (white, middle-class) people connected over their sadness, rather than their cynicism.

This is akin to what Carolyn Pedwell deems 'confrontational empathy', which is not 'premised on care, concern and sympathy' towards an 'Other' and 'works not to enable "privileged" subjects to put themselves in "the other's shoes"' (2016). In Pedwell's definition, confrontational empathy is 'a mode of affective perspective-taking adopted by those usually viewed as the postcolonial "objects" of empathy', which 'calls various transnational subjects to account for their role in perpetuating damaging neo-colonial and neoliberal relations' (2016). Of course, neither Bird nor her speakers are postcolonial objects of empathy – they are, in Pedwell's terms, the subjects. As such, Bird's poetry calls into question an apathetic and ambivalent approach to life which perpetuates nihilism and invites its readers to question their own positionality. Perhaps, as Pedwell suggests, this confrontational empathy invites shame (2016), which enables us to 'rethink how we wish to live in proximity to others' (Probyn in Pedwell, 2016).

Bird returns to sadness and connection in her 2017 collection, *In These Days of Prohibition*, particularly in the poem 'Public Resource' in which 'There is a place called The Open | where brave people put things' (2017, p. 49). Into 'The Open', people offer their sorrow: 'Things they can no longer carry' and 'Big things. Or little things | they fear are growing' (2017, p. 49). Bird warns that The Open is 'always hungry' for these offerings of sadness, and that sharing pain with strangers does not come with 'rising smoke' or a 'bell-ringer | in a tower grabbing a rope'; for Bird, there is 'no consequence unless | you dive in with it' (2017, p. 49). Here, Bird acknowledges that sharing pain or sadness is not enough, does not necessarily do anything but become an act of sharing unless one follows through – seeking change for the greater good, to keep diving into the sadness, unpacking its origins and pursuing reform. Sadness itself cannot hold the answers, as Bird writes in 'SS Suppression': *'doing nothing is not an option | for much longer'* (2017, p. 18).

Inertia and Ennui

In Bird's work, the emotional impact – or resonance – of a poem is hidden underneath layers of zaniness and characters. By refracting experiences

Sadness in Caroline Bird   127

and emotions through a lens of furtherance, which amplifies emotions and pain, and then offering moments that remove the lens of furtherance, Bird heightens the emotional affect, offering a moment of emotional clarity where the emotion, rather than the situation, is prioritised. As such, Bird speaks to the (presumed white, middle-class) reader's emotions, invoking a sadness that feels firstly resonant and then requires the reader to turn inwards, reflecting on their own emotions and, importantly, what they might do to enact change. Indeed, this is a tricky relationship to establish: how can one be certain that the reader will do this work? How does the sadness not invoke a self-centred pity? Perhaps the poet cannot guarantee any of this: they can only lead the way.

In the poem 'Fantasy Role-Play' (from *The Hat-Stand Union*), the characters take on various, shifting roles to escape from their lives and thereby their pain. The poem's speaker addresses a (mostly) unnamed 'you' who has two young children, Lionel and Greta (their names evidently echoing Hansel and Gretel), described as 'present, like crickets | too young to do anything but lie there and feel', and a husband who is 'a reactive blink to an inappropriate comment' (2013, p. 34). The 'you' of the poem seems to lead an idyllic life: she is part of a nuclear family, with a 'lucky' house, archways and roses – it is a hyperbolic image of stereotypical idyllic American suburbia. However, this is not entirely what it seems: the speaker's partner's children are not viewed as real people – they can only passively experience life, and feel its emotions; the children's names suggest a story with sinister twists and turns, where adults cannot be trusted; the need for multiple guard dogs is not explained; the husband is detached and barely able to comprehend what is happening to him. The idyllic life is on the edge of a knife.

Bird's poem evidently recalls the setting and premise of television series *Desperate Housewives* (2004–12), which follows a group of women and their families, friends and foes living on the fictional Wisteria Lane, a supposedly idyll of American suburbia – white picket fences, immaculate lawns and blooming gardens. In *Desperate Housewives*, this façade falters quickly in the first episode with the suicide of housewife and series narrator Mary Alice Young. As Kim Akass writes (2006, p. 50), there is a deep connection between *Desperate Housewives* and Betty Freidan's influential *The Feminine Mystique*, in which Freidan writes of the 'mystique of feminine fulfilment' which 'became the cherished and self-perpetuating core of contemporary American culture' (2010, p. 8). Women were meant to be 'selfless, never complaining, always happy' and, as a wives and mothers, 'put her husband, her children, and the cleanliness of her house first' (Douglas and Michaels in Akass, 2006, p. 51). Sharon Sharp notes that the series 'showcases a decidedly

128 *Whiteness, Feminism and the Absurd in Contemporary Poetry*

ambivalent take on "retreatism"' (2006, p. 122), which Negra and Tasker characterise as a scenario in which 'a well-educated white female professional displays her "empowerment" and caring nature by withdrawing from the workforce (and symbolically from the public sphere) to devote herself to husband and family' (in Sharp, 2006, p. 122).

While post-feminism would have it that choosing to devote oneself to husband and children is a form of empowerment, *Desperate Housewives* suggests that this is not necessarily the case, and women might strive to have it all (becoming Can-Do Girls in the process). Yet *Desperate Housewives* is far from feminist critique: it reinforces cultural clichés and conservative middle-class politics (Pozner and Seigel, 2006; Wang, 2021), focuses – largely – on white women, and the only non-white main character, Gabrielle Solis, is a reiteration of many clichés and stereotypes of Latina women (Pozner and Seigel, 2006; Merskin, 2007).

'Fantasy Role-Play' adopts a hyberbolic image of stereotypical idealised American suburbia, undercut with tragedy, unhappiness and pain, much like Wisteria Lane. The 'you' of Bird's poem is ostensibly leaving her husband, but this seems to be met with anguish: she screams as she opens and closes the door, and tellingly leaves it open, as if she might return. She also takes a satchel of apples 'from the tree [she was] married under' (2013, p. 34), so that, symbolically, she is carrying her marriage with her. The biblical allusions are apparent: the apples are symbols of the woman's sins and indiscretions, and are constantly with the speaker and the woman throughout their role-play. Notably, the credits of *Desperate Housewives* also centre around the fall of Eve, with red apples, once again symbolising transgressions, tumbling into the hands of the titular wives.

In the first stanza of 'Fantasy Role-Play' the speaker's identity is oblique, and Bird only reveals that he loves the 'you' of the poem and appears to be helping her leave her husband. As the poem continues, the speaker's identity becomes more unclear as he takes on various disguises, wearing a 'plastic Spider-Man mask' when his partner refuses to let him kiss her for 'the first two weeks' of their road trip (2013, p. 34). While the Spider-Man mask adds a level of humour and juvenility to the disguise, it also suggests that the speaker is hiding something painful, denying the sadness of the situation. The mask becomes a hyperbolic, amusing and gauche metonym for the ways in which the couple are hiding from one another or concealing the truth of their relationship through disguises (literally and metaphorically).

The woman also takes on various disguises, which at once help her hide from, then finally reveal, her identity. She reveals that her name is Marcella, and that she 'worked as a maid in the Jeffersons' household'

Sadness in Caroline Bird   129

(2013, p. 34). She admits to being 'a cold and passive mother' with a 'needy, disloyal and collapsible' husband; they 'were always fighting, throwing plates, cleaning products, fridges I at each other' (2013, p. 34). In a more hyperbolic and darkly humorous turn, the woman describes the couple 'mushing Lionel's face into his broccoli' and 'shunting Greta around like a mini vacuum cleaner' (2013, p. 34). Her new partner, it seems, has provided her with 'a chance to give them a better life' (2013, p. 34). The woman oddly feels a need to introduce herself and her job title to the speaker, and even more mysteriously describes herself as 'the woman you loved' (2013, p. 34), as though she has reinvented herself, which creates a baffling mystery for the reader to unpick. As such, while Bird misdirects the reader from the pain of the characters' lives with bizarre details, the characters misdirect themselves from their pain by creating new lives. In this way, Bird recreates the misdirection and distraction the speaker and his partner are creating, bothering themselves with disguises while trying to run away from their sadness, and also catches the reader in their willingness to be distracted from sadness.

Bird pushes the absurdity of the characters' role-play even further, to the point of confusion. The woman refers to the speaker as 'Mr Jefferson', her boss, telling him she is 'still very angry with you', while the speaker reveals himself to not be Mr Jefferson after all, but 'their gardener, Alejandro' (2013, p. 35). Just as the reader begins to think that Marcella is the woman's name, the real identities of the characters are revealed: the couple are married (they are the Jeffersons), their relationship is unhealthy and they have neglected their children. To deal with their sadness and save their relationship, they have been re-enacting stereotypes from US soap operas, much like *Desperate Housewives*, pretending, in turn, to be the maid and the gardener having affairs with the husband and wife. This dynamic is a key part of *Desperate Housewives*, in which Gabrielle Solis, a former model and now trophy wife to Carlos Solis, has an affair with her teenage gardener; Carlos has an affair with the couple's maid; both take part in a fantasy of shirking the bonds of marriage and asserting sexual power over one's employee.[12]

In 'Fantasy Role-Play', even as the sun comes up (perhaps suggesting a 'new dawn' for the couple) and quiet settles on the chaos of keeping up with the new identities, the sunlight highlights their 'battered faces' (2013, p. 35), and the physical (and thereby emotional) damage becomes apparent, inescapable. As their pain becomes obvious, the speaker tries to hide the couple's hurt again by suggesting a new disguise, becoming 'Alejandro', who stands in for another sexual stereotype-fantasy, that of the 'Latin lover' (Mastro et al., 2007, p. 348; Pérez, 2009, p. 37), who is 'constructed around the synthesis of eroticism, exoticism, and danger'

(Pérez, 2009, p. 38). The speaker's appeal to the 'Latino lover' stereotype reinforces that the fantasy role-play is a desperate, ill-informed and hopeless endeavour. Even the speaker seems to want to return to their original life, as he offers, immediately after, thinking better of the idea: 'Let's wake up the children and go home' (2013, p. 35). As the couple's pain is highlighted by the rising sun, the woman bites into an apple, reconnecting with her undisguised self. As much as the characters try to mask and escape their pain, it is ever-present.

The characters' all-encompassing sadness stems from their inability to acknowledge and discuss their pain (and attempt to repair the relationship); the disguises only deflect the pain. What might Bird be pointing her readers towards, then? She is certainly pointing them *away* from distraction and from letting sadness seep in and take hold. Sadness without movement – sadness that forces us to try to reinvent ourselves, but not really (in the way her characters do) – is pointless. The characters of 'Fantasy Role-Play' cannot change; this is not because they are sad, it is because they insist on repeating their behaviours in new guises, even when they feel they are doing something different.

In 'Far From Civilisation' (from *In These Days of Prohibition*), a group of women arrive at unnamed location – although it is not 'India' as Elle, one of the women, suggests and they are not at 'Buddha's temple' (2017, p. 15). It is clear that they are there to detox and recover from their addictions and illnesses; the speaker explains that they all 'dumped our pills and powders | behind a cactus', while a woman named Gemma declares that she has 'left Anna in the airport toilets' (2017, p. 15); Anna is the 'name of her eating disorder' (2017, p. 15), the speaker explains. The poem opens with a chaotic situation, as each woman tries to declare her feelings, her new self, or to understand where they are geographically. The women fundamentally misunderstand: they do not listen to each other, so some continue to believe that they are in India, and fixate on seeing Buddha's temple – even though such a place does not exist; Gemma, immediately upon finding herself in a new location, declares that she has recovered from her eating disorder and no longer needs to be treated, though the recovery from an eating disorder is a lifelong endeavour; Elle looks forward to being 'clean', but has already smuggled 'a secret rock [. . .] sewn into her sleeve' (2017, p. 14); Jewel hopefully explains that 'enlightenment comes at the end of | dust – and there's dust all over' (2017, p. 14).

The speaker's distinction between Gemma being not 'dishonest although certainly a liar' (2017, p. 14) unlocks the sadness in this poem: despite Gemma's apparently genuine intentions to recover from her eating disorder, the likelihood of her recovering is hampered by the fact that she is a liar – both to herself and others. The women's declarations, then, are devastating because they are consumed by false hope and promise, and this is not yet evident to them. Moreover, the women have been literally ostracised from society because of their sadness, mental health and trauma. Their failure to communicate and their inability to truly face and work on their issues leads them back to sadness: they cannot recover if they are still in denial. When the women think they have found Buddha's temple (which they believe to be the key to their recovery), the speaker opines: 'What can we learn | from a little fat man anyway?' (2017, p. 15), evidently recalling the loss of faith from 'Genesis'.

In a review of *In These Days of Prohibition*, poetry critic John Field writes that 'the collection satirises popular culture', noting that the line breaks around Gemma's introduction to the poem 'force [. . .] the reader to consider, for a moment, that there might actually be something wrong with Gemma', but 'Bird makes us wait for line two before delivering a satirical punch and exposing Gemma's vacuous hyperbolous vanity' (2017). Field misses the evident references to rehabilitation and recovery, and assumes that 'Gemma, Jewel, Elle and Pixie are on a modelling shoot, but they could just as easily be on a "gap yah"' (2017), making the women subjects of sexist ridicule, rather understanding Bird's oeuvre more broadly. Field fails to notice any techniques other than 'irony' (2017) in Bird's poems, and takes them at face value, rather than approaching them with the sensitivity they require. Indeed, at the end of his review, Field comments: 'If Brett Easton Ellis wrote poems, I'd like to think they'd be poems like these' (2017), completely missing the point of the collection; it is a collection about sadness, addiction, mental health and how these can specifically affect (white) women.

Although the Absurd in contemporary poetry has, as I demonstrated in Chapter 1, in large part privileged the white woman's experience, this does not mean that this experience is inherently worthless, especially when Bird's poetry works through ideas of privilege and sadness with nuance, trying to disrupt its readers' established ways of thinking, hoping to evoke a movement from languor and inertia into movement and change. If Broder's posts dampen the transformative potential of sadness by refusing connection, Bird's poems attempt to effectively resonate with the reader – not through the characters' literal experiences, but through the sadness they feel and how this hampers them; Bird wants her readers to take notice of this and reflect on their own despondency and apathy. However, Field's review does suggest that the message of Bird's poems can go unnoticed, that – if the reader is unwilling or unaware – sadness retains its stasis. As such, there is a trial-and-error approach at play, not just in Bird's poems, but in all poetry that attempts to grapple with wanting to enact change. Bird seems to be telling her readers – the complacent, the nihilistic – to do something about it. There is no other choice. What can sadness do, then? If we harness its potential, Bird seems to say, it can move us out of indifference and into activity. We must stop ourselves from being distracted; we must, as Thelandersson and Institute for Precarious Consciousness argue, turn our sadness into a chance for connection; out of that connection, we must offer something better and different.

Chapter 6

Reality and Imagination in Emily Berry's *Dear Boy*

In the previous chapter, I offered an explication of the Sad Girl internet movement to demonstrate how sadness can be a site for movement and change, which in turn can be used to understand Caroline Bird's collections *The Hat-Stand Union* (2013) and *In These Days of Prohibition* (2017). Bird's poems act like parables, in which Bird warns her (presumed white, middle-class) reader against their own ennui and inaction. In this chapter, I explore the blurring of imagination and reality in white British poet Emily Berry's debut poetry collection, *Dear Boy* (2013). Such blurring is a famed characteristic of the surrealist movement (Gascoyne, 2003), and here I understand it further through its connection to Freud's *The Uncanny* (2003). I argue that Berry's poems replicate a dream-state, ultimately creating an awareness of artifice for both the reader and poet – one that speaks to blurring memory and objective reality. Through close readings of Berry's poems, I reveal her work's links to trauma writing – particularly 'perpetual troping', as understood by Roger Luckhurst (2008) – and how Berry's poems use nightmarish situations to comment on gender roles, privilege and British politics. I compare Berry's work to an additional poem by British poet Mona Arshi to demonstrate how contemporary Absurdist poets subvert depictions of motherhood to unsettle evocations of empathy, and therefore how contemporary Absurdist poets can neglect empathy as a method for social change. Following on from Berry's use of the uncanny, I further develop an exploration into Berry's engagement with tropes of horror films and the Southern Gothic, with particular reference to the horror film *The Woman* (Lucky McKee, 2011), to investigate Berry's engagement with issues of gender and race.

Artifice and *The Uncanny*

David Gascoyne has noted that the 'avowed aim of the Surrealist movement' was 'to reduce and finally dispose altogether of the flagrant contradictions that exist between dream and waking life, the "unreal" and the "real", the unconscious and the conscious' (2003, p. 23). Gascoyne's assertions about reducing the distance between 'unreal' and 'real' are key to understanding the Absurd: as the surrealists agreed, blurring reality and imagination allows strange, new worlds to emerge. After all, Freud stated that 'an uncanny effect often arises when the boundary between fantasy and reality is blurred' (2003, p. 150); and, as Schelling notes, *unheimlich* is the name for 'everything that was intended to remain secret, hidden away, and has come into the open' (in Freud, 2003, p. 132). The Absurd replicates this dreamlike (or nightmarish) state, where the meandering imagination is working as it would in a dream: scenes, images and people can change within an instance.

In his review of Emily Berry's *Dear Boy* for the *Guardian*, Ben Wilkinson writes that the collection is 'immediately striking for its sophisticated awareness of [. . .] artifice' (2013). Wilkinson seems to damn Berry with faint praise here: while her awareness of artifice is sophisticated, it is artifice all the same. As Nick Groom comments, authenticity, particularly in literature, is 'worshipped as a fetish, embraced as a virtue' (2002, p. 293). In Chapter 2, I discussed the general privileging of the 'confessional' in poetry, Berry's response to this and how the Absurd sits ambivalently, wanting to communicate 'honestly' while also exploring other avenues for connection – autobiography does not necessarily equal emotional 'truth'. For Groom, attempts to forge 'authenticity' offer an opportunity to 'create a hybrid realism, both true and false' (2002, p. 15), so, in Berry's poems, a blurring of reality and imagination can produce an awareness of artifice not only for the writer, but for the reader as well. When Berry merges the true and the false (imagination and reality) in her poems, she blurs the boundaries between what might be real and not real.

In the titular poem of the collection, 'Dear Boy', Berry places this blurring and uncanniness upfront. The speaker declares: 'You know perfectly well I believe | nothing worthwhile is explainable' to the 'boy' (her partner). She tells him, 'don't be so literal', and ponders the fallibility of her memories: 'I'm not sure if you were there or not. | Did you want to be? We can make something up' (2013, p. 7). Berry's slippage between reality and imagination moves the reader swiftly from the reality of the boy's desperate phone calls to an almost paradise-like setting of a holiday. The speaker recalls fond memories with her partner (with whom she has ostensibly had an argument) – 'Perhaps it was you I parasailed with above the Mediterranean?' (2013, p. 7) – and then undercuts undermines the strangeness of the situation with a banal, very real, very literal and embarrassing detail: 'You complained that the harness was hurting your balls' (2013, p. 7). Yet the reader cannot trust that Berry's speaker is remembering correctly. Might her claim, 'I'm not sure if you were there or not', act as a way to undermine the titular boy, who has called her 'three times' to 'explain everything' (2013, p. 7)? It seems as though she is pretending that she does not remember him – that she has many other lovers to remember – and only recalls him through a gauche incident. The speaker's final question, 'remember?', is an appeal for the boy to corroborate her final, romanticised version of events ('We had such plans. We were slung between sea and sky. I I tangled your legs in mine' (2013, p. 7)), so the whole episode becomes unreliable.

Berry's 'Questions I Wanted to Ask You in the Swimming Pool', which is constructed entirely of questions, charts the speaker's memory of a quotidian day with her partner in which they go swimming. The questions might be rhetorical: the answers might always obviously be 'yes', and this is why we cannot hear (or see) the answers of the other person. However, as in 'Dear Boy', the speaker appeals for reassurance through each of her queries, suggesting she is unsure of what is real and imagined. The speaker asks questions that the other person simply cannot answer, such as: 'Didn't you see me standing in the shallow end, looking out at you I from blue goggles with alien eyes?' (2013, p. 48). The significant other cannot answer this because it is too convoluted: the speaker's partner might have seen her in the shallow end, but the description of her 'alien eyes' is completely hers – does the partner see the world (and her) in exactly the same way? The clumsy structuring of the image of the 'alien eyes', the way Berry builds details of the speaker's situation to reach a disappointing, conversational, almost clichéd image, expose a perceived 'failure' (or fear of failure), and is a fundamental means by which to read this poem. As the speaker's image fails, so is she afraid of her relationship failing.

In the final lines of the poem, Berry suggests that all is not well in the relationship, the speaker remembering that she and her partner laughed, 'worn out enough to relax with each other I for once', as they forgot 'that everything was actually fucked' (2013, p. 48). Questions such as, 'Didn't you promise, whatever I happened, you would always find me attractive?' (2013, p. 48) appear to be seated in reality: this might be a conversation that the couple have had, perhaps many times. Other questions, such as, 'Didn't I take too long I in the shower as usual' (2013, p. 48), suggest that the scenario might be imagined, that the speaker is visualising herself repeating usual behaviours or routines with her partner. If we suppose that the relationship has ended, then the speaker's constant questioning takes on a tragic dimension as she revisits and

136 *Whiteness, Feminism and the Absurd in Contemporary Poetry*

recalls a day, trying to pore over it to understand it and the end of her relationship. Considering Freud's notions of the uncanny as being 'that species of frightening that goes back to what was once well known and had long been familiar' (2003, p. 124), the uncanny is bound up in repetition and excavation of memories. Indeed, for Roger Luckhurst, trauma enacts a '"perpetual troping" around a primary experience that can never be captured' (2008, p. 7). This is not to say that Berry's speaker is conflating a break-up with a traumatic event per se, but that the idea of 'perpetual troping' – of revisiting an event to better understand it, but not gaining further clarity – is a key characteristic of Berry's poetry.[1] Indeed, this takes on a menacing effect elsewhere in the collection – an argument I will return to later in this chapter.

Gender Role-Play and Empathy

Berry's poems establish remembering and memory as crucial sites for power dynamics: in 'Dear Boy', the speaker seems to hold all the power as she willingly 'forgets' the 'boy'; she acquiesces when she invites him into the act of remembering, asking him to corroborate. In 'Questions I Wanted to Ask You in the Swimming Pool', the speaker's questions set up distance – where is the partner, and why is the speaker asking him so many questions? In her constant probing, the speaker becomes vulnerable, wanting to verify her memories, her emotions and the partner's love, even if it no longer exists. In an interview with Rachael Allen for *Granta*, Berry has said that she is 'more interested in the idea of gender as role-play than as something intrinsic' (Allen and Berry, 2011), which clearly echoes Judith Butler's conception of gender as being culturally constructed and borne not from 'a singular act, but a repetition and a ritual' (2014, pp. 9, xv). Whalley notes that a 'sense of uneasy and faintly ludicrous sexual menace' runs through *Dear Boy*, creating a dynamic that the reader understands to be 'a product of the absurd male desire within which the female speakers must accommodate themselves' (2016). Berry's collection, then, is distinctly concerned with gender roles and how they open up possibilities for authority, control and rebellion.

In the poem 'The Incredible History of Patient M.', the speaker is subjected to a doctor's strange, inappropriate and manipulative methods. The speaker recalls how the doctor 'straps his velcro cuff to my bicep' and 'pumps it till I'm breathless', then says, 'You need to breathe more' (2013, p. 14). The doctor also 'bites' his patient and 'leaves a mark', goes swimming with her and, in an extremely gauche and degrading move, slaps her 'face with his penis' (2013, p. 15). As such, the doctor appears to be more disturbed than his patient (who does not yet reveal their need for treatment) and performs his role as a doctor while crossing professional boundaries. The doctor abuses his authority (provided by his job title – a fact the reader is reminded of, since he is only referred to as 'The Doctor') to undermine the speaker, and to assault and oppress her.

In the sequel to this poem, 'Manners', the speaker declares with remarkable impassivity that her 'mother is dead' and 'it's classic' (2013, p. 51) – yet she refuses to speak to the doctor about this, knowing that he is 'recording me on tape so he can sell my story I to a documentary-maker when I'm famous' (2013, p. 51). In this poem, the speaker is undoubtedly childlike or at least pretending to be so; she makes a comic for the Doctor's birthday, a gesture which oversteps the professional doctor–patient relationship (not that the Doctor has not already done this). The reader expects the aphoristic first line of the poem ('The hand that bites is the maternal hand' (2013, p. 51)) to be spoken by the Doctor, but it is actually spoken by the 'dog-protagonist' of the comic and thereby the speaker, who outwardly assumes a submissive position, enabling the tape recordings and taking part in the doctor's increasingly worrying treatments, while rebelling against him in subtle ways.

Berry uses concrete observations in the poem, slipping from the bizarre situation of the Doctor's treatments to grounded memories, such as: 'In my one memory of my mother I am filling her I belly-button with shingle on the beach in Brighton' (2013, p. 51). So, while Berry's speaker superficially agrees with the doctor, reiterating his ideas about maternity, she internally cultivates a relationship with her mother through this single, powerful memory. In the final line of the poem – 'He doesn't notice that the last page is torn off' (2013, p. 51) – the speaker performs a subtle rebellion: she is keeping secrets (or, literally, a page of the comic) from the Doctor and, by extension, the reader. Therefore, as Webb writes, Berry's speakers resist straightforward categories of 'victimhood, fragility, or enfeeblement' (Webb and Berry, 2017) and become embroiled in power plays based around stereotypes of gendered behaviour. While the Doctor is exploitative, abusive and misogynistic, the speaker asserts her autonomy by showing the reader that she knows this and is playing her own manipulative game in return. Indeed, Webb notes that the speaker's 'cognizance and forthrightness underscores their autonomy', which consequently allows the speaker to gaze 'back at readers' (2017) during these games of authority.

Berry's approach to the reader–writer–speaker relationship is exemplified in 'Bad New Government',[2] in which the speaker wakes 'in an empty flat to a bad new government' (2013, p. 57). The speaker tries to find small moments of hope in the day, in spite of the political turmoil she gestures towards; she wishes to email her absent partner about 'the following | happy circumstances: early rosebuds, a birthday party, a new cake recipe' (2013, p. 57), three things which are ultimately hopeful: new life; continuing life; new discoveries. Yet these small moments of happiness come up against the realities of the government: she has an 'austerity breakfast' (2013, p. 57) – clearly recalling the UK Coalition and Conservative governments' fiscal policy, which ran from 2010 to 2019 – and her 'toast burns in protest' (2013, p. 57), a cruel riposte to the joy brought on by the cake. The speaker tells her absent partner that she will call him later 'to tell you about the new | prime minister the worrying new developments' and 'You light up my chambers' (2013, p. 57), offering hope in moments of darkness.

The speaker declares that she is 'writing my first political poem', which is presumably 'Bad New Government' itself. Yet, for Berry's speaker, the political poem is 'also (always) about my love for you' (2013, p. 57). Here, the move towards hope seems to stick: the poem ends, without punctuation, as though the hopeful turn towards love – and the intermingling of politics and love – might offer the solution. So, then, for Berry, to talk about politics involves talking about interpersonal relationships: political poems are 'always' about love, so they are inherently a blurring of despair and hope;[3] political poems must be about interpersonal relationships: the people we love – or are supposed to love (mothers, children), or the people who are supposed to care for us (doctors, governments) – and the power they hold over us.

It might be tempting to say that the romantic relationship in 'Bad New Government' provides the reader with a point of empathy – something for the reader to cling onto and make sense of, during this less than exact 'political' poem. *Love is the answer!* the presumed, privileged, white, middle-class reader might want to declare. Yet, as Pedwell writes, 'empathy – understood in shorthand as the affective ability [to] "put oneself in the other's shoes" – can easily become a kind of endpoint' because 'it is so widely and unquestioningly viewed as "good"', and subsequently it comes to 'represent a conceptual stoppage in conversation or analysis' (2016). Indeed, such positioning of empathy as 'good' tends to privilege 'individual expressions of emotionality than structural analyses of how well-being and suffering are linked' (Patel, 2016, p. 82). As Pedwell argues, when empathy is understood as an experience of 'co-feeling', it invites 'problematic appropriations or projections on the part of "privileged" subjects' and 'risks obscuring their complicity in the wider relations of power in which marginalisation, oppression and suffering occur' (2016).

While the presumably white, middle-class speaker of 'Bad New Government' frets over austerity, her 'cold' flat and 'empty' fridge (2013, p. 57), she is still privileged: able to live in a flat alone (while her partner is away), and still able to go to birthday parties and make cakes. Life has not fallen apart, totally. So, while the final line is certainly about the enduring nature of love through times of political turmoil, Berry is simultaneously making a knowing nod towards her speaker's relative privilege, and how her 'worry' might be considerably less than someone else's. Indeed, the 'bad new government' could be *any* British government throughout history – ones which have imposed austerity measures, stripped people of rights or colonised people. What the speaker of Berry's poem deems 'bad' might be the things she notices materially – rising heating bills, fewer trips to the supermarket – rather than the things that might have more destructive consequences. As such, Berry problematises a straightforward approach to empathy in *Dear Boy*, using gender power dynamics and 'political' material to show how, as Pedwell writes, 'empathy reaches its limit point [. . .] or simply makes no sense (or difference) in the midst of given social conditions and political hierarchies' (2016). Berry's approach deliberately evokes what Hemmings deems a '"visceral reaction" in the White feminist reader' (in Cooke, 2020, p. 51), drawing the reader in with a seemingly resonant experience, and then denies or problematises empathy to expose its limits.

In her Royal Society of Literature lecture for the Newcastle Poetry Festival (presented on 13 May 2023), 'Motherhood, Whiteness and Empathy', Parmar read three poems by Kim Moore, Fiona Benson and Hannah Sullivan to examine how motherhood is employed as a universalising collective gaze, so that inequalities caused by race are seen as secondary to – and eliminated by – mothering. As I demonstrated earlier in this book, the male speakers and characters of Edson's and Tate's poems are permitted to embrace nihilistic dislocation and strangeness in heteronormative domestic situations, and contemporary British Absurdist poetry has used motherhood as an essential landscape through which to challenge stereotypical depictions of women and their inner lives. As such, I now wish to explore how Berry and fellow British poet Mona Arshi eschew empathy through their depictions of motherhood, and thereby reject empathy as a 'solution'.

In 'My Perpendicular Daughter', Berry immediately defamiliarises motherhood in the opening line (which runs on from the title): 'grew taller than they said she would | when I got her' (2013, p. 20), suggesting that she has purchased this daughter, or that the pregnancy is the result of unusual circumstances. Indeed, the pregnancy is not smooth, with the speaker commenting that she 'thought a daughter would be | light and

140 *Whiteness, Feminism and the Absurd in Contemporary Poetry*

quiet', but that she has been 'hung [. . .] | upside down inside me' and now 'she sticks | straight out, gets in the way' (2013, p. 20). Indeed, the utter strangeness of the speaker's pregnancy casts light on how normative narratives about motherhood cannot provide solace; the speaker notes that she has been lied to about her daughter (2013, p. 20) and her misconceptions about having a daughter suggest that she has accepted at face value – from an unidentified 'they', who appear throughout the poem – a narrative of positive transformation through motherhood.

Indeed, the unidentified 'they' perpetuate misogyny throughout the poem, telling the speaker when she tries to 'take her [daughter] back' that she 'should be glad a man had | known me' and 'I'd only got what I'd been | begging for' (2013, p. 20); their language inhabits the same register as victim-blaming discourse surrounding sexual assault.[4] The speaker recalls being asked, 'Would I like a booklet?' (2013, p. 20), which trivialises the speaker's ordeal by imagining that all her worries can be resolved by a simple pamphlet; at the same time, 'known', a biblical term, creates a comical exaggeration and reverence for pregnancy – so the pregnancy itself becomes more important than the speaker, the person having the baby. As such, the 'they' of Berry's poem mimic right-wing anti-abortion rhetoric (Pollack Petchesky, 1981; Beckman, 2017),[5] and the humour of the term 'known' is undercut by the lack of humanity in the entire episode, which culminates in the offer of the booklet. 'They' therefore become the (unknown) faces of a totalitarian, misogynistic regime.

Berry's speaker instead asks for a glass of milk. Milk is noticeably linked to comfort: we are given it as newborns, through infancy and into childhood. Berry's speaker, then, appeals for her childhood to return to her at the moment she is leaving her childhood and starting another person's. However, the speaker describes the milk as a 'long white screech' which leaves her 'tongue all feathery' (2013, p. 20), suggesting that this milk no longer provides the comfort it did when the speaker was a child, and becomes symbolic of the adult role the speaker must take as a mother. The rejection of milk is a denial of lactation – the screech mirroring that of a child – and thereby a refusal of or an aversion to motherhood. This may seem to initially echo earlier Absurdist poems, like Edson's 'The Mother of Toads', in which a strange pregnancy wreaks havoc on a domestic situation, but Berry's depiction of such a situation is more subversive.

Adrienne Rich has distinguished two meanings of motherhood: 'the *potential relationship* of any woman to her powers of reproduction – and to children; and the *institution* – which aims at ensuring that that potential – and all women – shall remain under male control' (1976, p. 13; original emphasis). Rich identifies the former as 'mothering' which

Reality and Imagination in Emily Berry **141**

is 'potentially empowering to women', while the latter refers to 'the patriarchal institution of motherhood that is male-defined and controlled and is deeply oppressive to women' (O'Reilly, 2004, p. 2). Berry's speaker's aversion, then, is to the patriarchal version of motherhood, which does not care for her body or well-being but uses her status as an expectant mother to oppress her. In realising this, the speaker finally turns on the tyrants: '"This | is how the end begins," I said, and aimed' (2013, p. 20). By aiming her perpendicular daughter (herself a rebellious girl, it seems) at the 'they', and threatening them, Berry's speaker calls to an end their reign of terror – she will no longer accept this oppressive, patriarchal version of motherhood, and the abuses it brings.

Returning to Pedwell's idea of empathy 'making no sense (or difference) in the midst of given social conditions and political hierarchies' (2016), Berry's poem moves away from empathy as a given method for 'political' poems, or a solution to social and political issues. Berry's speaker presumably obliterates the oppressors at the end of her poem, allowing the reader to imagine a better future in which motherhood and womanhood do not carry with them all the trappings of the patriarchy. But the reader is also unable to empathise with the speaker. This does not necessarily mean that the reader does not read the poem with interest, laugh at its jokes or feel a sense of triumph at the speaker's rebellion, but the speaker is not empathetic in the traditional sense – the reader is unable to put themselves in the speaker's shoes.

In the poems I have read thus far, there is always a moment where, as in Caroline Bird's poetry, the lens of furtherance is pulled back and the emotional resonance of the poem comes to the fore – the shingle in the mother's belly-button, for example, or how the accumulation of questions reveals fear and failure. Yet in 'My Perpendicular Daughter', Berry refuses to break the reader's immersion in the bizarre scenario or blur imagination and reality, and thereby denies the reader the moment of connection they have been expecting. As Patel writes, empathy 'does not require realignment of social relations' (2016, p. 83), and while this is not to say that empathy cannot be a part of social reform, Berry's poem tries to steer its reader away from it and towards a more critical analysis of power dynamics. Rather than sitting in empathy, which might steer readers towards affect and inaction, Berry's poem denies empathy and literally points its readers towards rebellion.

Therefore motherhood, in its patriarchal sense, has become a space in which poets use Absurdist characteristics and techniques to critique empathy as a solution to gender inequality and harms caused by those in positions of responsibility and care. In Arshi's 'Large and Imprecise Baby', the speaker gives birth to the titular baby, and admits it 'was quite

142 *Whiteness, Feminism and the Absurd in Contemporary Poetry*

a shock [. . .] on account | of that fact I didn't even go to term' (2015, p. 44). The speaker declares her reactions but does not allow the reader to share in them: they are reported, not felt, in much the way the baby is described as 'passively feeding | from the bottom of the ocean' (2015, p. 44). As in Berry's poem, the baby's body, as well as the mother's, does not act as it should and later in the poem, when she seeks medical advice, the doctor says, 'It's not him it's you' and eyes her 'suspiciously' (2015, p. 44), echoing Berry's doctor and the unnamed 'they'. Moreover, the speaker is emotionally removed from her child, whom she describes as having a 'feeble mouth' and making 'a jittery noise like a broken gull, | or the scrape of a heavy chair' (2015, p. 44), so that the baby seems creature-like, not real, or frighteningly uncanny – made up of familiar sounds, but not the ones the speaker would expect her baby to emit. The speaker accepts that she must be a mother to the large and imprecise baby, but her maternal instincts are evidently not natural: she 'decide[s]' to kiss the baby and, rather than this being an epiphanic moment of connection, 'thin rain starts to fall' (2015, p. 44), leaving the reader without a clear sense of the speaker or baby's reaction to the kiss.

If empathy, as Pedwell writes, 'is now framed as an affective "solution" to a wide range of social ills' (2016), then what does Arshi's poem do by denying empathy? Certainly, it does not sit in nihilism – there is a sense of something having changed at the end of the poem, a sense of movement and the speaker persevering in her attempts to connect with her strange child. As in Berry's poem, Arshi denies that love (or empathy) is the answer, and this hinges on the fact that the doctor denies the speaker any support, advice or consideration. Just as the speaker is denied care, Arshi refuses the reader a clear sense of connection with the speaker, mirroring the speaker's feelings of isolation and disconnection. In doing this, she demonstrates how empathy, 'understood by liberals as a universal human quality', ultimately fails when it is 'framed as an affective bridge between subjects, cultures or societies' (Pedwell, 2016); for Berry and Arshi, empathy cannot redirect or change the patriarchal system of motherhood, or a society in which women are treated with suspicion. It must be reconceived.

The Southern Gothic and Horror Films

In a blog post for *Peony Moon*, Berry writes that she thinks of a sequence of her poems – which she deems the 'Arlene poems' ('Sweet Arlene', 'Arlene's House', 'Arlene and Esme') – as having 'an American Gothic theme' (2013). She continues:

America does the Unheimliche – Freud's idea about the eeriness of the unfamiliar familiar – really well. [. . .] American domestic scenes are so familiar to British people of my generation because of film and TV, and just embedded in the imagination [in] some intractable way, but at the same time it's not really our culture, so it remains somehow other. (2013)

The Southern Gothic is a literary subgenre transformed from the British Gothic 'into an American idiom' (Greven, 2016, p. 474). For Louis Palmer, the standard 'traditional Gothic novel tends to refer to three elements: a setting in an ancestral house, real or perceived occult events and a woman at risk', and the occult happenings can be 'explained rationally or accepted as supernatural' (2006, p. 123). Indeed, for Palmer, Southern Gothic novels are a 'direct appropriation of the British Gothic', allowing issues of class and race to come to the fore (2007, pp. 122, 125). Palmer argues that the Southern Gothic reflects 'a cultural shift to a positive, pejorative whiteness – positive in the sense of visible and obvious rather than invisible, and pejorative in the sense of taking on some of the negative characteristics of the raced Other' (2007, p. 120). For Teresa Goddu, the American South 'serves as the nation's "other", becoming the repository for everything from which the nation wishes to dissociate itself' (in Castillo Street and Crow, 2016, p. 2), so that the genre is thoroughly aware 'of the impossibility of escaping racial haunting and the trauma of a culture that is not just informed by racial history, but also haunted and ruptured by it' (Wester in Donovan-Condron, 2016, p. 340).

So, what is Berry, a British poet, doing when she invokes the Southern Gothic as inspiration for the Arlene poems? As Meredith Miller has argued, late eighteenth- and nineteenth-century British Gothic 'drew heavily on the culture of slavery and the uncanny return of the colonial other to the centre of culture' (2009, p. 135), so the Southern Gothic might not be entirely alone in its considerations of race. Yet Berry is insistent that her poems belong to a distinctly American tradition, which suggests that she perceives the genre to hold potentialities that its British antecedent does not. If, as Donovan-Condron writes, 'history, both personal and national, haunts Southern Gothic' writing (2016, p. 340), the genre might open up space for a confluence of Berry's main concerns: gender power dynamics, authority and trauma.

The Arlene poems centre around Arlene, a monstrous woman who has entrapped the poem's speaker and, later, the speaker's younger sister, Esme. In 'Sweet Arlene', the reader learns that Arlene lives in a house with a 'mutilated floor' (2013, p. 11), which the speaker repeatedly tries and fails to escape throughout the poem. Arlene keeps the speaker 'in one room', in which the speaker 'smother[s] the window with a system of blankets' (2013, p. 11), ironically trying to keep something frightening away as she is haunted by Arlene from inside the house. Arlene can be a maternal figure, whom the speaker refers to as 'Sweet Arlene', but who also terrifyingly shifts into 'a devil' (2013, p. 11); the speaker declares: 'we couldn't | trust her. We were scared and we'd been up all night' (2013, p. 11). Arlene is an archetypal Southern Gothic monstrous woman, as Donovan-Condron describes: 'neither explicitly monstrous nor explicitly Southern' (2016, p. 339). Crucially, Arlene is monstrous because her actions 'cross, refute, and re-write the categorical distinctions by which patriarchal society would control [her]' (Donovan-Condron, 2016, p. 349). Indeed, I have shown that Berry's poems are deeply concerned with authority and gender power dynamics; if Southern Gothic monstrous women 'demonstrate how power warps those who wield it and those whom it subjects', then Arlene exposes 'the consequence of the patriarchy's association of women with domestic spaces' (Donovan-Condron, 2016, pp. 349, 347): Arlene is a terrible surrogate mother who wreaks havoc upon her ward.

Several of the poems in *Dear Boy* mention and think through the death or absence of a mother. Sitting next to 'Sweet Arlene' in the collection is 'The House by the Railroad', to which Berry gives an epigraph from Norman Bates, the antagonist of Alfred Hitchcock's film *Psycho* (1960): 'This place? This place happens to be my only world' (in Berry, 2013, p. 14). The quote, in full, concludes: 'I grew up in that house up there. I had a very happy childhood. My mother and I, we were more than happy' (1960). In the film, Bates is emotionally abused by his mother, who prevents him from engaging with the world. What, then, does Berry's call to Bates suggest about her speaker's relationship to both house and mother? In 'The House by the Railroad', the speaker talks to a house which is haunted 'by the decadent shape of an absent woman' (2013, p. 14). Following the epigraph, we might assume the poem to reveal something about the mother–daughter relationship that pushes it off its pedestal. But the house is the issue here: it is 'full of dirty tricks', hiding the absent mother from the speaker, who finds – in the final moments of the poem – a woman with 'neat grey hair' (2013, p. 14), who may or may not be her mother.

As such, Berry's poems can reinforce the idea of a true, ideal mother – the mother who might save the trapped daughter or be miraculously found after many years. To be left alone with one's true mother is the dream. The nightmare is Arlene: she is far from a suitable replacement, and, although the Arlene poems never explicitly mention a mother, Berry seems to think through the absence of a mother through the very unsuitability of Arlene.

Indeed, this makes the speaker monstrous also, for being motherless is, for Donovan-Condron, 'a key aspect of [. . .] women's monstrosity' in the Southern Gothic, because a motherless woman is 'tethered to a past they did not shape' and becomes 'bereft of a future of their own making, literally and metaphorically' (2016, p. 347).

This bind creates a sense of trauma or troping, a movement from imagination to reality and back again, without will. The circularity of 'Sweet Arlene' is an alarming blur of reality, imagination and calls to other poems. The speaker listens to a tape, on which 'a doctor's voice said: I Imagine a place. We did and that place was Arlene's house' (2013, p. 12). The doctor evidently recalls the Doctor from 'The Incredible History of Patient M' and 'Manners' in *Dear Boy*, and even when offered a moment of reprieve from Arlene, the speaker returns to her abuser and the false sense of security her authority allows. Later in the poem, the speaker suggests she has escaped, waking 'on a plane and my head was on my baby's lap and I thought Arlene had left us', but then Arlene finds her again, and the speaker 'shushed her and rocked her, I just like she taught us' and carries 'her back to our house' (2013, p. 12), presumably now taking on the role of the mother instead. As such, Arlene appears like the ghost or demon in a horror film: the reader thinks she has been defeated or banished, and then she returns in the final moments, creating a sense of dread (and a cliffhanger). Luckhurst's idea of 'trauma time', in which a '"traumatic event is persistently re-experienced" – through intrusive flashbacks, recurring dreams, or later situations that repeat or echo the original' (2008, p. 1) is entirely applicable to 'Sweet Arlene', as the speaker returns to Arlene and the house, time and time again. As with nightmares, what is real and what is imagined in the Arlene poems is not discernible. Is Arlene's house an imaginary space, as suggested by the speaker's reaction to the tape? Is Arlene real? Which is the true Arlene: the devil, or Sweet Arlene?

Indeed, the speaker's 'baby' is a sketched figure, and therefore arouses uncertainty – it is possible that he might be entirely imagined. The speaker only mentions 'baby' when she wants to escape. She pleads twice with her 'baby', 'take me home' and mentions 'baby' again when she does not feel 'safe' in her 'bones' (2013, p. 11); her body itself becomes like the haunted house: 'We rattled and kept ourselves awake. We knocked and knocked' (2013, p. 11). For Xavier Aldana Reyes, 'the female monstrous body in horror is intrinsically connected to patriarchal constructions of pregnancy, birthing and menstruation as dirty' (2020, p. 396), and so we see the speaker's body as starting to react to Arlene's influence, becoming haunted and faltering as Arlene refuses to allow her to mature. While the speaker 'tried to be I cheeks and hips and

146   *Whiteness, Feminism and the Absurd in Contemporary Poetry*

everything you need in a woman' (2013, p. 12), thinking of being sexually alluring for 'baby', Arlene cradles the speaker like a mother would cradle a child, thwarting her independence and adulthood, and reiterating a patriarchal control over the speaker's body. When the speaker becomes motherlike to Arlene, she seems to be playacting, like a child playing with a baby doll.

Yet, as Reyes notes, it is important not simply to conflate mothering, menstruation and pregnancy with monstrosity (2020, p. 396): Arlene is frightening because she poses a real threat to the speaker. In 'Arlene's House', the speaker reveals that 'Arlene lives in our house now and she won't leave' (2013, p. 42); the house, despite the 'doormat I and rugs and a room each' has become haunted again, thanks to Arlene, who 'just turned up and knew I all the house's tricks, the way the wind sucks doors shut' (2013, p. 42). Arlene's hatred of 'baby' becomes clearer as she declares, 'Haven't I loved you with every force?' if the speaker mentions him (2013, p. 42). The speaker once again uses 'baby' as an imaginary escape, admitting, 'sometimes something clangs open and I can't help myself, I I'll remember how we lay in bed as the wonky blinds delivered light' (2013, p. 42), a line which recalls a more frightening image from 'Sweet Arlene': 'this shaft of light lying like a plank across the floor' (2013, p. 11). Such echoes cast aspersions once again on whether 'baby' is real: does the speaker have a lost love she might return to, or has she created him as a rebellion, a way to assert her sexuality and maturity? She declares: 'I'm oldest so I've been out in the world' and has therefore 'seen other ways of doing things' (2013, p. 42). The irony here is, of course, that Arlene's way of doing things *is* different – or, at least, ostensibly different from a patriarchal household or existence defined by romantic relationships. But in trying to set up her matriarchy, Arlene falls into the traps of patriarchy: control, abuse and (sexual) repression.

The creation of a new matriarchal family unit is also the focus of Lucky McKee's horror film, *The Woman* (2011), in which a feral woman wreaks revenge on Chris Cleek, a lawyer who lives on a rural farm and captures her while hunting, and in the name of freeing the woman 'from her baser instincts', bathes her in boiling water, washes her with a pressure washer and rapes her; his son, Brian, after witnessing the rape, tortures and sexually assaults her too. Chris beats his wife, Belle, and the film insinuates that he has raped his eldest daughter, Peggy, who is secretly pregnant. Chris and Brian also feed Peggy's teacher, Ms Raton – who is suspicious that Peggy might be pregnant – to their vicious German Shepherd dogs and Chris and Belle's secret daughter, Socket, who is eyeless and they have raised as a dog. Darlin', the youngest daughter, is

Reality and Imagination in Emily Berry **147**

told off for attempting to kiss boys, and sets out to befriend The Woman. She is angelic and entirely impervious to any sort of prejudice.

In *The Woman*, women are victims, stereotypes, jokes or (at the very worst, the film seems to suggest) independent, and a threat to patriarchy. In the final scenes of the film, The Woman, who has killed Chris, Belle and Brian, constructs a new family. She gives Darlin' her finger, inviting her to ingest the blood of her original family, clearly refiguring an earlier scene in which The Woman bites off Chris' finger and his wedding ring. Now that The Woman has destroyed the patriarchal, heteronormative family, she can build her own. Darlin' accepts, and so The Woman, Darlin' and Socket walk across the farmlands and back to the forest. Peggy follows slowly behind. It is not very difficult to read the ideas behind this image: this is a monstrous new kind of family, which has destroyed the patriarchy and, most threateningly, does not require men.[6]

In Berry's Arlene poems and *The Woman*, the matriarchy is threatening and flawed because the matriarch reinscribes the violence and oppression of the patriarchy: as Arlene is controlling and thwarts the speaker's maturity and relationships, The Woman creates her own family out of people she can easily manipulate. In the film, Peggy is left trailing behind because she is already marked by the patriarchy, and older, thereby less easy to influence. While McKee's vision of a 'feminist' horror film is unclear, Berry's is a more certain continuation of themes explored in *Dear Boy*: the frightening and terrifying experience of living under abuse of power. As the speaker of 'Bad New Government' is concerned about 'worrying new developments' (2013, p. 57), the speaker of 'Sweet Arlene' considers 'the worrisome nature of details' (2013, p. 11), an echo which places the poems in conversation. Though ostensibly very different, both poems land on the same ambivalence: the enduring nature of romantic love, even if it cannot answer questions or solve problems, and abuses of power. Like 'Bad New Government', 'The Incredible History of Patient M.', 'Manners' and 'My Perpendicular Daughter', the Arlene poems explore the speaker's response to authoritarian power.

The speaker's attempts to overthrow Arlene or escape her are continuously thwarted by her own lack of faith. In 'Sweet Arlene', the speaker wishes 'we had faith' and sends out a 'prayer, a faithless one', which is 'too weak' (2013, p. 11), and does not work. As the ennui and stasis of the people in Caroline Bird's 'Genesis' becomes a subtle criticism of those who complain about their position and yet do nothing to change it, Berry begins to show how the speaker's suffering – while certainly wrought by Arlene – cannot be remedied by her own reluctance to change matters. Indeed, the speaker's declaration of having 'seen other ways of doing things' in 'Arlene's House' (2013, p. 42) is undercut by the

148 *Whiteness, Feminism and the Absurd in Contemporary Poetry*

poem's title, which suggests Arlene's consuming hold over the speaker, and the final lines of the poem, which act as a capitulation:

> Heaven help those girls, Arlene says, if they take my broken
> spirit for a role model. As if heaven would ever get any
> kind of look in. We're far away now. The house is smaller than
> the light in Arlene's eye. We rock, knees to chest, and put
> ourselves to bed. We don't know what we'd do without her. (2013, p. 43)

At first, Berry refutes Arlene's own slide into existential dread and stasis by having Arlene (at least ostensibly) hope for more for her captives. Yet the speaker is also embittered, casting off any hope for redemption ('heaven') as she comes to recognise Arlene's power. The speaker then suddenly implies that she has escaped Arlene through a series of staccato images: she is 'far away', and she seems to be looking at the house from a distance, scared of being discovered. But the escape is once again imagined: the speaker feels she would be at a loss without Arlene, inferring that she has not escaped at all. The idea of the house being 'far away' is imagined, an image of her desire to escape as Arlene's influence traps her irreversibly. The likening of the house to 'the light in Arlene's eye' suggests that the speaker might never escape. When she tries to leave (even by imaginary means), she is always brought back to Arlene.[7]

'Arlene and Esme', published in the January 2014 edition of *POETRY* magazine, offers a tentative solution to the speaker's surrender and existential dread: her younger sister, Esme. Esme 'has a plan', which involves imagining 'a future' and doing 'what she likes' (2014), despite Arlene's rules. The speaker frets, listening to Arlene as she tells her '*You're not strong*', to which the speaker wants to reply, but does not: 'I'm in charge now' (2014). Esme is decidedly more positive than the speaker, as she sees things from 'an un-given-up perspective', telling the speaker, '*You are a whole person*' (2014). This statement signals a slight shift for the speaker, who responds, 'A row of mornings fan out' (2014), and in the final moments of the poem, turns her attention to the pancakes her sister has made, so that Arlene appears banished. After the first half of the poem, Esme laughs, releasing the tension created by Arlene, and consequently vanquishes her. This is the only positive ending to a poem in the sequence, and the only one in which Arlene does not reappear or reassert herself at the end. It is also the only poem in the sequence in which the speaker's 'baby' is not mentioned, which suggests that the speaker has finally accepted he is not going to save her.

Esme does not have any direct interactions with Arlene, which suggests – as the whole sequence has done – that Arlene is a creation of the speaker's imagination, a stand-in for grief or anxiety as the speaker lies 'awake watching over my sisters and I listen to them breathe' (2014). Even when the speaker sleeps, she says, 'I dream I can't sleep and I'm standing there looking | down at them, the night pouring from my hands' (2014), a nightmarish image that demonstrates how much reality and imagination have become blurred for the speaker. Esme offers a way out, through small gestures of positivity, through the way 'she tries things out' (2014). Esme is 'unafraid', while the speaker admits: 'I don't know if I can live my life' (2014). By ending the poem on a moment of hope – Arlene's potential disappearance, a minute of peace for the speaker and Esme – Berry suggests that movement from paralysing stasis, moving away from abusive power, is possible. However, this movement is ultimately curtailed by excluding 'Arlene and Esme' – each other's counterparts, hopelessness and hopefulness – from *Dear Boy*. If one does not go looking, the speaker remains stuck in her troping, becoming a haunted house, more and more like Arlene.

I have spent some time discussing here how Berry's sequence enacts tropes of horror films and the Southern Gothic to think about gender roles and overthrowing oppressive power structures, so I now wish to return to the question of whiteness. If, as Palmer writes, the Southern Gothic can render whiteness visible, then how might Berry's sequence be engaging with this crucial element of the genre? In her influential *Playing in the Dark*, Toni Morrison writes of the importance of investigating the 'impact of racism of those who perpetuate it' and to refute the idea that 'literature is . . . "universal"' and 'race-free' (1993, pp. 11, 12). At first glance, the Arlene poems are apparently 'unraced', and thereby white, focused on gender power dynamics, taking the presumed whiteness of the reader at face value. Yet, for Miller, the Southern Gothic is 'a facility for expressing the relationship between structures of masculine and feminine sexuality and structures of race and culture' (2009, p. 137). 'Sweet Arlene' and 'Arlene's House' do not necessarily engage with questions of race – or class – eschewing them to create an otherworldly nightmare that could only be inhabited by a privileged white person: where race and class do not exist. While Arlene *is* horrific, the world outside is not so threatening, full of neighbours who 'try to ask | if we're all right' (2013, p. 42).

Yet, in 'Arlene and Esme', Berry begins to point to Britain's colonising in the form of 'black mould' which 'has made a map of Australia' (2014).[8] Berry's image clearly connotes decay and infestation, which ostensibly mimics the devastating impact of colonisation and gives the speaker 'trouble breathing' (2014). Of course, black mould is literally dangerous to the respiratory system, but the speaker's fear seems to come from the fact that Australia is 'so far away' (2014). Here, Berry's speaker is awestruck by the largeness of the world – its possibilities, all that could happen out there if she got away from Arlene – and by the idea of being very far away from Arlene and how frightening that would be. Berry's image – and Arlene's insistence that the speaker look at this mould by the window – inscribes the mould with evil, so that the decay becomes a metonym for another, more widespread and no less devastating abuse of power. Certainly, Berry's gesture towards this historical context is oblique, and perhaps not yet fully fledged – though Miller concedes that, 'even in literature, one can only think oneself halfway out of any ideological structure' (2009, p. 139). Once Arlene is banished by Esme's laughter, Berry's attempts to reckon with race and colonisation dissipate, and the poem returns to the domestic. This might, however, be a gesture towards how Esme's positivity – like the speaker's in 'Bad New Government' – can only solve so many problems. The black mould will continue to spread, Arlene may return and the speaker will need to find some way to vanquish her, and all that she stands for, for good.

Afterword: Failing Better

In white American poet Anne Boyer's 'The Revolt of the Peasant Girls', published in 2014 on the *PEN America* website, the titular peasant girls engage in guerrilla warfare against men. 'Peasant', of course, suggests low social status, a harkening back to a feudal system in which girls come last in the social pecking order. Towards the end of the poem, Boyer states their oppression explicitly with the repetition of 'class':

> We were of three classes: female, children, poor. We were of two more classes: farmers, rebels. We were of one more class: who fought their own fathers. We were of one more class: who betrayed their own mothers. (2014)

This repetition and furtherance emphasise the illogicality of class as a social marker, and of social inequality. The text also emphasises the amount of strain the girls are under: first, by the society they live in, which has classed them as 'female, children, poor' – presumably the worst three things they could be; second, for taking part in a revolution, which ultimately begets pain and destruction of the status quo and family unit, through fighting 'their own fathers' and betraying 'their own mothers' (2014).

To counter this, the peasant girls celebrate their girlhood: they hug 'Care Bears', wear 'aquamarine-and-heart stud earrings' and write their list of demands 'in a pen with four-colored ink' (2014).[1] The peasant girls are connected by their girlishness; throughout the poem, they refer to themselves collectively as 'we' and use this union as a source of strength. Indeed, the peasant girls gain literal supernatural powers – 'dreams and visions' from an 'oracular sow', and form a matriarchal society in which they are supervised by 'Mom', who may or may not be mother to all of the girls (2014).

The girls are descended from oppressed communities – 'indigenous people', 'escaped slaves' and 'witches' (2014) – and these historical connections to the land they inhabit, and the oppression and violence their

152 *Whiteness, Feminism and the Absurd in Contemporary Poetry*

ancestors experienced, provide them with insight and power. The girls receive their first visions 'In the earliest July of the decade, immediately preceding a series of multi-township Pioneer Days' (2014). Pioneer Day, an official holiday celebrated on 24 July in the American state of Utah, commemorates the entry of Brigham Young and the initial group of Mormon pioneers into the Salt Lake Valley on that day in 1847. As such, Boyer's poem reminds the reader of colonial practices – the pioneers violently displacing Native Americans (Herbets, 2020) – and the continued celebration of such historical events, a practice which centres whiteness and the experience of settlers, and remains ignorant to the realities of such holidays.

Indeed, that the girls receive their visions at this time suggests some higher call to social change, one that must be a collective endeavour. The girls' visions come in a series of dreams as they turn ten years old, while they are still children. Boyer at once makes the dreams a powerful invocation of collective intent, while also highlighting the perceived gaucherie of girlhood: the dreams are focused on popular culture and their pets. Boyer pre-empts sneers at the girls' visions, so that the reader who laughs at the girls' endeavours must question why they laugh: what prejudices do they have against a set of hopeful, imaginative (and powerful) girls? From where have these intolerances been inherited? Boyer's tactic is exemplified in the oracular sow, who 'explained black magic, class struggle, seasonality, theories of gender, the | agricultural optic' (2014). The girls are just children, after all, and should be allowed to be concerned with ponies (which they would prefer to the sow, they admit), and fantasising about shopping in 'the new mall' (2014), rather using it as their base to engage in warfare against the patriarchy. The poem, then, offers a critique of the way girls are conditioned to mature early, and how oppression is inherited and unavoidable. It is notable that boys do not feature in the warfare – they are spared this experience.

The dream-visions ostensibly suggest that the girls will be victorious, since their brothers' jeans crumble (there might be a suggestion here that their *genes* crumble, since the significance of the Levi 501s is not explored, and the vision depicts the fall of men entirely). The visions are imbued with feminine power: the little sisters have the agency and the ability to route train tracks, literally changing the course of events; the girls are 'bricks', which suggests that they might be able to build something in the wake of destroying their patriarchal society. However, their visions are Macbethian[2] and might not be all that they seem, since the speakers seem to be vocalising the poem from beyond the grave, telling us: 'we wait for the earth to open and spit out our bodies to the statisticians. || Now we are like any heroes: forgotten' (2014). The girls imagine themselves resurrected, in their 'decayed Kangas, crawling out from under the mounds of Playtex and Wet-n-Wild they bulldozed over us' (2014).

Even in their supernatural resurrection, the girls are seemingly defeated – returned to their childhood trainers, emerging under the detritus of a capitalist patriarchy that forces them to wear bras. This seems to be a knowing nod towards the myth of feminists being preoccupied with burning their bras, which originates from a 1968 protest against a Miss America pageant in New Jersey, in which women threw a number of objects, including lipstick and high-heeled shoes, into a 'Freedom Trash Can'; Robin Morgan, one of the protest's organisers, asserts in an interview with the BBC that it was not set alight (BBC News, 2018). Morgan opines that the myth serves to belittle the women's efforts and trivialise the protest (2018). Considering how the poem charts many of the ways the peasant girls are patronised, infantilised and underestimated, Boyer seems to be pointing to yet another history of oppression – of undermining attempts to assert feminist causes. Indeed, the Miss America protest has become synonymous with second-wave feminism, which is highly criticised for its focus on white, middle-class women's issues; Boyer also seems to be suggesting that the girls' fixation on bras might be a misguided interest, one they will grow out of as their politics develop. The reference to 'Wet-n-Wild' is twofold: to a brand of water parks across the United States, Brazil and Mexico, originally opened in 1977 and owned by SeaWorld creator George Millay, which highlights the capitalist drive to bulldoze land and use it for personal financial gain; and to the term in common parlance, which is used to describe someone who is sexually promiscuous, which suggests the girls will be resurrected into a society which sexualises them prematurely. Even at ten years old, they have been taught to be ashamed of their sexuality and bodies, of 'walking around without tops at the town pool' (2014).

The girls' defiant warfare takes the form of a series of inventive and brilliant suits, including ones made from 'the skins of dads', 'the downy hair of varsity athletes' and 'the canvas pants of the man who worked at Casey's General Store' (2014). At moments when it seems as though the girls may be defeated or outsmarted because their suits are unsuitable for combat, the undercutting dark humour of the suits' materials reasserts the girls' authority through wit and their murder of the dads, the man who worked at Casey's General Store and varsity athletes, reaffirming their cause and conviction, and reminding the reader that the girls are equipped in some ways to fight the war – they are not to be pitied.

Even their own warfare exposes their oppression, with 4H banning one of their suits 'because it was made of illicit skyscapes' and is therefore deemed 'sexual' (2014). 4H is a US-based network of organisations that promotes 'hands-on learning and positive youth-adult partnerships' and helps 'youth acquire knowledge and develop life skills that enable them to find and focus their energy into their passions while also giving back to the community' (University of California, 2023).[3] The joke here seems to be that the girls have created their own version of 4H, which *actually* promotes positive youth–adult relationships (say, with 'Mom'), and has provided them with a cause and community. 4H itself is under the control of the patriarchy, sexualising the girls' endeavours and turning their creativity into shame.

Throughout the poem, the girls are infantilised and patronised. Rather than listening to their demands or cause, the president provides them with 'coloring books' to meaninglessly distract them (2014). He does not take their demands seriously *because* they are girls. Simultaneously, upon hearing their opponents are girls, the sheriffs' deputies try to rape them (the insinuation here being that girls are weak, and that girls deserve to be raped). Others are 'just killed' (2014). The poem therefore ends on a sense of circularity: many girls have died for their cause, and nothing has changed – they are still oppressed by men.

Yet the speaker asserts that to tell this story of political corruption 'in plural is to deny the intimacy of facts', and the final line of the poem, 'The Intimacy of the Facts: DEAR FUTURE GIRLS,' (2014) with its centre-alignment and comma, suggests that a new story is about to be told, that more will be revealed. While this is not necessarily a triumphant end – the bleak ending of the poem confirms that the new story will still contain oppression, rape, threats, corruption and the patriarchy – there is a glimmer of hope. The girls, like so many before them, have tried to defy their oppressors, and the future girls – who may suffer the same fate – at least have the solidarity of the girls before them. Each time they try, they inch closer. Boyer concludes the poem with an open-ended invitation for the reader to imagine a better future, one in which we learn from our mistakes, one in which change will come, even if slowly, if we keep on trying.

When I began this research into contemporary Absurdist poetry in Britain and the US, I was focused on an investigation into feminine and feminist iterations of the Absurd. But, while undertaking that research, I have pursued a necessary investigation into how race, gender and class might be working together in several contemporary Absurdist poems. In this book, I have demonstrated how contemporary Absurdist poetry written by white poets has tended to foreground issues of gender, and how this has ultimately opened up space for poets to consider race – and, in some cases, their own whiteness, or the pervading issue of whiteness.

Often, this work has been oblique, with the poets' attentions to race being communicated through their investigations of privilege, cultural capital, class, popular culture references and gender politics. This suggests, as Parmar has argued, a reluctance towards discussing whiteness in British poetry – perhaps for fear of recentring whiteness or getting it wrong – and that whiteness is clearest to these writers when they take other aspects of identity into consideration. As Park Hong has argued, the avant-garde (in both Britain and the US) has been taken over by white poets, marginalising important works by writers of colour. Focusing on whiteness has meant that I must write about white writers, but I hope to have brought their work into conversation with writers of colour. Yet decentralising whiteness also means, as Magi points out, 'studying how texts written by people of color might not fulfill political expectations, or should *not only* be instrumentalized toward political aims' (2017); I hope to have begun this work here, too.

My own investigations have called into question the 'success' of such challenges to whiteness. If, as a critic, it has taken much investigation to unearth some potential meanings of these poems, how is the white poet's presumed white, middle-class reader meant to learn from them if they do not approach the poems with this lesson in mind? There are notable exceptions, of course, which I have highlighted throughout the book. Yet I have landed, many times, on the question of how didactic a poem should be, cautioning against 'emotionally non-directive' writing, while also acknowledging the need for poets to leave space for their readers to come to their own conclusions. Is it the poet's or poem's job to ensure the reader learns something from the poem? I am still uncertain.

I would like to propose, then, in this vein, that this book is about failure. It is about white people's failure to recognise whiteness as a present and active part of life, literature, society and politics; about white people's failure to acknowledge that whiteness is not the 'default' or 'universal', and how that finds its way into poetry; it is about the poetry establishment and its members' failure to make 'rooms' not white. It is about how political upheaval is borne from the systems which fail to take care of us; it is about our failure to look after the world and, thereby, it is about the apocalypse, and imagining a better future. It is also about the endeavour of trying to create change and failing, and so trying again; of trying to upset the status quo and realising one's own prejudices, ignorance and need to learn. It is about how failure can, at times, be an ultimately positive action, since it inherently sets up subsequent actions: learning, and trying again. As Kayo Chingonyi writes, 'If, in writing about race, white writers cannot make space for shame, for history, then they participate in a literary culture that is either hyperdefensive or one so laden with apology as to obscure the possibility for meaningful exchange' (2020, p. 46).

Boyer's poem, then, is a paean to hopeful failure: to the possibility of trying to change things, failing and trying again. One might read her poem as a nihilistic view of US history (and let us not forget Western history), which has oppressed uncountable numbers of people and continues to do so today. The ending of the poem might be a suggestion of how things cannot change, and history is doomed to repeat itself. But, to my mind, Boyer's poem resists such a reading in her persistent attempts to bring whiteness into the conversation. Indeed, this is a poem about girlhood, about how being a girl brings untold amounts of pressure, oppression and violence upon a person; but it is also a poem about how whiteness throughout history has created a narrative of triumph and endeavour at everyone's expense, but particularly girls of colour, who – should they survive – become women of colour and live through oppression every day. Whiteness has wreaked havoc, and this is what has borne the patriarchy. Make whiteness visible, write poems that wrongfoot the reader and ask them to reflect on their own privileges and prejudices, and we will edge closer to a better future, Boyer seems to say.

At its most successful, contemporary Absurdist poetry enacts an important reversal of power, constantly shifting authority and honesty, destabilising gendered, classed and raced expectations. It engages with popular culture as a means of rejecting elitism in poetry, and thereby highlights class structures, using bathos, gaucherie and self-effacing humour as a route to Menippean satire, calling its reader to reflect and change. In many cases, the Absurd imagines the end of the world as a truly hopeful space for reform – to accept the Absurd into one's life, and from there do something different. Historically, the Absurd has been bound up in nihilism, existential dread, stasis or looping structures which cannot change. The contemporary Absurdist poetry I have explored in this book sees this nihilism and understands it, but is beginning to comprehend that this is, ultimately, a futile endeavour.

Naturally, writers' work begins somewhere and develops over the course of a career, as does the critic's thinking about a range of issues or their specialism. To say that the poems selected for this book are the poets' last words on race, gender, class, inequality and politics would be entirely unfair, and I hope to have offered readings that open potentialities. In writing about race, specifically whiteness, we need – both critics and poets – to be allowed to fail, although not with impunity. As political movements evolve from the mistakes and shortcomings of their forebears, poetry and criticism inherently must fail if they are to advance; all critical and creative writing must fail if we are to keep on writing.

This is most likely why Beckett's famous quote, 'Ever tried. Ever failed. No matter. Try again. Fail again. Fail better', taken from his penultimate prose work, *Worstward Ho* (1983),[4] has become so popular. As Ned Beauman (2012) and Mark O'Connell (2014) investigate, the quote has been misappropriated to the point that it has been adopted by 'the entrepreneurial class [. . .] with particular enthusiasm, as a battle cry for a startup culture in which failure has come to be fetishized, even valorized' (O'Connell, 2014), and 'is now [. . .] flayed completely of meaning and turned into a successful brand with no particular owner' (Beauman, 2012). Therefore, in some guises, failure has become a sort of endpoint for critical thinking, as sadness and empathy have done. As Beauman notes, 'when Beckett talks about failure, he's often talking about how *language* can't withstand the weight of the meaning you want to put into it' (2012; emphasis mine), and therefore 'his unintended ubiquity is ideal: What better argument for the feebleness of determinate meaning than the tawdry afterlife of "fail better"?' (2012).

Poetry is the endeavour of finding the right language for expression, of finding the right words in the right order to capture a particular experience and make it emotionally resonant or affective for a reader. It is made out of the frustration with language that Beckett describes, and endures because writers, learning from their peers and predecessors, hope that their poems might enact change, however subtle. I understand this is an ultimately utopian description of poetry, since poems fail to do this all the time, and all poets do not share a utopian ideal of a 'better future'. Not all poets want to tackle their prejudices (in poem form). Not all poems are (nor can they be) about politics, society and race. When poems like Emily Berry's 'Bad New Government' go viral, they are usually taken at face value, or twisted to serve a particular purpose, popular in their quotability and seeming ubiquity – how they resonate with white readers. As with Beckett's quote, they are flattened, lose their ambivalences and shortcomings, and become enshrined as examples of 'great poems'. For Beauman, this is the logical conclusion of the Absurd, because 'there's no demonstration of life's futility or language's emptiness that is so profound, it can't one day be turned into a reassuring fridge magnet, and that thankfully helps put pessimism back in its place' (2012).

As O'Connell writes, the 'entrepreneurial fashion for failure with which [Beckett's quote] fits so snugly is not really concerned, as Beckett was, with failure per se' (2014), but with 'failure as an essential stage in the individual's progress toward lucrative *self*-fulfillment' (2014; emphasis mine). Beckett's quote, when appropriated in this way, is about individualistic, capitalistic striving towards betterment, not the 'greater good' kind of bettering I discussed in Chapter 5. The meme-ification of poems like Berry's 'Bad New Government' leads us logically back to failure but not pessimism, I would argue. Indeed, the poem has failed to do what it really needed to do, and readers have failed to respond to the poem in the way it requires. So, the poet must try again. This is the poet's most hopeful state: understanding the ways in which one's poem has failed, sitting with a blank page before them, ready to try again, imagining an ideal reader who responds in exactly the way the poem needs.

Notes

Introduction

1. My full-length poetry collections are *Fortune Cookie* (2017) and *Museum of Ice Cream* (2021).
2. The venue of publication is especially important here. While a US publication was willing to publish an investigation into race and British poetry, a British publication was not – a fact Preti Taneja highlighted in her introduction to Parmar's Royal Society of Literature lecture at the Newcastle Poetry Festival on 13 May 2023.
3. This is a fitting approach considering Esslin's assertion that the playwrights of the Theatre of the Absurd 'do not form part of any self-proclaimed or self-conscious school or movement' (2023, p. 4).
4. The Poetry Book Society's Next Generation Poets list names twenty poets once every ten years who are expected to influence the poetry landscape of the coming decade. The most recent list was released in 2014. See Chapter 1 for further discussion of the landscape of contemporary British poetry and the Absurd.
5. Returning to Cornwell's assertion that 'textual inclusion of the word "absurd" ... may not constitute any guarantee that a work is to be regarded with justification as fully, or solely, belonging to what we may choose to consider "literature of the absurd"' (2006, p. 100), it is evident that Whalley is not referring to the literary Absurd but absurdity in widely understood forms.
6. Indeed, Cornwell notes that the Absurd 'enjoys far more currency in literature' (2006, p. 2).
7. The text was first published in 1959.
8. The Faber New Poets scheme was launched in 2009 by Faber & Faber, and was funded by Arts Council England. The scheme aimed to 'identify and support emerging talents at an early stage in their careers' through 'a programme of mentorship, bursary and pamphlet publication' (Burnett, 2009). Each year until 2016, the scheme selected four poets to support.
9. The play was first performed in 1955.
10. The text was first published in 1955.

Chapter 1

1. For further discussion of reviewing culture and race in British poetry, I recommend reading Parmar's two articles cited in this chapter. Readers may also be interested to read Dave Coates and Parmar's qualitative report, *The State of Poetry and Poetry Criticism* (2018). Parmar has founded the Ledbury Poetry Critics scheme, a national mentorship programme for poetry reviewers founded in collaboration with Ledbury Poetry Festival and Sarah Howe to encourage diversity in poetry reviewing culture. For further discussion and data for reviewing culture and gender in the US, readers may be interested in reading VIDA's annual reports.
2. Indeed, as Juliana Spahr and Stephanie Young evidence in 'The Program Era and the Mainly White Room' for the *Los Angeles Review of Books* (2015), the majority of poets and readers in literal rooms (i.e. readings, conferences, etc.) are white. Spahr and Young are writing about a specifically US context, but, as Parmar's work shows, the British poetry establishment follows a similar pattern, in which rooms – literal and figurative – are mainly white.
3. Caroline Bird, 2002; Luke Kennard, 2005; Heather Phillipson, 2008; Sam Riviere, 2009. Other poets in this book have also been awarded an Eric Gregory Award: Jack Underwood, 2007; Emily Berry, 2008; Sophie Collins, 2014 and 2019; Rachael Allen, 2017 (Society of Authors, 2022). These poets have also been individually shortlisted for, and awarded, other poetry prizes in the UK. Allen is poetry editor at *Granta*, Berry held tenure as the *Poetry Review*'s editor from 2016 until the end of 2022, while Collins, Kennard, Riviere and Underwood teach at British universities. This is to say that the poets mentioned in this chapter hold significant influence over the British poetry establishment, whether through publications, editorship or teaching the 'next generation' of poets.
4. The Costa Book Awards were a set of annual literary awards recognising English language books by writers based in UK and Ireland; there was a special category for poetry collections. When the prize abruptly ended in 2022, the Nero Book Awards were established in 2023, but without a poetry category. As Rishi Dastidar explains in an article for the *Guardian*, a spokesperson for Caffè Nero stated: 'The chosen categories reflect the main genres readers are most likely to find/see when they visit a bookshop or online retailer' (2023), and, according to Meryl Halls, managing director of the Booksellers Association, 'the new prizes' focus will be on "commercial books with wide appeal"' (2023). Although these claims about the commerciality of poetry are specious, as Dastidar argues in his article, the decision to eschew poetry from the Nero Awards acts as further evidence of a wider public opinion that poetry is elitist, and not for the general reader.
5. Further to these individual prizes, in 2014, the Poetry Book Society announced its latest 'Next Generation' poets, which includes poets featured in this book: Emily Berry, Luke Kennard, Heather Phillipson and Jane Yeh (who has also been shortlisted for the Whitbread, Forward and

Aldeburgh poetry prizes). The Poetry Book Society intends for its Next Generation poets to lead 'our national cultural conversation for many years to come' (McMillan in Flood, 2014).

6. JT Welsch's *The Selling and Self-Regulation of Contemporary Poetry* (2021) is an authoritative study of the contemporary poetry industry, and offers incisive thought on prize culture, 'debut fever' and the professionalisation of poetry, including how higher education institutions and the study of creative writing have created a penchant for the critical-creative approach to poetry. I do not have space to investigate the relationship between the emergent popularity of this new aesthetic in the Absurd and higher education in this book, but recommend Welsch's study for consideration of a UK higher education context, and Mark McGurl's *The Program Era: Postwar Fiction and the Rise of Creative Writing* (2011) for a study of the US context.

7. The above list of highly decorated poets does not reflect the number of British poets who are writing poetry one might deem Absurdist, many of them published by esteemed publishers, such as Bloodaxe and Carcanet, or with smaller, independent presses, such as Broken Sleep Books. *Mercurius Magazine* regularly features poets under its online 'Surreal-Absurd Sampler' feature, and provides a helpful insight into the array of poets writing Surreal and/or Absurdist poetry today, demonstrating the sheer range of idiosyncratic approaches to the aesthetic.

8. See Chapter 2 for further discussion of post-internet poetry and how this relates to this aesthetic of the Absurd.

9. Following Vrushali Patil (2013), I use the term 'patriarchy' to refer to the concept of patriarchy and gender oppression more broadly.

10. In Sam Riviere's 2021 novel, *Dead Souls*, the unnamed narrator listens to the monologue of a poet, Solomon Wiese, who is found guilty of plagiarism twice (a criminal offence in the near-future world of the novel). *Dead Souls* is an invective against the small and ineffective British poetry scene, and a damning look at what poetry *cannot* do; it suggests that poetry, and publishing it, is a fools' game; it offers little hope or sense of redemption for poets, publishers – and probably, by extension, its readers. At the centre of Riviere's novel are ideas of authenticity, forgery and plagiarism. Weise's tale is one in which he tries – and fails – to forge work and is caught. This preoccupation – of forgery and plagiarism – is a constant element in Riviere's poetry; his most recent collection, *After Fame* (2020) uses the Roman poet Martial's material to create his own; *Kim Kardashian's Marriage* (2015) is created entirely from Google searches.

11. I refer to VIDA counts because Allen and Collins cite this work in their Introduction to issue 1 of their journal, *Tender* (2012). VIDA is an US organisation 'dedicated to creating transparency surrounding gender imbalances and the lack of diversity in the literary landscape' (2017); their main activity is producing yearly 'counts' which highlight how many women, non-binary, transgender and people of colour have been published by major publications in the US. There is no equivalent in the UK, save Coates

and Parmar's *The State of Poetry and Poetry Criticism* (2020), which concluded that between 2011 and 2018 in the UK and Ireland 'poetry reviewing is more diverse than ever, due to the work done in the last two years by initiatives such as the Ledbury Emerging Poetry Critics and The Complete Works, as part of an ongoing fight for an inclusive poetry culture dating much further back'. In both cases, VIDA counts and *The State of Poetry and Poetry Criticism* consider race in their data, and demonstrate how writers of colour are under-represented. Riviere's poem, then, sits uncomfortably in this evolving conversation, at once highlighting that women are under-represented in poetry (while never looking at the issue of race), ridiculing the institution of poetry and, simultaneously, creating a fantasy in which this speaker proves that poetry is very silly indeed.

12. This is not true of Caroline Bird or Luke Kennard, whom both identify their work as belonging to a surrealist and/or Absurdist tradition.

13. In her correspondence with Copus, Hill writes: 'I object to the idea of "*bending* reality into a *different* shape". Different from what? I feel I am not bending but straightening or unfolding' (2022). Copus responds, 'As the poems unfold, hidden surfaces become unhidden; brought to the light' (2022). This does not seem a far cry from André Breton's definition of surrealism: 'Psychic automatism in its pure state, by which one proposes to express – verbally, by means of the written word, or in any other manner – the actual functioning of thought' (in Gascoyne, 2003, p. 57).

14. *Violet* was published earlier than many of the books in this study, which were mostly published through the years 2010–20. I have chosen *Violet* as an exemplification of Hill's oeuvre and also to demonstrate her influence over many of the other poets in this book, who often cite Hill's work as inspiration, of which there are too many instances to list.

15. As Lucy Winrow writes in her thesis on Hill's poetry, Gregson's is a 'barbed critique' (2013, p. 15) of Hill's work. Gregson writes of the 'uproarious sing-song of [her] flaky carnival' (2011, p. 9), which somewhat diminishes the work in the same breath as trying to understand it.

16. British publisher Salt published a paperback edition of the collection in 2010, from which I am quoting.

17. Kennard's poem parallels Jennifer L. Knox's poem 'Small on Sunday' (published in *A Gringo Like Me*, 2007) in which the speaker and her companion are shrunk by a god after travelling to see a false god, 'The Sleepy Hippo'. The speaker's epiphany that she and her companion have been praying to the wrong god is ultimately defeatist and nihilistic: the speaker accepts her fate, and Knox suggests that humans are doomed to repeat their destructive behaviours. See Clake (2021) where I write about the poem, nihilism and its relation to US television series *Atlanta*.

18. The article is a review of four US poetry collections: *I Know Your Kind* by William Brewer (2017, Milkweed Editions); *Wonderland* by Matthew Dickman (2018, W.W. Norton & Co.); *The Second O of Sorrow* by Sean Thomas Dougherty (2018, BOA Editions); *The Cold and the Rust* by Emily Van Kley (2018, Persea Books).

Chapter 2

1. Flarf is a now-defunct school of poetry. It was founded by Gary Sullivan, Nada Gordon, Drew Gardner, Mitch Highfill, Jordan Davis, Carol Mirakove, K. Silem Mohammed, Katie Degentesh, Maria Damon and Erik Belgum in May 2001, as a response to a scam poetry competition sponsored by Poetry.com (Sullivan, 2011). The movement involves 'heavy usage of Google search results in the creation of poems, plays', and is community-based, 'in the sense that one example leads to another's reply' (Sullivan, 2011). The poems are 'created, revised, changed by others, incorporated, plagiarized, etc., in semi-public' (Sullivan, 2011). Joyelle McSweeney notes that the poems are characterised by 'jangly, cut-up textures, speediness, and bizarre trajectories' (2006), and Sullivan notes their willingness to be 'kind of corrosive, cute' or employ a 'cloying awfulness' (2011).
2. I cannot provide a full account of post-internet poetry here, including Alt-Lit, but recommend readers engage with Charles Whalley's Post-Internet Poetry project (https://postinternetpoetry.tumblr.com/). David Kauffman's *Reading Uncreative Writing: Conceptualism, Expression, and the Lyric* (2017) offers an in-depth exegesis of the Uncreative Writing movement.
3. It is worth noting that Merrett King claims that her work is indebted to Sad Girl Theory and Sick Girl Theory (2022, p. 8), concepts I will return to in Chapter 5.
4. Michael Brown, an eighteen-year-old Black man, was shot and killed by white police officer Darren Wilson in Ferguson, Missouri, on 9 August 2014. Brown's killing prompted protests in Ferguson, international outrage and broader discussions about police violence and structural racism under the banner of Black Lives Matter (Lowery, 2017). For further details about Michael Brown's killing and its aftermath, I recommend Wesley Lowery's article, 'Black Lives Matter: Birth of a Movement' (2017).
5. Kim Calder provides a thorough account of Place's projects in her 2015 article, 'The Denunciation of Vanessa Place' for the *Los Angeles Review of Books*.
6. Cooke's book focuses on prose life-writing, memoir and autobiography. In her conclusion to the book, Cooke writes that she is 'reticent to approach lyric poetry from a primarily autobiographical perspective', and acknowledges that lyric poetry is broadly considered as being separate to life-writing (2020, p. 203).
7. Collins takes a generous view of translation, which includes ekphrasis.
8. For further information about 4chan and its controversies, I recommend Caitlin Dewey's 2014 article for *The Washington Post*, 'Absolutely Everything You Need to Know to Understand 4chan, the Internet's Own Bogeyman' and Mike Wendling's *Alt-Right: From 4chan to The White House* (2018).
9. As Skeggs's *Formations of Class and Gender: Becoming Respectable* (2002) demonstrates, this denial of working-classness is not unusual, for the 'label working class when applied to women has been used to signify all that is dirty, dangerous and without value' (2002).

10. As Skeggs writes, McRobbie found 'a complete absence of class discourse from the general talk of the young women she studied, arguing: "[b]eing working-class meant little or nothing to these girls – but being a girl over-determined their every moment"' (2002).

11. This does not mean I am only understanding class through this dynamic. Class is, as Biressi and Nun write, 'a shadowy and dubious concept at the best of times' (2013, p. 1). Following Biressi and Nun, I understand social class as being 'formed through material conditions and economic (in)securities and the uneven distribution of life chances and opportunities which these conditions create' (2013, p. 1). Class is also a complex and 'ongoing social process' (2013, p. 1) which changes throughout our lives – hence Allen's ambivalence to class.

12. I have chosen not to represent line breaks in prose poems in this chapter and throughout the book, as prose poems are intended to be read as blocks or paragraphs of prose, rather than line-broken poems.

13. Skeggs notes that being dependent on one's parents for clothing can be viewed by (working class) women as the 'ultimate sign of immaturity' (2002), so we might see the speaker's top as a symbol of her desire to be independent and construct her appearance for herself.

14. Gina G represented the United Kingdom at the Eurovision Song Contest in 1996 with the song, which reached number one in the UK Singles Chart. The song also reached the US top 20 in 1997 and earned her a 1998 Grammy Award nomination for Best Dance Recording. The song belongs to Susan Sontag's definition of camp, which 'discloses innocence, but also, when it can, corrupts it' and 'turns its back on the good-bad axis of ordinary aesthetic judgement' (2018, pp. 15, 22); in other words, '(Ooh Ahh) Just a Little Bit' is 'good' because it is delightfully bad.

15. As Skeggs notes, white middle-class femininity is defined as the ideal, and is always coded as respectable (2002).

16. 'Safe for Work' – content that is appropriate to view in a formal setting – and 'Not Safe for Work' – content that is not appropriate to view in a formal setting, respectively.

17. As Skeggs notes, both Black women and men have been 'designated as the dangerous, atavistic sexual other' (2002). As such, definitions of sexuality have become irrevocably linked to class and race because 'sex is regarded as that thing which *par excellence* is a threat to the moral order of Western civilization. Hence one is civilized at the expense of sexuality, and sexual at the expense of civilization' (Mercer and Julien in Skeggs, 2002).

18. I believe that this title is a reference to *When Harry Met Sally* (1989), in which the character Harry (Billy Crystal) calls himself a 'wildman' while wearing a white knitted jumper.

19. For Mikaela Pitcan, Alice E Marwick and danah boyd, respectability politics are rooted 'in resistance to racist imagery of Black people, particularly Black women', who 'adopted self-presentation strategies that downplayed sexuality and emphasized morality and dignity to reject White America's stereotypes of them' (2018, p. 164). However, they note that 'behaviors are

Notes   165

judged respectable by comparing them to racist, sexist, and classist norms that idealize upper–middle class versions of White womanhood' (2018, p. 164).

20. I do not have space here to list numerous policies and their effects; for a full list of Trump's policies and how they have affected civil and human rights, see the Leadership Conference on Human Rights's 'Trump Administration Civil and Human Rights Rollbacks' (2021).

Chapter 3

1. I unfortunately do not have adequate space here to explain why both plays are, indeed, of the Absurd, but would like to point readers to a number of the texts in this book's bibliography for further considerations of these plays and their situating within the Theatre of the Absurd.

2. Notably, in the opening of *Endgame*, Hamm wonders if there can be misery 'loftier than mine' (2006, p. 93), and, considering his mother and father, thinks: 'I am willing to believe they suffer as much as such creatures can suffer. But does that mean their suffering equals mine? No doubt' (2006, p. 93). In this speech, Hamm goes back and forth on this idea of suffering, and concludes, 'The bigger a man is the fuller he is. [*Pause. Gloomily.*] And the emptier' (2006, p. 93). Beckett seems to suggest that perhaps if Hamm had been able to conclude and understand his parents' own suffering, he might have 'ended' their suffering.

3. At times, there is a first-person narrator, in addition to characters named 'Sara' and Sara's 'partner', who disappears and reappears throughout the collection and remains unidentifiable. The identity of the 'I' in Nørth's collection is also not revealed, but several clues suggest it is the partner. It is also not evident whether this 'I' narrates all the poems, or only some. I would like to consider this in detail, but unfortunately this is not the scope of this chapter, and I am using Nørth's work here to show the dynamic of denial, acceptance and rebellion in contemporary Absurdist poetry. The partner's infrequent appearances might suggest poor communication and an inability to connect, which is a recurring theme in Nørth's collection.

4. I take Sparks Lin's proposition that 'both a machine and a human can become a cyborg contextually without changes to the physical body', and that 'within discourses of the cyborg, it is vital to understand that mechanization and humanization are both strategic cognitive processes used to enforce global stratifications of power such as white supremacy and patriarchy' (2022, p. 9). As such, I am referring to robots, androids and cyborgs throughout the chapter, as they seem to take on very similar roles in contemporary Absurdist poetry.

5. British poet Bhanu Kapil's *Incubation: A Space for Monsters*, first published in 2006 by US publisher Leon Works and reissued in 2023 by British publisher Prototype, undertakes similar concerns. The hybrid text follows Laloo, a 'Punjabi-British hitchhiker on a J-1 visa' (2023, p. 13), who is at

once 'cyborg', 'monster', a baby, a child, a woman, pregnant, not pregnant, an immigrant and the daughter of immigrants. Laloo is seemingly the victim of a horrific procedure in an American hospital, and as she tries to escape the realities of this by hitchhiking across the country, she is met with racism, with drivers asking if she is 'from one of those shit-hole countries' (2023, p. 40), treated with suspicion ('How can we keep tabs on these J-1 visa holders, who come over here and . . .' (2023, p. 45)) and turns into a series of numbers: 'My alien number is A#786334901. My social security number is 102-70-5846. My phone number is +1 970 290 6292' (2023, p. 53). The reader is reminded, however, that 'real England' is not much better; the narrative suggests that Laloo began her hitchhiking when she was a child, escaping a 'local festival' in her 'dad's Ford Cortina' (2023, p. 25) and reaching Dover, with 'its scone and jam emporiums and holding centres, complete with their certified interpreters' (2023, pp. 25–6), where she is 'no longer what a person could call a girl or even British', and she is 'mistakenly detained' (2023, p. 26). Despite being treated with suspicion, Laloo describes herself as being like an American, showing how she has 'changed from one kind of girl to another as a result of my experiences' (2023, p. 53). Laloo's journey is underlined with the threat of travelling alone as a woman. The text also explores cultural and gendered expectations – such as marriage, pregnancy and desirability. The dreamlike, shifting realities of the text suggest Laloo's attempts to reconcile all these parts of herself; as Donna Haraway notes, 'to be other is to be multiple, without clear boundary, frayed, insubstantial' (2016, p. 26). At the end of the narrative Laloo disappears, perhaps because 'Her body is very vulnerable tonight, there is the forest next to the highway', but also perhaps because she is 'darkness in a dress' and therefore able to transform herself into 'a shiver, moving through the trees' (2023, p. 110). Laloo's disappearance can be read as a hopeful act of transcendence and, as Cheryl Higashida has written, Kapil's writing pushes 'against neoliberalism's hegemonic consolidation and its legacies: the grotesque inequalities growing within but especially between nations', and 'the cooptation and commodification of "identity politics," the xenophobic and heteronormative calls for stronger nationalisms' (2012, p. 39). In the coda for the British edition, Kapil writes that the difference between a monster and a cyborg is 'repetition' (2023, p. 119), yet her work perhaps has less to do with Absurdist iterations of apocalypse and fears of technology – which I explore at length in this chapter.

6. In an interview with Mike Sakasegawa for the podcast *Keep the Channel Open* (2018), Choi notes: 'As a Korean American there are politics of taking a Japanese woman's voice that I haven't fully addressed and haven't fully worked out', yet Sakasegawa points out that because Kyoko is fictional, it is a 'different proposition' to assuming the voice of a real Japanese person. In a later interview with Levi Todd for *The Rumpus* (2019), Choi notes: 'I'm not really interested in inhabiting a persona that isn't secretly me. I really understand and respect the move to

separate author from speaker; at the same time, it's important for me to make others reconcile with the fact that every speaker is me, no matter how discordant it might seem' (2019), so Choi seems to reconcile herself to her choice to provide Kyoko with a voice by making that voice – however obliquely – her own, imbued with her own experiences (rather than appropriating their experiences). It is not the scope of this chapter to think through Choi's use of a fictional Japanese-appearing cyborg, but I include Choi's comments here to show that thinking through race and representation is a troubling and complex endeavour, one that is much more complex than whiteness to a broad stroke of 'people of colour'.

7. In her interview with Todd, Choi notes that the project began with poems about or voiced by Kyoko, but now there is 'only one poem in the book that remains in her voice' (2019). Choi sees the Kyoko poems as writing she needed to do 'to get things going', but that 'the book ended up outgrowing her' (2019).

8. 'The Turing Test' or the 'imitation game', as first proposed by Turing, would involve a remote human interrogator distinguishing between a computer and a human subject based on their replies to a range of questions. After several of these tests, a computer's success at 'thinking' could be measured by its probability of being misidentified as the human subject (Encyclopaedia Brittanica, 2024).

9. As Brian Massumi writes: 'If we are unable to separate ourselves from our fear, and if fear is a power mechanism for the perpetuation of domination . . . our unavoidable participation in the capitalist culture of fear [may be] a complicity with our own and other's oppression' (in Ngai, 2001, p. 7).

10. It is not the scope of this chapter to explore this in detail, but the repeated criticism and evaluation of Beyoncé's politics demonstrates how Black women's beliefs and conduct are subject to unparalleled scrutiny – one of the main subjects of Claudia Rankine's *Citizen* (2015). One of the main criticisms aimed at Beyoncé is how her music and music videos exploit 'negative stereotypes' of Black women; how this is received – as either an assertion of 'control over the representation' of these negative stereotype or reaping 'the benefits of it' as bell hooks contends (2014, p. 65) – varies wildly, and is the subject of much debate. Indeed, Beyoncé's feminism is often criticised for being a 'popular' or post-feminist – which 'encourages female strength and independence' (Thelandersson, 2022, p. 133) and glorifies 'freedom of choice', 'empowerment' and sexual freedom (Tasker and Negra, 2007, p. 2).

11. The poem's title is taken from an episode of *Star Trek: The Next Generation*.

12. Howard D. Weinbrot also believes that satire has two tones: that of 'the sever, in which the angry satirist fails and becomes angrier still' or 'the muted, in which the threatened angry satirist offers an antidote to the poison he knows remains' (in Quintero, 2011, p. 8); these tones evidently run parallel to Kaufman's definitions of feminine and feminist humour.

Chapter 4

1. 'White trash' is a derogatory term. As Newitz and Wray write, 'stereotypes of white trash can be traced to a series of studies produced around the turn of the century by the U.S. Eugenics Records Office' (1997, p. 2). Stereotypes of 'white trash' rely on images of people who are 'poor, dirty, drunken, criminally minded, and sexually perverse' (Newitz and Wray, 1997, p. 2). As Newitz and Wray argue, these stereotypes serve as a 'useful way of blaming the poor for being poor. The term white trash helps solidify for the middle and upper classes a sense of cultural and intellectual superiority' (1997, p. 2). John Waters also states that the term is 'not just a classist slur – it's also a racial epithet that marks out certain whites as a breed apart, a dysgenic race unto themselves' (in Newtiz and Wray, 1997, p. 2).

2. The poem's title most likely refers to Levittown, the postwar housing project in Long Island, New York, constructed by Levitt and Sons from 1947 to 1951. It was (and remains) a controversial development, known as one of the first mass-produced suburbs and a symbol of the capitalist American dream. The majority of Levittown's population is white (Marshall, 2015). Colin Marshall's 2015 article for the *Guardian*, 'Levittown, the prototypical American suburb – a history of cities in 50 buildings, day 25', provides some helpful context. Alluding to Levittown in her poem reinforces Knox's technique of blurring high and low culture, and suggests whiteness is a part of the poem – however latent that might be.

3. During her keynote paper at the 'Poetry and TV' conference at the University of Birmingham in 2018, Knox commented that the speaker of the poem is supposed to be a white man.

4. As the American Civil Liberties Union (ACLU) writes in 'A Tale Of Two Countries: Racially Targeted Arrests in the Era of Marijuana Reform' (2020), Black people are 3.6 times more likely than white people to be arrested for marijuana possession, despite similar usage rates.

5. For further reading on fatphobia, I recommend Susie Orbach's *Fat is a Feminist Issue* (Arrow, 2016) and Aubrey Gordon's article, 'Aubrey Gordon on Dealing With Aggressive Fatphobia' (2020).

6. Notably, Knox's and Gordon's poems appear to be very similar on the page – both poets build to a use of all upper-case utterances.

7. As Sontag writes, 'Camp art is often decorative art, emphasising texture, sensuous surface and style and the expense of content' (2018, p. 6).

Chapter 5

1. I do not have adequate space here to fully describe the characteristics and postings of the Sad Girl movement, but recommend Thelandersson's thorough exegesis of the Sad Girl and the other texts cited in this chapter for fulsome accounts.

Notes   169

2. A search on X (formerly Twitter) brings up three instances of Broder using this phrase: May 2016, June 2016 and February 2019. Many of the posts mentioned in this chapter have appeared in Broder's account on multiple occasions. Broder's willingness to recycle her own content (presumably for likes and followers) casts aspersions on how genuinely she can be communicating moments or feelings of sadness. Perhaps Broder repeats these behaviours, but still, the act of recording them and repeating them for an audience suggests they are performed – and perhaps not even genuine.

3. Broder has published a related book of essays, *So Sad Today* (Grand Central, 2016).

4. A typical Tumblr Sad Girl post might look something like: 'a picture of Uma Thurman in *Pulp Fiction* smoking a cigarette, displayed on a background of crystals and pink pills. Surrounding, and on top of, this image are phrases like "I hate everything," "anti-you," and "you little shit" in various figurations' (Thelandersson, 2022, p. 163).

5. As Gill and Kanai write, 'the "confidence cult" and the relatable self are two integral parts of how women especially are urged to express their feelings' (in Thelandersson, 2022, p. 160).

6. According to Thelandersson, Instagram Sad Girl posts 'generally focused on making fun of mental distress through memes and other comedic portrayals. Astrology, leftist politics, and the disappointment of heterosexual men were also popular topics' (2022, p. 176).

7. Hannah Williams notes that, despite being sad, the Sad Girl 'is desirable, funny, sexy' (2017).

8. As David F. Crew writes, the 'wartime food shortages, the continuation of the Allied blockade after the armistice, postwar transportation problems, the dismantling of state rationing, and the effects of soaring inflation [. . .] produced a decade-long deterioration of nutrition' in the Weimar Republic (1998, p. 166). Wilfried Rudloff explains that 'poverty levels [. . .] increased enormously in comparison to the years prior to 1914' (2017, p. 107). As the Los Angeles County Museum of Art notes, artists grouped under the term *Neue Sachlichkeit*, or New Objectivity, produced 'sober, unsentimental, and graphic' work that highlighted the sense of alienation, fear of moral decay and scepticism of social change that dominated this era (2019, pp. 1, 3).

9. Of course, there are several parallels between *Endgame* and *Waiting for Godot*, as MacNeice points out, particularly the looping nature of time and the characters' inability to accept the Absurd into their lives or change their circumstances. As Beckett is not the focus of this chapter, I do not have space to compare the two plays at length, and would direct readers to the bibliography for readings of these plays.

10. This is not atypical of the Theatre of the Absurd; Cornwell notes that Harold Pinter's work dissects 'the foibles and discourse of the middle classes' (2006, p. 134) in *A Slight Ache* (1959), *The Collection* (1961) and *The Lover* (1963).

11. As Olivier Guiberteau writes, British people are generally considered 'reserved, repressed, resilient, unemotional and self-controlled' (2020).

170   *Whiteness, Feminism and the Absurd in Contemporary Poetry*

12. As Mersken explores, 'sex, passion, manipulation, and physical beauty' (2007, p. 138) are common stereotypes afforded to Latina women. As a 'Vamp', Gabrielle Solis uses her 'intellectual and devious sexual wiles to get what she wants' (2007, p. 138). For Mersken, the tension between Carlos and Gabrielle centres around 'power and autonomy' and the two are 'exaggerated examples of macho/ machismo – macha/ marianisma' (2007, p. 140). Indeed, the racial stereotypes in *Desperate Housewives* do not end with the Solis family. Xiao-Mei, the maid of the Solis household, is an illegal immigrant who was sold as a domestic servant by her uncle. Xiao-Mei embodies many of the sexual stereotypes of Asian women discussed in Chapter 3: 'misunderstanding' Gabrielle and Carlos's plans to keep her from being deported by having her act as a surrogate, Xiao-Mei embarks on an affair with Carlos.

Chapter 6

1. In her second collection, *Stranger, Baby* (2017), Berry explores a mother's death as a traumatic incident, using this 'perpetual troping' to capture the experience in an 'apparently personal' manner – Berry's mother died when she was young, but this does not necessarily mean the poems are 'straight' autobiography. My review of the collection for *Review 31*, 'Apparently Personal', was published in 2017, and explores these ideas in further detail.
2. The poem has proven particularly popular in response to the British government, with the poem often shared online when a new Prime Minister and Conservative Party cabinet is announced.
3. In a review of Berry's third collection, *Unexhausted Time* (2022), Will Shaw writes that Berry's poems chart the 'failures of present-day Britain with weary pessimism and deadpan humour', but that while the book is 'bleak', it is 'not hopeless' (2022). Indeed, Shaw claims that 'to close off failure as a subject for British poetry is to abandon any hope of writing about politics' (2022).
4. As Evans writes: 'All too frequently, governmental responses to sexual harassment and violence against women is to put the onus on the behaviour (and dress) of individual women themselves' (2015, p. 46).
5. In England, Scotland and Wales, abortions are granted on the grounds of two registered medical practitioners being 'of the opinion, formed in good faith' that any one of the following grounds apply: risk to the life of the pregnant person; preventing permanent, serious injury to their physical or mental health; risk of injury to the physical or mental health of the pregnant person or any existing children of their family (up to a term limit of twenty-four weeks of gestation); or substantial risk that, if the child were born, they would 'suffer from such physical or mental abnormalities as to be seriously handicapped' (Smith, 2022). Abortion remains a criminal offence in Britain under the Offences Against The Person Act 1861.
6. McKee's work is often championed as feminist, although McKee himself does not claim to identify as a feminist (McWeeny, 2011). McKee's film

suggests that it is inevitable that an 'untamed' woman who is brought into a patriarchal family will cause upset and destroy the family unit. This idea is perpetuated in the unsubtle images of the woman biting off Chris' ring finger and spitting out his wedding ring: she is independent and hates the patriarchy, and she is therefore a threat. Indeed, the viewer is invited to partake in the male gaze directed at the woman, when Chris first sees her bathing in the river. As Laura Mulvey states: 'The determining male gaze projects its phantasy on to the female figure which is styled accordingly. In their traditional exhibitionist role women are simultaneously looked at and displayed, with their appearance coded for strong visual and erotic impact so that they can be said to connote to-be-looked-at-ness' (1999, pp. 808–9). This particular scene is filmed in slow motion, so that the shots can linger on the woman's breasts and the way she moves. At points, the image of the woman is viewed through the scope of Chris' gun, as though we are complicit in his voyeurism. Carolina Stopenski claims that due to the female bodies in horror films being centred as objects 'of the depraved, exposed to a variety of tortures and destructions' (what Carol J. Clover deems the 'Final Girl' (1987, p. 207)), a 'female enactor of violence may become a feminist antihero' (2022, p. 2). Yet McKee's film does very little with the 'female mutilator' to advance ideas about gender power dynamics.

7. As Miller writes, 'action and passivity, mobility and imprisonment, and their relation to positions of gender, remain one of the abiding concerns' of Gothic writing (2009, p. 143).

8. During the American Revolutionary War (1775–83), the British government investigated whether Captain James Cook's first landing place on the east coast of Australia might be a place of transportation for thousands of convicts who could no longer be transported to American colonies (Glyn Williams, 2018). As Shayne T. Williams writes, Cook's landing is 'symbolic [. . .] because it portended the end of [the Dharawal people's] cultural dominion over our lands. [. . .] With the First Fleet came the legal fiction terra nullius, a fiction that was applied to justify colonial subjugation of us' (2018).

Afterword

1. The poem is ostensibly set in 1981, with references to toys and clothes popular during the decade, actress and singer Olivia Newton John – famous for her role as Sandy in *Grease* (1978) and her single 'Physical' (1981) – and Rick Springfield, famous for his single 'Jesse's Girl' (1981). However, Boyer's invocation of a feudal system and the rural setting (the girls identify themselves as 'farmers' (2014)) provide an almost timelessness to the poem. This is particularly fitting considering Boyer's attempts to show how history repeats itself, with slight variation, and how oppression is passed down to later generations; it almost does not matter when the poem takes place, since the oppressions the girls face are reiterations of the oppressions their ancestors suffered.

2. In Act 1, Scene III of *Macbeth*, three witches predict Macbeth's future. The first witch names Macbeth 'thane of Glamis!', his current title, while the second witch names him 'thane of Cawdor', and the third witch names him 'king hereafter', prophesying his promotions. The witches' visions are not all they seem, however, disguising the true circumstances behind Macbeth's changes in title, and set up the tragic events of the play.

3. In 2002, the Bush administration began a civil rights investigation into the use of Native American symbols and tribal names in West Virginia's 4-H Club chapter, which resulted in all 4-H chapters changing their practices (*Washington Times*, 2002). As well as demonstrating that 4-H is couched in misogyny, then, Boyer also continues highlighting colonisation and racist practices, showing how the two function together.

4. The work's title is a parody of Charles Kingsley's historical novel *Westward Ho!* (1855).

Bibliography

ACLU (2020). *A Tale of Two Countries: Racially Targeted Arrests in the Era of Marijuana Reform*. New York: ACLU

Ahmed, S. (2007). A Phenomenology of Whiteness. *Feminist Theory*, 8(2), 149–68. https://doi.org/10.1177/1464700107078139

——. (2014). *The Cultural Politics of Emotion*. Edinburgh: Edinburgh University Press

Akass, K. (2006). Still Desperate After All These Years: The Post-Feminist Mystique and Maternal Dilemmas. In: McCabe, J. and Akass, K. (eds.), *Reading Desperate Housewives: Beyond the White Picket Fence*. New York: I.B. Tauris & Co, pp. 48–58

Aldana Reyes, X. (2020). Abjection and Body Horror. In: Bloom, C. (ed.), *The Palgrave Handbook of Contemporary Gothic*. Cham: Palgrave Macmillan. https://doi.org/10.1007/978–3-030–33136–8_24

Alexander, E. et al. (2000). What's African American about African American Poetry? *Fence*. Available at: https://fenceportal.org/whats-african-american-about-african-american-poetry (Accessed: 20 July 2022)

Allen, R. (2014). *Faber New Poets 9*. London: Faber & Faber

——. (2016). Wallpapers/General: /wg/. In: Collins, S. (ed.), *Currently & Emotion*. London: Test Centre, p. 203

—— and Berry, E. (2011). Interview: Emily Berry. *Granta*. Available at: http://granta.com/interview-emily-berry/> (Accessed: 11 March 2016)

—— and Collins, S. (2012). Introduction. *Tender*, 1, p. 3. Available at: www.tenderjournal.co.uk/previousissues (Accessed: 11 March 2016)

——. (2013). Introduction. *Tender*, 2, p. 2. Available at: www.tenderjournal.co.uk/previousissues (Accessed: 11 March 2016)

—— and Johnson, L. (2019). An Interview with Rachael Allen. University of Liverpool (website). Available at: www.liverpool.ac.uk/new-and-international-writing/poetry-class/rachael-allen/ (Accessed: 13 February 2023)

Alpers, P. (1996). *What Is Pastoral?* London: University of Chicago Press

Alsadir, N. (2022). *Animal Joy*. London: Fitzcarraldo Editions

Andes, E. (2020), The Gurlesque Poetry Movement. EAWrites (website). Available at: www.ecawrites.com/post/2018/07/03/the-gurlesque-poetry-movement (Accessed: 21 July 2022)

Andrews, H. and Parker, M. (2018). It's About Multiplicity: A Conversation with Morgan Parker. *MELUS*, 43(3), 148–62. www.jstor.org/stable/10.2307/26566157

Arshi, M. (2015). Large and Imprecise Baby. In: Arshi, M., *Small Hands*. Liverpool: Liverpool University Press, p. 44

Attlee, E. (2015). Click, Click, Click: Cliché in the Poetry of Emily Berry, Heather Phillipson and Sam Riviere. *Dandelion: Postgraduate Arts Journal and Research Network*, 5(2), 1–13. https://doi.org/10.16995/ddl.319

Baker, J.R. and Timm, A.M. (2021). Zero-Tolerance: The Trump Administration's Human Rights Violations Against Migrants on The Southern Border. *Drexel Law Review*, 13(3), 581–661. http://dx.doi.org/10.2139/ssrn.3559908

Baker, P. and Levon, E. (2016). 'That's what I call a man': Representations of Racialised and Classed Masculinities in the UK Print Media. *Gender and Language*, 10(1), 106–39

Bakhtin, M. (1984). *Rabelais and His World*. Trans. by Hélène Iswolsky. Bloomington: Indiana University Press

Baraka, A. (1988). Henry Dumas: Afro-Surreal Expressionist. *Black American Literature Forum*, 22(2), 164–6. www.jstor.org/stable/2904491

BBC News. (2018). 100 Women: The Truth Behind the 'Bra-Burning' Feminists. BBC (website). Available at: www.bbc.co.uk/news/world-45303069 (Accessed: 26 April 2023)

Beauman, N. (2012). Fail Worse. *The New Inquiry*. Available at: https://thenewinquiry.com/fail-worse/ (Accessed: 28 April 2023)

Beckett, S. (2006). *Endgame*. In: *Samuel Beckett: The Complete Dramatic Works*. London: Faber & Faber, pp. 89–134

——. (2006). *Waiting for Godot*. In: *Samuel Beckett: The Complete Dramatic Works*. London: Faber & Faber, pp. 7–88

Beckman, L.J. (2017). Abortion in the United States: The Continuing Controversy. *Feminism & Psychology*, 27(1), 101–13. https://doi.org/10.1177/0959353516685345

Bennett, M.Y. (2015). *The Cambridge Introduction to Theatre and Literature of the Absurd*. Cambridge: Cambridge University Press

Berkow, I. (2005). Spinning the Globe: Ball Hog Heaven. *The New York Times*. Available at: www.nytimes.com/2005/07/24/books/review/spinning-the-globe-ball-hog-heaven.html (Accessed: 25 August 2020)

Berny, M. (2020). The Hollywood Indian Stereotype: The Cinematic Othering and Assimilation of Native Americans at the Turn of the 20th Century. *Angles: New Perspectives on the Anglophone World*, 10, 1–26. https://doi.org/10.4000/angles.331

Berry, E. (2013). A Sculpture about a Phone Call. *Peony Moon*. Available at: https://peonymoon.wordpress.com/2013/06/17/emily-berry-a-sculpture-about-a-phone-call/ (Accessed: 22 September 2017)

——. (2013). *Dear Boy*. London: Faber & Faber

Bibliography 175

——. (2014). Arlene and Esme. Poetry Foundation (website). Available at: www.poetryfoundation.org/poetrymagazine/poems/detail/56688 (Accessed: 14 July 2016)

——. (2022). Silent as a Fire Alarm. *The London Review of Books*. Available at: www.lrb.co.uk/the-paper/v44/n19/emily-berry/silent-as-a-fire-alarm (Accessed: 1 February 2023)

——. et al. (eds.) (2012). Selima Hill. Poetry Archive (website). Available at: www.poetryarchive.org/poet/selima-hill (Accessed: 4 December 2017)

Best, C. (2016). *Faber New Poets 14*. London: Faber & Faber

——. (2019). *Hello*. Oxford: Partus Press

——. and Perry, R. (2015). Peer Review: Ornate Resignation – Crispin Best Interviews Rebecca Perry. *The Quietus*. Available at: http://thequietus.com/articles/17342-rebecca-perry-beauty-beauty-poetry-interview-crispin-best (Accessed: 12 September 2016)

Bird, C. (2013). *The Hat-Stand Union*. Manchester: Carcanet

——. (2017). *In These Days of Prohibition*. Manchester: Carcanet

Biressi, A. and Nunn, H. (2013). *Class and Contemporary British Culture*. London: Palgrave Macmillan

Blakely, M.K. (1980). Dear Gloria. In: Kaufman, G. and Blakely, M.K. (eds.), *Pulling Our Own Strings: Feminist Humour and Satire*. Indiana: Indiana University Press, pp. 9–12

Bloomberg-Rissman, J. (2010). Review: Gurlesque: The New Grrly, Grotesque, Burlesque Poetics, eds. Lara Glenum and Arielle Greenberg. *galatea resurrects 14*. Available at: http://galatearesurrection14.blogspot.com/2010/04/gurlesque-new-grrly-grotesque-burlesque.html (Accessed: 21 July 2022)

Bond, H. (2017). Crispin Best. *[smiths] Magazine*. Available at: www.smithsmagazine.co.uk/2017/12/21/londons-oddest-poet-an-interview-with-crispin-best/ (Accessed: 21 December 2017)

Borzutzky, D. (2014). Delusions of Progress. Poetry Foundation (website). Available at: www.poetryfoundation.org/harriet-books/2014/12/delusions-of-progress (Accessed: 26 July 2022)

Bourdieu, P. (1986). The Forms of Capital. In: Richardson, J. (ed.), *Handbook of Theory and Research for the Sociology of Education*. Westport, CT: Greenwood, pp. 15–29

——. (2010). *Distinction: A Social Critique of the Judgement of Taste* (8th ed.). Trans. from French by Richard Nice. Abingdon: Routledge

Boyer, A. (2014). The Revolt of the Peasant Girls. PEN America (website). Available at: https://pen.org/the-revolt-of-the-peasant-girls/ (Accessed: 4 December 2017)

Broder, M. (2017a). 'i came, i saw, i hid in the bathroom'. X (26 October). Available at: https://x.com/sosadtoday/status/730446818237022209 (Accessed: 21 March 2023)

——. (2017b). 'you say potato, i say inevitable death'. X (26 October). Available at: https://x.com/sosadtoday/status/1000223782106099713 (Accessed: 21 March 2023)

——. (2017c). 'she died as she lived: kind of ready for it but not really'. X (29 October). Available at: https://x.com/sosadtoday/status/924722152347193344 (Accessed: 21 March 2023)

——. (2018). 'crying internally'. X (4 December). Available at: https://x.com/sosadtoday/status/1070055165586235392 (Accessed: 21 March 2023)

——. (2021). 'i feel bad for all of us'. X (27 November). Available at: https://x.com/sosadtoday/status/1464476769054953477 (Accessed: 21 March 2023)

——. (2022a). 'charcuterie board: vibrator, twizzlers, empty pack of cigarettes belonging to a dead man, crystal that didn't heal me, therapy copay'. X (21 October). Available at: https://x.com/sosadtoday/status/1583513170462711808 (Accessed: 21 March 2023)

——. (2022b). 'i was born to give up'. X (15 April). Available at: https://x.com/sosadtoday/status/1514757645726629890 (Accessed: 21 March 2023)

Bromwich, K. and Broder, M. (2016). So Sad Today's Melissa Broder: 'I just want to rip that chapter out'. *Guardian*. Available at: www.theguardian.com/books/2016/may/08/so-sad-today-melissa-broder-poet-twitter-book-mental-health> (Accessed: 14 November 2017)

Brontë, C. (1992). *Jane Eyre* (2nd ed.). Hertfordshire: Wordsworth Editions

Brown, C. and Tyga. (2015). *Ayo* (official video). YouTube. Available at: www.youtube.com/watch?v=zKCrSN9oXgQ (Accessed: 10 August 2017)

Burnett, C. (2009). Faber New Poets. *Frieze*. Available at: www.frieze.com/article/faber-new-poets (Accessed: 13 February 2023)

Burns, L. and Whalley, C. (2018). Positions of Cute in Post-Internet Poetry. *Hotel*. Available at: https://partisanhotel.co.uk/Lucy-Burns-Charles-Whalley> (Accessed: 22 August 2018)

Butler, J. (2014). *Gender Trouble: Feminism and the Subversion of Identity* (2nd ed.). London: Routledge. Available at: https://ebookcentral.proquest.com/lib/st-andrews/detail.action?docID=180211 (Accessed: 2 February 2016)

Calder, K. (2015). The Denunciation of Vanessa Place. *Los Angeles Review of Books*. Available at: https://lareviewofbooks.org/article/the-denunciation-of-vanessa-place/ (Accessed: 9 February 2023)

Caleshu, A. (2011). *Reconfiguring the Modern American Lyric: The Poetry of James Tate*. Bern: Peter Lang

Camus, A. (1955). *The Myth of Sisyphus*. Trans. from French by Justin O'Brien. New York: Vintage. Available at: https://postarchive.files.wordpress.com/2015/03/myth-of-sisyphus-and-other-essays-the-albert-camus.pdf (Accessed: 1 March 2023)

——. (1989) *The Stranger*. Trans. from French by Matthew Ward. London: Vintage Books

Carr, K. (2011). Interview: Lucky McKee Talks About 'The Woman' Walk-Outs, Feminist Directing, and Why He's Not Directing 'iCarly'. *Film School Rejects*. Available at: https://filmschoolrejects.com/interview-lucky-mckee-talks-about-the-woman-walk-outs-feminist-directing-and-why-he-s-not-49dc5c105375#.s4jvljt8s (Accessed: 14 July 2016)

Carroll, H. (2011). *Affirmative Reaction: New Formations of White Masculinity*. London: Duke University Press

Castillo Street, S. and Crow, C.L. (eds.) (2016). Introduction: Down at the Crossroads. *The Palgrave Handbook of the Southern Gothic*. London: Palgrave Macmillan, pp. 1–6

Chanter, R. and Hawlin, T. (2016). Faber New Poets in Conversation. *The London Magazine*. Available at: https://thelondonmagazine.org/faber-new-poets-in-conversation/ (Accessed: 23 February 2023)

Chasar, M. (2012). *Everyday Reading: Poetry and Popular Culture in Modern America*. New York: Columbia University Press

Chingonyi, K. (2020). Whitely: Race and Lyric Subjectivity in Clare Pollard's Poetry. *Wasafiri*, 35(3), 43–7

Choi, F. (2015). AI v.2.1. Asian American Writers' Workshop (website). Available at: https://aaww.org/imaginary-lineage/ (Accessed: 11 March 2023)

——. (2019). *Soft Science*. New York: Alice James Books

Cixous, H. (1976). The Laugh of the Medusa. Trans. from French by Keith Cohen and Paula Cohen. *Signs*, 1(4), 875–93. Available at: www.jstor.org/stable/3173239 (Accessed: 21 February 2016)

——. and Clement, C. (1986). *The Newly Born Woman*. Trans. from French by Betsy Wing. Minneapolis: University of Minnesota Press

Clake, J. (2017). Apparently Personal. *Review 31*. Available at: http://review31.co.uk/article/view/486/apparently-personal (Accessed: 30 March 2023)

——. (2017). *Fortune Cookie*. London: Eyewear Publishing

——. (2021). *Museum of Ice Cream*. Hexham: Bloodaxe Books

——. (2021). Rat Phones, Alligators, Lemon Pepper Wet: The New Absurd of Atlanta. In: Winckler, R. and Huertas-Martín, V. (eds.), *Television Series as Literature*. Singapore: Palgrave Macmillan, pp. 167–84

Clayton, D.M., Moore, S.E and Jones-Everseley, S.D. (2019). The Impact of Donald Trump's Presidency on the Well-Being of African Americans. *Journal of Black Studies*, 50(8), 707–30

Cloke, P. and Little, J. (1997). *Contested Countryside Cultures: Otherness, Marginalisation and Rurality*. London: Routledge

Clover, C.J. (1987). Her Body, Himself: Gender in the Slasher Film. *Representations*, 20, 187–228. https://doi.org/10.2307/2928507

Coates, D. (2013). Caroline Bird – The Hat-Stand Union. *Dave Poems*. Available at: https://davepoems.wordpress.com/2013/11/11/caroline-bird-the-hat-stand-union/ (Accessed: 8 October 2017)

——. (2017). Caroline Bird – In These Days of Prohibition. *Dave Poems*. Available at: https://davepoems.wordpress.com/2017/09/28/caroline-bird-in-these-days-of-prohibition/ (Accessed: 8 October 2017)

——. (2019). Jane Yeh – Monsters, Detectives and The Truth of Masks. *Dave Poems*. Available at: https://davepoems.wordpress.com/2019/08/12/

jane-yeh-monsters-detectives-and-the-truth-of-masks/ (Accessed: 10 March 2023)

—— and Parmar, S. (2020). *The State of Poetry and Poetry Criticism in the UK and Ireland, Jan 2012 – Mar 2018*. University of Liverpool (website). Available at: www.liverpool.ac.uk/new-and-international-writing/emerging-critics/poetry-report/ (Accessed: 30 June 2020)

Collins, S. (2015). Essay: Wallpapers/General. *PracCrit*. Available at: www.praccrit.com/poems/wallpapersgeneral/ (Accessed: 16 February 2023)

——. (ed.) (2016). *Currently & Emotion: Translations*. London: Test Centre

Collinson, D. and Hearn, J. (1996). 'Men' at 'Work': Multiple Masculinities / Multiple Workplaces. In: Mac an Ghaill, M. (ed.), *Understanding Masculinities: Social Relations And Cultural Arenas*. Buckingham: Open University Press, pp. 61–76

Colquhoun, I. (2006). Surrealism. *artcornwall.org*. Available at: www.artcornwall.org/features/Surrealism_Ithell_Colquhoun.htm (Accessed: 26 February 2018)

Connelly, D.R. (2016). Faber New Poets 13–16: A Review of Pamphlets by Crispin Best, Rachel Curzon, Sam Buchan-Watts and Elaine Beckett. *Lotus-Eater*, 4, 41–6

Cooke, J. (2020). *Contemporary Feminist Life Writing: The New Audacity*. Cambridge: Cambridge University Press

Cornwell, N. (2006). *The Absurd in Literature*. Manchester: Manchester University Press

Corrigan, T. (2011). *Film and Literature: An Introduction and Reader* (2nd ed.). London: Routledge

Cowart, D. (1994). Tragedy and the 'Post-Absurd': *Hamlet* and *Rosencrantz & Guildenstern Are Dead. Literary Symbiosis: The Reconfigured Text in Twentieth-Century Writing*. Athens: University of Georgia Press, pp. 27–45

Crawford, J. (2018). The Female Romantic Poets who used Opium for its 'tranquilising power'. University of Exeter (website). Available from: https://news-archive.exeter.ac.uk/featurednews/title_645441_en.html (Accessed 28 April 2023)

Crenshaw, K. (1989). Demarginalizing the Intersection of Race and Sex: A Black Feminist Critique of Antidiscrimination Doctrine, Feminist Theory and Antiracist Politics. *University of Chicago Legal Forum*, 1989(8). https://chicagounbound.uchicago.edu/uclf/vol1989/iss1/8

Crew, D.F. (1998). *Germans on Welfare: From Weimar to Hitler*. New York: Oxford University Press

Crosby, D. A. (1988). *The Specter of the Absurd: Sources and Criticisms of Modern Nihilism*. New York: State University of New York Press

Cunningham, P. and Nørth, N.A. (2015). The Existence of Fire: An Interview with Sara Woods. *Fanzine*. Available at: http://thefanzine.com/the-existence-of-fire-an-interview-with-sara-woods/ (Accessed: 30 January 2017)

Curtis, B. (2014). The Wet Stuff: Jeff Henry, Verrückt, and the Men Who Built The Great American Water Park. *Grantland*. Available at: https://grantland.com/features/the-wet-stuff-verruckt-waterslide-schlitterbahn/ (Accessed: 26 April 2023)

Darcy, A. (2016). Knows It Knows Too Much: Jennifer L. Knox, Elliptical Compromises, and the Resolution of Humor. *Critical Flame*. Available at: http://criticalflame.org/jennifer-l-knox-elliptical-compromise-humor (Accessed: 23 September 2017)

Dastidar, R. (2023). No Rhyme or Reason: Why Is Poetry Missing from the new Caffè Nero Book Awards? *Guardian*. Available at: www.theguardian.com/books/2023/may/24/no-rhyme-or-reason-why-is-poetry-missing-from-the-new-caffe-nero-book-awards (Accessed: 6 February 2024)

Delville, M. (1998). *The American Prose Poem*. Florida: University Press of Florida

Derksen, C. (2002). A Feminist Absurd: Margaret Hollingsworth's *The House That Jack Built*. *Modern Drama*, 45(2), 209–30. https://doi.org/10.1353/mdr.2002.0049

Derrida, J. (2006). *Specters of Marx: The State of the Debt, the Work of Mourning and the New International* (2nd ed). Trans. from French by Peggy Kamuf. London: Routledge

Dewey, C. (2014). Absolutely Everything You Need to Know to Understand 4chan, the Internet's Own Bogeyman. *The Washington Post*. Available at: www.washingtonpost.com/news/the-intersect/wp/2014/09/25/absolutely-everything-you-need-to-know-to-understand-4chan-the-internets-own-bogeyman/ (Accessed: 10 February 2023)

DiAngelo, R. (2016). White Fragility. *Counterpoints*, 497, 245–53. www.jstor.org/stable/45157307

Donovan-Condron, K. (2016). Twisted Sisters: The Monstrous Women of Southern Gothic. In: Castillo Street, S. and Crow, C.L. (eds.), *The Palgrave Handbook of the Southern Gothic*. London: Palgrave Macmillan, pp. 339–50

Dyer, R. (2017). *WHITE* (2nd ed.). London: Routledge

Easterling, A. (1982). *Shakespearean Parallels and Affinities with the Theatre of the Absurd in Tom Stoppard's Rosencrantz and Guildenstern are Dead*. Available at: www.diva-portal.org/smash/get/diva2:610866/FULLTEXT02.pdf (Accessed: 16 May 2016)

Edson, R. (1994). *The Tunnel: Selected Poems*. Oberlin: Oberlin College Press

Edwards, S. (2018). Wearing the Poppy Has Always Been a Political Act – Here's Why. *The Conversation*. Available at: https://theconversation.com/wearing-the-poppy-has-always-been-a-political-act-heres-why-106489 (Accessed: 16 February 2023)

Ehrenstein, D. (2007). 'Magic Negro' Returns. *Los Angeles Times*. Available at: www.latimes.com/archives/la-xpm-2007-mar-19-oe-ehrenstein19-story.html (Accessed: 22 February 2023)

Encyclopaedia Britannica (2024). Turing Test: Artificial Intelligence. *Encyclopaedia Britannica*. Available at: www.britannica.com/technology/machine-learning (Accessed: 3 April 2024)

Epstein, A. (2018). Funks of Ambivalence: On Flarf. *Los Angeles Review of Books*. Available at: https://lareviewofbooks.org/article/funks-of-ambivalence-on-flarf/ (Accessed: 6 August 2018)

Esslin, M. (2023). *The Theatre of the Absurd*. London: Bloomsbury Academic

Etter, C. (2013). Review: *Instant-flex 718* by Heather Phillipson. *Guardian*. Available at: www.theguardian.com/books/2013/sep/13/instant-flex-718-heather-phillipson-review (Accessed: 15 March 2017)

Evans, E. (2015). *The Politics of Third Wave Feminisms: Neoliberalism, Intersectionality, and the State in Britain and the US*. Basingstoke: Palgrave Macmillan

Evans-Bush, K. (2016). TS Eliot Prize Row: Is Winner Too Young, Beautiful – and Chinese? *Guardian*. Available at: www.theguardian.com/books/2016/jan/23/deranged-poetess-sarah-howe-ts-eliot-prize-media (Accessed: 23 January 2016)

Ex Machina (2015). Directed by A. Garland. Available at: Prime Video (Accessed: 13 March 2023)

Fama, B., Rabbit White, R. and Simonds, S. (2020). Be Gay, Do Crimes: On the Gurlesque, Lana Del Rey, and Teen Girl Theory. Poetry Foundation (website). Available at: www.poetryfoundation.org/harriet-books/2020/04/Be-Gay-Do-Crimes (Accessed: 21 July 2022)

Field, J. (2014). Land of Confusion: Heather Phillipson's *Instant-flex 718*. *Poor Rude Lines*. Available at: https://johnfield.org/2014/12/17/heather-phillipson-instant-flex-718 (Accessed: 15 March 2017)

——. (2017). John Field Reviews the Shortlist: Caroline Bird. *T.S. Eliot Prize Newsletter* Available at: http://mailchi.mp/tseliotprize/carolinebird (Accessed: 3 November 2017)

Fischer, B.K. (2011). Hello Kitty. *Boston Review*. Available at: https://bostonreview.net/articles/b-k-fischer-lara-glenum-arielle-greenberg-gurlesque/ (Accessed: 21 July 2022)

Fisher, M. (2014). *Ghosts of My Life: Writings on Depression, Hauntology and Lost Futures*. Winchester: John Hunt Publishing

Flood, A. (2014), 'Next Generation' of 20 Hotly-Tipped Poets Announced by Poetry Book Society. *Guardian*. Available at: www.theguardian.com/books/2014/sep/11/next-generation-20-poets-poetry-book-society-kate-tempest (Accessed: 16 August 2022)

Fournier, L. (2018). Sad Girls, and Selfie Theory: Autotheory as Contemporary Feminist Practice. *a/b: Auto/Biography Studies*, 33(3), 643–62. https://doi.org/10.1080/08989575.2018.1499495

Francis, T. (2013). Close-Up: Afrosurrealism: Introduction: The No-Theory Chant of Afrosurrealism. *Black Camera: An International Film Journal*, 5(1), 95–112. https://muse.jhu.edu/article/525947

Bibliography 181

Freud, S. (2003). *The Uncanny*. Trans. from German by David McLintock. London: Penguin Books

Friedan, B. (2010). *The Feminine Mystique*. London: Penguin Classics

Gamer, M. and Porter, D. (eds.) (2008). *Lyrical Ballads 1798 and 1800: Samuel Taylor Coleridge & William Wordsworth*. Plymouth: Broadview Editions

Gascoyne, D. (2003). *A Short Survey of Surrealism*. London: Enitharmon Press

Gavins, J. (2013). *Reading the Absurd*. Edinburgh: Edinburgh University Press

Gazeta, R. and Davydenko, V. (2014). Pistols at Dawn: The Soviet Eastern versus the Classic Western. *Russia Beyond*. Available at: www.rbth.com/arts/2014/04/08/pistols_at_dawn_the_soviet_eastern_versus_the_classic_western_35681.html (Accessed: 26 July 2022)

Gillis, S. (2007). Neither Cyborg Nor Goddess: The (Im)Possibilities of Cyberfeminism. In: Gillis, S., Howie, G. and Munford, R., *Third Wave Feminism: A Critical Exploration* (2nd ed.). London: Palgrave Macmillan, pp. 168–81

Glenum, L. (2010). Theory of the Gurlesque: Burlesque, Girly Kitsch, and the Female Grotesque. In: Glenum, L. and Greenberg, A. (eds.), *Gurlesque: the new grrly, grotesque, burlesque poetics*. Pennsylvania: Saturnalia Books, pp. 11–24

Goddard, K. (2013). Dear Racist in the Queue in Tesco. *Squawk Back* (June 2013). Available at: www.thesquawkback.com/2013/06/dearracistinthequeueattesco.html (Accessed: 18 April 2018)

Goldsmith, K. (2015). Post-Internet Poetry Comes of Age. *The New Yorker*. Available at: www.newyorker.com/books/page-turner/post-internet-poetry-comes-of-age (Accessed: 9 February 2023)

Gordon, A. (2020). Aubrey Gordon on Dealing with Aggressive Fatphobia. *Literary Hub*. Available from: https://lithub.com/aubrey-gordon-on-dealing-with-aggressive-fatphobia/ (Accessed: 25 March 2023)

Greenberg, A. (2003). On the Gurlesque. Small Press Traffic (website). Available at: www.sptraffic.org/html/news_rept/gurl.html (Accessed: 23 May 2018)

——. (2010). Some Notes on the Origin of the (Term) Gurlesque. In: Glenum, L. and Greenberg, A. (eds.), *Gurlesque: the new grrly, grotesque, burlesque poetics*. Pennsylvania: Saturnalia Books, pp. 1–10

——. (2013). Some (of My) Problems with the Gurlesque. The Volta (website). Available at: www.thevolta.org/ewc38-agreenberg-p1.html (Accessed: 25 August 2020)

Greenwald Smith, R. (2019). Fuck the Avant-Garde. Post45 (website). Available at: https://post45.org/2019/05/fuck-the-avant-garde/ (Accessed: 21 July 2022)

Gregson, I. (2011). Post/Modernist Rhythms and Voices: Edith Sitwell and Stevie Smith to Jo Shapcott and Selima Hill. In: Dowson, J. (ed.),

The Cambridge Companion to Twentieth-Century British and Irish Women's Poetry. Cambridge: Cambridge University Press, pp. 9–23

Greven, D. (2016). The Southern Gothic Film: An Overview. In: Castillo Street, S. and Crow, C.L. (eds.), *The Palgrave Handbook of the Southern Gothic*. London: Palgrave Macmillan, pp. 473–86

Grobe, C. (2017). Interlude: The Unbearable Whiteness of Being Confessional. In: Grobe, C., *The Art of Confession: The Performance of Self from Robert Lowell to Reality TV*. New York: New York University Press, pp. 37–44

Groom, N. (2002). *The Forger's Shadow: How Forgery Changed the Course of Literature*. London: Picador

Guiberteau, O. (2020). The Truth about British Stoicism. BBC (website). Available at: www.bbc.com/travel/article/20201101-the-truth-about-british-stoicism (Accessed: 29 March 2023)

Gurnow, M. (2014). No Symbol Where None Intended: A Study of Symbolism and Allusion in Samuel Beckett's *Waiting for Godot*. Way Back Machine (website). Available at: https://web.archive.org/web/20141007231614/http://themodernword.com/beckett/paper_gurnow.html (Accessed: 29 March 2023)

Hairston, T. and Parker, M. (2017). Poet Morgan Parker on Why Beyoncé Is a Metaphor for Every Black Woman. *The Cut*. Available at: www.thecut.com/2017/02/morgan-parker-poetry-beyonce-and-black-womanhood.html (Accessed: 10 March 2023)

Haraway, D.J. (2016). A Cyborg Manifesto: Science, Technology, and Socialist-Feminism in the Late Twentieth Century. In: Haraway, D.J., *Manifestly Haraway*. Minneapolis: University of Minnesota Press, pp. 3–90

Harpalani, V. (2020). Racial Stereotypes, Respectability Politics, and Running for President: Examining Andrew Yang's and Barack Obama's Presidential Bids. *Race and the Law Prof Blog*. Available from: https://bit.ly/3UTSuIy (Accessed: 22 February 2023)

Harris, F.C. (2014). The Rise of Respectability Politics. *Dissent*, 61(1), 33–7. https://doi.org/10.1353/dss.2014.0010

Hartigan, J., Jr. (1997). Name Calling: Objectifying 'Poor Whites' and 'White Trash' in Detroit. In: Wray, M. and Newitz, A. (eds.), *White Trash: Race and Class in America*. London: Routledge, pp. 41–56

Heffernan, G. (2014). 'J'ai compris que j'étais coupable' ('I understood that I was guilty'): A Hermeneutical Approach to Sexism, Racism, and Colonialism in Albert Camus' *L'Étranger/The Stranger*. In: Francev, P. (ed.), *Albert Camus's* The Stranger: *Critical Essays*. Newcastle upon Tyne: Cambridge Scholars Publishing, pp. 1–25

Herbets, A. (2020). At Least One Native American Group Views Pioneer Day as a Racist Symbol of Colonialism. Fox13 Salt Lake City. Available from: https://bit.ly/4dN6Env (Accessed: 26 April 2023)

Hermosillo, C. (humdog). (2012). pandora's vox: on community in cyberspace. Available at: https://gist.github.com/kolber/2131643 (Accessed: 9 January 2017)

Higashida, C. (2012). Reponses [Responses] to Bhanu Kapil, 'Writing/Not-Writing: Th[a][e] Diasporic Self: Notes towards a Race Riot Scene'. *English Language Notes*, 50(1), 39–41. https://doi.org/10.1215/00138282-50.1.39

Hill, S. (1997). *Violet*. Newcastle upon Tyne: Bloodaxe Books

—— and Berry, E. (2021). Selima Hill talks to Emily Berry. Available at: https://soundcloud.com/poetrysociety/selima-hill-talks-to-emily-berry-1 (Accessed: 2 February 2023)

—— and Copus, J. (2022). 'Telling You The Truth, As Best As I Can.' Selima Hill and Julia Copus in Correspondence. *Poetry London*. Available at: https://bit.ly/4bJ4GTq (Accessed: 1 February 2023)

—— and Vianu, L. (2006). Sometimes Autobiography is Not Enough. *Desperado Essay-Interviews*. Available at: http://lidiavianu.scriptmania.com/selima_hill.htm (Accessed: 4 December 2017)

Hinchliffe, Arnold P. (1969). *The Critical Idiom: 5 – The Absurd*. London: Methuen Drama

Hoffman, Steven K. (1978). Impersonal Personalism: The Making of a Confessional Poetic. *ELH*, 45(4), 687–709. www.jstor.org/stable/2872583

Holloway-Smith, W. (2014). *Factions and Class Fictions: Investigating Narratives of Resistance in Representations of Lower-Class Men in Post-War British Literature in the New Wave & Thatcherite Years*. Available at: https://bura.brunel.ac.uk/bitstream/2438/13791/1/FulltextThesis.pdf (Accessed: 3 August 2016)

hooks, b. (2014). Selling Hot Pussy: Representations of Black Female Sexuality in the Cultural Marketplace. *Black Looks: Race and Representation* (2nd ed.). London: Routledge, pp. 60–77

Hull, K. (2020). Lost and Found: Trump, Biden, and White Working-Class Voters. *Atlantish Perspectief*, 44(5), 11–16. www.jstor.org/stable/48600591

Iacovelli, S., Rabedeau, J., Koenig, M. et al. (2017). The 2016 VIDA Count – The Big Picture Gets Bigger: Commitment to Intersectionality. VIDA: Women in Literary Arts (website). Available at: www.vidaweb.org/the-2016-vida-count (Accessed: 20 October 2017)

Iglesias, H. (2004). *Boxing Inside the Box: Women's Prose Poetry*. Niantic: Quale Press

Institute for Precarious Consciousness. (2014). We Are All Very Anxious: Six Theses on Anxiety and Why It is Effectively Preventing Militancy, and One Possible Strategy for Overcoming It. Plan C (4 April) (website). Available at: www.weareplanc.org/blog/we-are-all-very-anxious/#f1 (Accessed: 22 March 2023)

Jones, O. (2019). The British Working Class is a Rainbow of Diversity: To Claim Otherwise is Dangerous and Wrong. *Medium*. Available from: https://owenjones84.medium.com/the-british-working-class-is-a-rainbow-of-diversity-to-claim-otherwise-is-dangerous-and-wrong-138ca4159c6 (Accessed: 18 June 2024)

Kapil, B. (2023). *Incubation: A Space for Monsters*. London: Prototype

Kaufmann, D. (2017). *Reading Uncreative Writing: Conceptualism, Expression, and the Lyric*. London: Palgrave Macmillan

Kaufman, G. (1980). Introduction. In: Kaufman, G. and Blakely, M.K. (eds.), *Pulling Our Own Strings: Feminist Humour and Satire*. Indiana: Indiana University Press, pp. 13–16

Keene, J. (2015). On Vanessa Place, Gone With the Wind, and the Limit Point of Certain Conceptual Aesthetics. *J's Theater*. Available at: http://jstheater.blogspot.com/2015/05/on-vanessa-place-gone-with-wind-and.html (Accessed: 9 February 2023)

Keller, C. (1996). *Apocalypse Now and Then: A Feminist Guide to the End of the World*. Boston: Beacon Press

Kempf, C. (2019). Poetics of Whiteness. *West Branch* (89). Available at: https://bit.ly/4bvWENQ (Accessed: 6 February 2023)

Kennard, L. (2010). *The Harbour Beyond the Movie* (2nd ed.). Cambridge: Salt

——. (2018). 'Man and Nature In and Out of Order': The Surrealist Prose Poetry of David Gascoyne. In: Monson, J. (ed.), *British Prose Poetry: The Poems Without Lines*. London: Palgrave Macmillan, pp. 249–64

Kharms, D. (2000). Elizaveta Bam. Trans. from Russian by Timothy Langen and Justin Weir. In: Langen, T. and Weir, J. (eds.), *Eight Twentieth-Century Russian Plays*. Evanston: Northwestern University Press, pp. 167–94

King, A. (2010). The Gurlesque. Amy King (website). Available at: https://amyking.org/2010/03/29/the-gurlesque/ (Accessed: 21 July 2022)

—— and Greenberg, A. (2010). Arielle Greenberg on 'Gynocentric Anthems,' The Gurlesque, and Creative Partnerships. VIDA (website). Available at: www.vidaweb.org/gynocentric-anthems/ (Accessed: 21 July 2022)

Kipnis, L. and Reeder, J. (1997). White Trash Girl: The Interview. In: Wray, M. and Newitz, A. (eds.), *White Trash: Race and Class in America*. London: Routledge, pp. 113–30

Klein, E.B. (2022). A New Feminist Absurd?: Women's Protest, Fury, and Futility in Contemporary American Theatre. *Modern Drama*, 65(1), 24–51. https://doi.org/10.3138/md-65-1-1187

Knox, J.L. (2007). *A Gringo Like Me* (2nd ed.). New Jersey: Bloof Books

——. (2015.) Our Robots. *Days of Shame and Failure*. New Jersey: Bloof Books, p. 83

——. (2016). Humor, Poetry, and Privilege. Indolent Books (15 May) (website). Available at: www.indolentbooks.com/humor-poetry-and-privilege (Accessed: 3 April 2017)

Kuehn, J. (2014). Exoticism in 19th-century literature. British Library, *English and Drama blog*. Available at: www.bl.uk/romantics-and-victorians/articles/exoticism-in-19th-century-literature (Accessed: 28 February 2023)

Jackson, M. (2007). A Mystifying Silence——Big and Black. *The American Poetry Review*, 36(5), 19–25. www.jstor.org/stable/20683641

Jameson, F. (1991). *Postmodernism, or, the Cultural Logic of Late Capitalism*. New York: Duke University Press

Lavery, C. and Finburgh, C. (eds.) (2015). *Rethinking the Theatre of the Absurd: Ecology, the Environment and the Greening of the Modern Stage*. London: Bloomsbury

Lavrentiev, S. (2013). The Balkan Westerns of the Sixties. *Frames Cinema Journal*. Available at: https://framescinemajournal.com/article/the-balkan-westerns-of-the-sixties/ (Accessed: 26 July 2022)

The Leadership Conference of Civil and Human Rights. (2021). Trump Administration Civil and Human Rights Rollbacks. The Leadership Conference of Civil and Human Rights (website). Available at: https://civilrights.org/trump-rollbacks/ (Accessed: 23 February 2023)

Lehman, D. (1999). *The Last Avant-Garde: The Making of the New York School of Poets*. New York: Anchor Books

——. (2003). *Great American Prose Poems: From Poe to the Present*. New York: Scribner Poetry

Leiby, S. (2011). I am Such a Failure: Poetry On, Around, and About the Internet. Pool (website). Available at: https://pooool.info/i-am-such-a-fail-ure-poetry-on-around-and-about-the-internet/ (Accessed: 19 April 2024)

Lerner, B. (2016). *The Hatred of Poetry*. London: Fitzcarraldo Editions

Loden, R. and Silem Mohammad, K. (2007). The Dangerfield Conundrum: A Roundtable on Humor in Poetry. *Jacket*, 33. Available at: http://jacket-magazine.com/33/humpo-discussion.shtml (Accessed: 17 December 2017)

Logan, W. (2013). Collateral Damage. *The New Criterion*, 42(9). Available at: www.newcriterion.com/issues/2013/6/collateral-damage (Accessed: 10 August 2017)

Los Angeles County Museum of Art. (2019). New Objectivity: Modern German Art in the Weimar Republic, 1919–1933: Exhibition Didactics. Available from: https://archive.org/details/NewObjectivityExhibitionDi-dactics/mode/2up (Accessed: 7 March 2024)

Lowery, W. (2017). Black Lives Matter: Birth of a Movement. *Guardian*. Available from: www.theguardian.com/us-news/2017/jan/17/black-lives-matter-birth-of-a-movement (Accessed: 19 June 2024)

Luckhurst, R. (2008). *The Trauma Question*. London: Routledge

Lyotard, J. (1984). *The Postmodern Condition: A Report on Knowledge*. Trans. from French by Geoff Bennington and Brian Massumi. Manchester: Manchester University Press

MacNeice, L. (2008). *Varieties of Parable*. London: Faber & Faber

Magi, J. (2016). Racing Stein: What Is Seen and Unseen in Taking a Hero Out for a Reread. In: Rankine, C., Loffreda, B. and King Cap, M. (eds.), *The Racial Imaginary: Writers on Race in the Life of the Mind*. Albany: Fence Books, pp. 159–69

——. (2017). Decoding/Recoding Whiteness: The Contemporary Moment, Some Theory, Some Autobiography. Poetry Foundation (website). Available at: www.poetryfoundation.org/harriet-books/2017/10/decoding-recoding-whiteness-the-contemporary-moment-some-theory-some-autobiography (Accessed: 7 February 2023)

Maguire, E. (2018). *Girls, Autobiography, Media: Gender and Self-Mediation in Digital Economies*. London: Palgrave Macmillan

Malone, M. (2016). Review of Faber New Poets 13–16 for *The Interpreter's House*, 62. Available from: www.academia.edu/24872356/Review_of_Faber_New_poets_13_16_for_The_Interpreters_House_62 (Accessed: 19 June 2024)

Manatakis, L. (2017). Why We Need Absurdist Art in Uncertain Times. *Dazed*. Available at: www.dazeddigital.com/art-photography/article/37995/1/delirious-art-new-york-absurdist-art-in-uncertain-times (Accessed: 20 July 2022)

Marso, L.J. (2010). Marriage and Bourgeois Respectability. *Politics & Gender*, 6(1), 145–53. https://doi.org/10.1017/S1743923X09990572

Marwick, A. (2013). memes. *Contexts*, 12(4), 12–13. https://doi.org/10.1177/1536504213511210

Mastro, D., Behm-Morawitz, E. and Ortiz, M. (2007). The Cultivation of Social Perceptions of Latinos: A Mental Models Approach. *Media Psychology*, 9(2), 347–65. http://dx.doi.org/10.1080/15213260701286106

Masud, N. (2022). A Horizon Line: Flat Style in Contemporary Women's Poetry. *Textual Practice*, 36(4), 542–61. https://doi.org/10.1080/0950236X.2022.2030512

Mayne, P. (2016). The Politicisation of the Poppy: The Misuse of the Poppy by the Far Right. Huffington Post (website). Available from: www.huffingtonpost.co.uk/philip-mayne/poppy-remembrance-day-britain-first_b_8490286.html (Accessed: 16 February 2023)

McDonald, P. (2017). 'Make Sure You Don't Murder Your Coffee!' Comedy and Violence in the Poetry of Luke Kennard. *Sillages Critiques*, 22. Available at: https://sillagescritiques.revues.org/4840 (Accessed: 23 September 2017)

McGurl, M. (2011). *The Program Era: Postwar Fiction and the Rise of Creative Writing*. Cambridge, MA: Harvard University Press

McMillan, D. (2012). Worstward Ho. In: Gontarski, S.E. (ed.), *On Beckett: Essays and Criticism*. London: Anthem Press, pp. 152–4. https://doi.org/10.7135/UPO9780857285805.015.

McSweeney, J. (2006). Petroleum Hat. Constant Critic (website). Available at: http://constantcritic.com/joyelle_mcsweeney/petroleum_hat (Accessed: 5 June 2018)

McWeeny, D. (2011). Sundance Review: Lucky McKee's 'The Woman' Outrages and Offends with Surgical Skill at Midnight. Hit Fix (website). Available at: www.hitfix.com/blogs/motion-captured/posts/sundance-review-lucky-mckees-the-woman-outrages-and-offends-with-surgical-skill-at-midnight (Accessed: 12 July 2016)

Merrett King, C. (2022). Unsure Theory: Ambivalence as Methodology. *Arts*, 11 (78). https://doi.org/10.3390/arts11040078

Merskin, D. (2007). Three Faces of Eva: Perpetuation of the Hot-Latina Stereotype in *Desperate Housewives*. *The Howard Journal of Communications*, 18(2), 133–51. https://doi.org/10.1080/10646170701309890

Meskimmon, M. (2003). *Women Making Art: History, Subjectivity, Aesthetics*. London: Routledge

The Met. (2017) Art and the Limits of Reason. *The Met*. Available at: www.metmuseum.org/exhibitions/listings/2017/delirious (Accessed: 20 July 2022)

Miller, M. (2009). 'I Don't Want to be a [White] Girl': Gender, Race and Resistance in the Southern Gothic. In: Wallace, D. and Smith, A. (eds.), *The Female Gothic: New Directions*. London: Palgrave Macmillan, pp. 133–51

Milligan, B. (2003). Introduction to Thomas de Quincey, *Confessions of an English Opium-Eater*. London: Penguin, pp. xiii–xxxviii

Moi, T. (2001). *Sexual/ Textual Politics: Feminist Literary Theory* (16th ed.). London: Routledge

Mooney, H. (2018). Sad Girls and Carefree Black Girls. *Women Studies Quarterly*, 46(3,4), 175–94. www.jstor.org/stable/26511338

Moore, F. (2016). Book review: U.S. and Us. The Poetry Society (website). Available at: http://poetrysociety.org.uk/publications-section/the-poetry-review/book-review-u-s-and-us/ (Accessed: 6 April 2016)

Moore, N. (2007). Imagining Feminist Futures: The Third Wave, Postfeminism and Eco/feminism. In: Gillis, S., Howie, G. and Munford, R. (eds.), *Third Wave Feminism: A Critical Exploration* (2nd ed.). London: Palgrave Macmillan, pp. 125–42

Morrison, T. (1993). *Playing in the Dark: Whiteness and the Literary Imagination*. New York: Vintage

Müller, J. (2017). *What is Populism?* (2nd ed.). London: Penguin

Mulvey, L. (1999). Visual Pleasure and Narrative Cinema. In: Braudy, L. and Cohen, M. (eds.), *Film Theory and Criticism: Introductory Readings*. New York: Oxford University Press, pp. 833–44

Murphy, M.S. (1992). *A Tradition of Subversion: Prose Poem in English from Wilde to Ashbery*. Amherst: University of Massachusetts Press

Myers, M. (2010). Gurlesque: The New Grrly, Grotesque, Burlesque Poetics. rain taxi (website). Available at: www.raintaxi.com/gurlesque-the-new-grrly-grotesque-burlesque-poetics/ (Accessed: 21 July 2022)

Nelson, M. (2007). *Women, the New York School, and Other True Abstractions*. Iowa City: University of Iowa Press

Newell-Hanson, A. (2015). 2015 the year of . . . sad girls and sad boys. *i-D*. Available at: https://i-d.vice.com/en/article/pabvk7/2015-the-year-of-sad-girls-and-sad (Accessed 21 March 2023)

Newman, Robert D. (1993). Cannibals and Clock-Teasers: Narrating the Postmodern Horror Film. *Transgression of Reading: Narrative Engagement as Exile and Return*. London: Duke University Press, pp. 59–81

Ngai, S. (2001). Bad Timing (A Sequel). Paranoia, Feminism, and Poetry. *differences: A Journal of Feminist Cultural Studies*, 12(2), 1–46. https://muse.jhu.edu/article/9623

——. (2005). *Ugly Feelings*. Cambridge, MA: Harvard University Press

Noel-Tod, J. (ed.) (2018). *The Penguin Book of the Prose Poem: From Baudelaire to Anne Carson*. London: Penguin Random House UK

Nolan, M. and Best, C. (2016). meet crispin best, london's most original and oddest poet. *i-D* (15 April). Available at: https://i-d.vice.com/en/article/9kyjnp/meet-crispin-best-londons-most-original-and-oddest-poet (Accessed: 23 February 2023)

O'Brien, S. (2016). Faber New Poets 13 to 16 review – Four Debuts with Promise and Punch. *Guardian*. Available at: www.theguardian.com/books/2016/apr/22/faber-new-poets-pamplets-13-to-16-review (Accessed: 06 August 2018)

O'Connell, M. (2014). The Stunning Success of 'Fail Better': How Samuel Beckett Became Silicon Valley's Life Coach. *Slate*. Available at: https://slate.com/culture/2014/01/samuel-becketts-quote-fail-better-becomes-the-mantra-of-silicon-valley.html (Accessed: 28 April 2023)

O'Hara, F. (2004). Personism: A Manifesto. In: Cook, J. (ed.), *Poetry In Theory: An Anthology 1900–2000*. Oxford: Blackwell Publishing, pp. 367–9

Oppenheimer, D.B., Cornillie, H., Smith, H.B. et al. (2018). Be Careful What You Wish For: Ronald Reagan, Donald Trump, The Assault on Civil Rights, and The Surprising Story of How Title VII Got Its Private Right of Action. *Berkeley Journal of Employment & Labor Law*, 39(1), 147–75. https://doi.org/10.15779/Z385M6270B

Orbach, S. (2016). *Fat is a Feminist Issue*. London: Arrow

O'Reilly, A. (ed.) (2004). *From Motherhood to Mothering: The Legacy of Adrienne Rich's of Woman Born*. Ithica: State University of New York Press

Oshinsky, S.J. (2004). Exoticism in the Decorative Arts. *The Met*. Available at: www.metmuseum.org/toah/hd/exot/hd_exot.htm (Accessed: 28 February 2023)

Owens, T. (2016). '@SandeepKParmar @msamykey She won a top literary prize for the political platitudes she represents. Reductive yet accurate. #derangedpoetess'. X (23 January). Available at: https://x.com/anukasan1977/status/690862524330348544 (Accessed: 21 March 2023)

Palmer, J. (1987). *The Logic of the Absurd: On Film and Television Comedy*. London: BFI Publishing

Palmer, L. (2006). Bourgeois Blues: Class, Whiteness, and Southern Gothic in Early Faulkner and Caldwell. *The Faulkner Journal*, 22(1/2), 120–9. www.jstor.org/stable/24908287

Park Hong, C. (2014). Delusions of Whiteness in the Avant-Garde. *Arcade*. Available at: https://arcade.stanford.edu/content/delusions-whiteness-avant-garde (Accessed: 20 July 2022)

Parker, M. (2017). *There Are More Beautiful Things than Beyoncé*. Oregon: Tin House Books

Parmar, S. (2015). Not a British Subject: Race and Poetry in the UK. *Los Angeles Review of Books*. Available at: https://lareviewofbooks.org/article/not-a-british-subject-race-and-poetry-in-the-uk/ (Accessed: 23 August 2022)

——. (2020). Still Not a British Subject: Race and UK Poetry. *Journal of British and Irish Innovative Poetry*, 12(1). https://doi.org/10.16995/bip. 3384

Patel, L. (2016). The Irrationality of Antiracist Empathy. *The English Journal*. 106(2), 81–4. www.jstor.org/stable/26450214

Patil, V. (2013). From Patriarchy to Intersectionality: A Transnational Feminist Assessment of How Far We've Really Come. *Signs*, 38(4), 847–67. www.jstor.org/stable/10.1086/669560

Pedwell, C. (2016). De-Colonising Empathy: Thinking Affect Transnationally. *Samyukta: A Journal of Gender and Culture*, 1(1), n.p. https://doi. org/10.53007/SJGC.2016.V1.I1.51

Penley, C. (1997). Crackers and Whackers: The White Trashing of Porn. In: Wray, M. and Newitz, A. (eds.), *White Trash: Race and Class in America*. London: Routledge, pp. 89–112

Pérez, D.E. (2009). *Rethinking Chicana/o and Latina/o Popular Culture*. New York: Palgrave Macmillan

Perloff, M. (2022). From Language Poetry to the New Concretism: The Evolution of the Avant-Garde. *Literature of the Americas*, 12, 10–36. https://doi.org/10.22455/2541-7894-2022-12-10-36

——. (1996). Whose New American Poetry? Anthologizing in the Nineties. *Diacritics*, 26, 104–23. www.jstor.org/stable/1566408

Petit, P. (2017). *Mama Amazonica*. Hexham: Bloodaxe Books

Phillipson, H. (2013). *Instant-Flex 718*. Hexham: Bloodaxe Books

Pickering, J. (2014). Classy Looks and Classificatory Gazes: The Fashioning of Class in Reality Television. *Film, Fashion & Consumption*, 3(3), 195–209. https://doi.org/10.1386/ffc.3.3.195_1

Pitcan, M., Marwick, A.E. and boyd, d. (2018). Performing a Vanilla Self: Respectability Politics, Social Class, and the Digital World. *Journal of Computer-Mediated Communication*, 23(3), 163–79. https://doi. org/10.1093/jcmc/zmy008

Plester, B. (2015). 'Take it like a man!': Performing Hegemonic Masculinity Through Organizational Humour. *Ephemera: Theory and Politics in Organization*, 15(3), 537–59

Poggioli, R. (1968). *The Theory of the Avant Garde*. Cambridge, MA: Harvard University Press

Pollack Petchesky, R. (1981). Antiabortion, Antifeminism, and the Rise of the New Right. *Feminist Studies*, 7(2), 206–46. https://doi. org/10.2307/3177522

Pozner, J.L. and Seigel, J. (2006). Desperately Debating Housewives. In: McCabe, J. and Akass, K. (eds.), *Reading Desperate Housewives: Beyond the White Picket Fence*. New York: I.B. Tauris & Co, pp. 206–14

Price, J.A. (1973). The Stereotyping of North American Indians in Motion Pictures. *Ethnohistory*, 20(2), 153–71. www.jstor.org/stable/481668

Quintero, R. (2011). Introduction: Understanding Satire. *A Companion to Satire: Ancient and Modern*. London: Wiley-Blackwell, pp. 1–11

Railton, D. and Watson, P. (2011). Music Video in Black and White: Race and Femininity. In: Railton, D. and Watson, P. (eds.), *Music Video and the Politics of Representation*. Edinburgh: Edinburgh University Press, pp. 87–107

Ramazani, J. (2019). Poetry and Race: An Introduction. *New Literary History*, 50(4), vii–xxxvii. https://doi.org/10.1353/nlh.2019.0050

Rankine, C. (2015). *Citizen: An American Lyric*. London: Penguin Random House

——. Loffreda, B. and King Cap, M. (eds.) (2016). *The Racial Imaginary: Writers on Race in the Life of the Mind*. Albany: Fence Books

Reed, A. (2014). *Freedom Time: The Poetics and Politics of Black Experimental Writing*. Baltimore: Johns Hopkins University Press

Rees-Jones, D. (2005). *Consorting with Angels: Essays On Modern Women Poets*. Newcastle upon Tyne: Bloodaxe Books

Rich, A. (1976). *Of Woman Born: Motherhood as Experience and Institution*. New York: W.W. Norton

Riggs, T. (2023). Salvador Dalí: Lobster Telephone – 1936. Tate (website). Available at: www.tate.org.uk/art/artworks/dali-lobster-telephone-t03257 (Accessed: 27 September 2017)

Riviere, S. (2011). 'Unlike': Forms of Refusal in Poetry on the Internet. Pool (website). Available at: https://pooool.info/unlike-forms-of-refusal-in-poetry-on-the-internet/ (Accessed: 18 June 2024)

——. (2012). *81 Austerities*. London: Faber & Faber

——. (2021). *Dead Souls*. London: W&N

Robinson, M. (1979). From Purgatory to Inferno: Beckett and Dante Revisited. *Journal of Beckett Studies*, 5, 69–82. www.jstor.org/stable/44782905

Robinson, S. (2000). *Marked Men: White Masculinity in Crisis*. New York: Columbia University Press

Rogers, J. (2020). Review: Hello by Crispin Best. *SPAM*. Available at: www.spamzine.co.uk/post/review-hello-by-crispin-best (Accessed: 8 February 2023)

Rooney, K. (2013). And Now, Deep Thoughts About 'Deep Thoughts'. *The New York Times Magazine*. Available at: www.nytimes.com/2013/04/14/magazine/and-now-deep-thoughts-about-deep-thoughts.html (Accessed: 30 September 2015)

Rosales, J. (2016). Of Surrealism & Marxism. *Blind Field*. Available at: https://blindfieldjournal.com/2016/12/01/of-surrealism-marxism/ (Accessed: 28 April 2023)

Rosemont, P. (2019). *Surrealism: Inside the Magnetic Fields*. San Francisco: City Lights Books

Row, J. (2014). Jess Row: Native Sons. *Guernica*. Available at: www.guernicamag.com/jess-row-native-sons/ (Accessed: 7 February 2023)

——. (2016). What Are White Writers For? *New Republic*. Available at: https://newrepublic.com/article/137338/white-writers-for (Accessed: 7 February 2023)

Rudloff, W. (2017). The Welfare State and Poverty in the Weimar Republic. In: Lutz, R. (ed.), *Poverty and Welfare in Modern German History*. Brooklyn: Berghahn Books, pp. 105–36

Ruston, S. (2014). Representations of Drugs in 19th-Century Literature. British Library (website). Available at: www.bl.uk/romantics-and-victorians/articles/representations-of-drugs-in-19th-century-literature (Accessed: 26 July 2022)

Rutherford, J. (1996). Who's That Man? In: Chapman, R. and Rutherford, J. (eds.), *Male Order: Unwrapping Masculinity* (2nd ed.). London: Lawrence & Wishart, pp. 21–67

Saïd, E.W. (1979). *Orientalism*. New York: Vintage Books

Sakasegawa, M. and Choi, F. (2018). Transcript – Episode 74: Franny Choi. *Keep the Channel Open*. Available at: www.keepthechannelopen.com/transcripts/2018/9/12/transcript-episode-74-franny-choi (Accessed: 10 March 2023)

Santos, M. (2013). *Verse, Voice and Vision: Poetry and Cinema*. Plymouth: The Scarecrow Press

Sartre, J.P. (1969). *Nausea*. Trans. from French by Lloyd Alexander. New York: New Directions Publishing

van der Schyff, K. (2011). Staging the Body of the (M)other: The 'Hottentot Venus' and the 'Wild Dancing Bushmen'. In: Gordon-Chipembere, N. (ed.), *Representation and Black Womanhood: The Legacy of Sarah Baartman*. Basingstoke: Palgrave Macmillan, pp. 147–63

Scot Miller, D. (2009). Call it Afro-Surreal. 48hills (website). Available at: http://sfbgarchive.48hills.org/sfbgarchive/2009/05/19/call-it-afro-surreal/ (Accessed: 28 April 2023)

__. (2016). Afrosurreal: The Marvelous And The Invisible 2016. Open Space (website). Available at: https://openspace.sfmoma.org/2016/10/afrosurreal-the-marvelous-and-the-invisible/ (Accessed: 28 April 2023)

Sharp, S. (2006). Disciplining the Housewife in *Desperate Housewives* and Domestic Reality Television. In: McCabe, J. and Akass, K. (eds.), *Reading Desperate Housewives: Beyond the White Picket Fence*. New York: I.B. Tauris & Co, pp. 119–28

Shaw, C. (2004). Welcome to the Wonderland of Dreams: Selima Hill's Portrayal of Madness in *Lou–Lou* and *Bunny*. Sheer Poetry (website). Available at: www.sheerpoetry.co.uk/advanced/dissertations/welcome-to-the-wonderland-of-dreams (Accessed: 4 December 2017)

Shaw, W. (2022). Review: *Unexhausted Time* by Emily Berry. *William Shaw Writer*. Available at: https://williamshawwriter.wordpress.com/2022/12/27/review-unexhausted-time-by-emily-berry/ (Accessed: 6 January 2023)

Skeggs, B. (2002). *Formations of Class and Gender: Becoming Respectable*. SAGE Publications Ltd. https://dx.doi.org/10.4135/9781446217597

Society of Authors (2022). Eric Gregory Awards. *The Society of Authors*. Available at: www2.societyofauthors.org/prizes/the-soa-awards/eric-gregory-awards/ (Accessed: 26 August 2022)

Sontag, S. (2018). *Notes on 'Camp'*. London: Penguin Random House

Smith, S. (2022). Are Abortion Rights at Risk in the UK? *Dazed*. Available at: www.dazeddigital.com/politics/article/56468/1/are-abortion-rights-at-risk-in-the-uk (Accessed: 5 April 2023)

Spahr, J. and Young, S. (2015). The Program Era and the Mainly White Room. *Los Angeles Review of Books*. Available at: https://lareviewofbooks.org/article/the-program-era-and-the-mainly-white-room/ (Accessed: 7 February 2023)

Sparks Lin, M. (2022). *Towards A Cyborg Poetics: Race, Technology, and Desire in Asian American Science Fiction Poetry*. Available at: https://repository.wellesley.edu/object/ir1769 (Accessed: 10 March 2023)

Stent, S. (2012). *Women Surrealists: Sexuality, Fetish, Femininity and Female Surrealism*. Available at: https://etheses.bham.ac.uk/id/eprint/3718/ (Accessed: 15 November 2015)

Stopenski, C. (2022). Exploring Mutilation: Women, Affect, and the Body Horror Genre. *(Un)common Horrors*, 2, 1–19. https://doi.org/10.15291/sic/2.12

Stoppard, T. (1999). *Rosencrantz and Guildenstern Are Dead*. London: Faber & Faber

Sullivan, G. (2011). A Brief Guide to Flarf Poetry. poets.org (website). Available at: www.poets.org/poetsorg/text/brief-guide-flarf-poetry (Accessed: 5 June 2018)

Sweeney, G. (1997). The King of White Trash Culture: Elvis Presley and the Aesthetics of Excess. In: Wray, M. and Newitz, A. (eds.), *White Trash: Race and Class in America*. London: Routledge, pp. 249–66

Tasker, Y. and Negra, D. (eds.) (2007). *Interrogating Post-Feminism: Gender and the Politics of Popular Culture*. Durham, NC: Duke University Press

Tate, J. (2012). *The Eternal Ones of the Dream: Selected Poems 1990–2010*. New York: HarperCollins

Taylor, D. (ed.) (2015). About. *Mslexia*. Available at: https://mslexia.co.uk/about/ (Accessed: 12 November 2015)

Thelandersson, F. (2022). *21st Century Media and Female Mental Health: Profitable Vulnerability and Sad Girl Culture*. London: Palgrave Macmillan

Thring, O. (2016). Born in the Rubbish Tip, the Greatest Poetry of Today. *The Times*. Available from: www.thetimes.com/article/born-in-the-rubbish-tip-the-greatest-poetry-of-today-8hzrknm30 (Accessed 23 January 2016)

Todd, L. and Choi, F. (2019). A Complicated, Shifting Subjectivity: Talking with Franny Choi. *The Rumpus*. Available at: https://therumpus.net/2019/05/28/the-rumpus-interview-with-franny-choi/ (Accessed: 10 March 2023)

Tunnicliffe, A. and Wollen, A. (2015). Artist Audrey Wollen on the Power of Sadness: Sad Girl Theory, Explained. *Nylon*. Available at: https://nylon.com/articles/audrey-wollen-sad-girl-theory (Accessed: 28 May 2018)

Underwood, J. (2018). On Poetry and Uncertain subjects. Poetry Foundation (website). Available from: www.poetryfoundation.org/poetrymagazine/articles/146494/on-poetry-and-uncertain-subjects (Accessed: 28 February 2023)

University of California. (2023). Young People in 4-H Are Uniquely Prepared to Step Up to the Challenges of a Rapidly Changing World. *University of California 4-H Youth Development Program*. Available at: https://4h.ucanr.edu/ (Accessed: 26 April 2023)

Walker, Nancy A. (1988). *A Very Serious Thing: Women's Humour and American Culture*. Minneapolis: University of Minnesota Press

Wang, Z. (2021). Disparaging vs. Recognizing the White Working Class in *Friends, Desperate Housewives*, and *The Big Bang Theory*. *American Journal of Economics and Sociology*, 80(3), 903–13. https://doi.org/0.1111/ajes.12408

Washington Times (2002). Administration Probes 4-H Indian Themes. *Washington Times*. Available from: www.washingtontimes.com/news/2002/jun/25/20020625-032408-7001r/ (Accessed: 26 April 2023)

Watercutter, A. (2015). *Ex Machina* has a Serious Fem-Bot Problem. *Wired*. Available at: www.wired.com/2015/04/ex-machina-turing-bechdel-test/ (Accessed: 14 April 2018)

Watson, L. and Wollen, A. (2015). How Girls are Finding Empowerment Through Being Sad Online. *Dazed*. Available at: www.dazeddigital.com/photography/article/28463/1/girls-are-finding-empowerment-through-internet-sadness (Accessed: 21 March 2023)

Webb, R. (2014). Review – *Faber New Poets 9* – Rachael Allen. *Ambit*. Available at: www.ambitmagazine.co.uk/review-faber-new-poets-9-rachael-allen/ (Accessed: 20 October 2015)

——. (2015). Thoughts on Jack Underwood's Happiness. *Ambit*. Available at: www.ambitmagazine.co.uk/thoughts-on-jack-underwoods-happiness/ (Accessed: 2 February 2016)

__ and Berry, E. (2017). Spectacular Endlessly: An Interview With Emily Berry. *Los Angeles Review of Books*. Available at: https://lareviewofbooks.org/article/spectacular-endlessly-an-interview-with-emily-berry (Accessed: 7 March 2017)

Welsch, J.T. (2020). *The Selling and Self-Regulation of Contemporary Poetry*. London: Anthem Press

Wendling, M. (2018). *Alt-Right: From 4chan to the White House*. London: Pluto Press

Whalley, C. (2014). IRL: Rachael Allen's 4chan poems. *The Missing Slate*. Available at: http://journal.themissingslate.com/2014/04/17/irl-rachael-allens-4chan-poems/view-all/ (Accessed: 13 February 2023)

——. (2016). Emily Berry. Poetry International Web (website). Available at: www.poetryinternationalweb.net/pi/site/poet/item/27677/Emily-Berry (Accessed: 3 January 2017)

———. [@charleswhalley] (21 January 2016). 'How did Sarah Howe win T.S. Eliot prize, asks Private Eye'. X. Available at: https://x.com/charleswhalley/status/690288465884401664 (Accessed: 21 January 2016)

———. (2017). I Was a Rickety House: A Commentary on 'Hennecker's Ditch'. Charles Whalley (website). Available at: www.charleswhalley.co.uk/2017/03/18/i-was-a-rickety-house (Accessed: 19 March 2017)

Wilkinson, B. (2013). Dear Boy by Emily Berry review. *Guardian*. Available at: www.theguardian.com/books/2013/mar/22/dear-boy-review (Accessed: 7 December 2015)

Williams, B. (2019). President Trump's Crusade Against the Transgender Community. *American University Journal of Gender, Social Policy & the Law*, 27(4), 525–51. https://digitalcommons.wcl.american.edu/jgspl/vol27/iss4/2

Williams, G. (2018). After Cook's Voyages: The Imperial Legacy. British Library (website). Available at: www.bl.uk/the-voyages-of-captain-james-cook/articles/after-cook-voyages-the-imperial-legacy (Accessed: 20 April 2023)

Williams, H. (2017). The Reign Of The Internet Sad Girl Is Over———And That's A Good Thing. *The Establishment*. Available at: https://theestablishment.co/the-reign-of-the-internet-sad-girl-is-over-and-thats-a-good-thing-eb6316f590d9 (Accessed: 8 October 2017)

Williams, L. (2016). How Hollywood Whitewashed the Old West. *The Atlantic*. Available from: www.theatlantic.com/entertainment/archive/2016/10/how-the-west-was-lost/502850/ (Accessed: 26 July 2022)

Williams, S.T. (2018). An Indigenous Australian Perspective on Cook's Arrival. British Library (website). Available at: www.bl.uk/the-voyages-of-captain-james-cook/articles/an-indigenous-australian-perspective-on-cooks-arrival (Accessed: 20 April 2023)

Williamson, A. (2006) Cynicism. *The American Poetry Review*, 35 (3), 39–43. www.jstor.org/stable/20683218

Winrow, L. (2013). *The Construction of Gender through Embarrassment, Shame and Guilt in the Poetry of Selima Hill*. Available at: https://salford-repository.worktribe.com/OutputFile/1497238 (Accessed: 4 April 2017)

Wise, D.W. (2019). Obama's legacy is as a disappointingly conventional president. *LSE*. Available at: https://blogs.lse.ac.uk/usappblog/2019/04/30/obamas-legacy-is-as-a-disappointing-conventional-president/ (Accessed: 22 February 2023)

The Woman (2011). Directed by Lucky McKee. Available at: Prime Video (Accessed: 20 April 2023)

Woods, S. (2014). *Sara or the Existence of Fire*. Michigan: Horse Less Press

Wray, M. (1997). White Trash Religion. In: Wray, M. and Newitz, A. (eds.), *White Trash: Race and Class in America*. London: Routledge, pp. 193–210

—— and Newitz, A. (1997). Introduction. *White Trash: Race and Class in America*, London: Routledge, pp. 1–14

Yeh, J. (2012). *The Ninjas*. Manchester: Carcanet

Yezzi, D. (1998). Confessional Poetry & the Artifice of Honesty. *New Criterion*. Available from: www.newcriterion.com/issues/1998/6/confessional-poetry-the-artifice-of-honesty (Accessed: 13 February 2018)

Yu, J. and Knox, J.L. (2019). 10 Rations = 1 Decoration: A Conversation with Jennifer L. Knox about Poetry's Strange Math. *Medium*. Available at: https://medium.com/emrys-journal-online/10-rations-1-decoration-a-conversation-with-jennifer-l-knox-about-poetrys-strange-math-22cd5dbbc95d (Accessed: 3 April 2023)

Index

Afro-surrealism, 11, 82
Ahmed, Sara, 27–8, 37, 54, 75–6
Allen, Rachael, 36, 48–9, 52–8
Alsadir, Nuar, 59
android *see* cyborg
apocalypse, 71–5, 78–9, 80–7, 112
Arshi, Mona, 133, 139, 141–2
Attlee, Edwina, 35–6, 48
avant-garde, 2–7, 9–11, 22, 25–7, 29,
    32, 39, 48, 96–7, 102, 105, 155

Bakhtin, Mikhail, 86
Baraka, Amiri, 11
Bartmaan, Sarah, 81
Beckett, Samuel, 1, 70–1, 119–23,
    157
Bennett, Michael Y., 2, 12, 14, 72
Berry, Emily, 6, 35, 39, 41, 48–9, 51,
    133–50
Best, Crispin, 45, 59–68
Beyoncé, 81
Bird, Caroline, 31, 37–9, 117–19,
    122, 125–32
Bourdieu, Pierre, 94, 105
Boyer, Anne, 101, 151–4, 156
Breton, Andre, 9, 11
Broder, Melissa, 114–16
Brown, Chris, 106
Burns, Lucy, 61, 103
Butler, Judith, 114, 136

Calder, Kim, 47
Caleshu, Anthony, 29
camp, 97, 101, 103, 104, 111
Camus, Albert, 1, 62, 70, 71, 122
Cixous, Hélène, 16
Coates, Dave, 84, 119, 160n
Coleridge, Samuel Taylor, 93, 95
Collins, Sophie, 36, 48–9, 52, 55–7
confrontational empathy, 126
Cooke, Jennifer *see* New Audacity
confessional poetry, 15, 49–51, 53
Cornwell, Neil, 2, 8–9, 12, 14, 69
Copus, Julia, 39
Chingonyi, Kayo, 155
Choi, Franny, 76–80
Crenshaw, Kimberlé *see*
    intersectional feminism
cute, 61–3, 67, 103–4
cyborg, 76–84, 87

Darcy, Ailbhe, 85, 96
del Rey, Lana, 113
Delville, Michel, 8, 12, 17, 28, 29,
    43
Derksen, Celeste, 14, 32
Desperate Housewives, 127–9
DiAngelo, Robin, 27
Dickman, Matthew *see* William
    Logan
Dyer, Richard, 56, 109

Edson, Russell, 2, 17, 18–19, 28, 31, 37, 41, 139, 140
emotionally non-directive writing, 46, 155
Elizaveta Bam see Daniil Kharms
Endgame, 70–1, 73–4, 78, 122; *see also* Samuel Beckett
Epstein, Andrew *see* Flarf
Esslin, Martin, 2, 7, 8, 12, 14, 15, 119–20, 124
Evans, Elizabeth, 15, 52, 74, 76
Ex Machina, 77

Faber Anxious Style, 7
female insanity, 17, 25, 28–9, 33–4, 37, 39, 42, 43
Field, John, 131
Fisher, Mark, 78–9; *see also* hauntology
Flarf, 6, 46, 163n
flat style, 48–50, 52, 59
Francis, Terri *see* Afro-surrealism
Freud, Sigmund *see* uncanny
Frost, Robert, 2, 99, 100

Garland, Alex *see Ex Machina*
Gascoyne, David, 12, 133
Gavins, Joanna, 1–2, 14
Gillis, Stacy, 52
Glenum, Lara *see* Gurlesque
Goldsmith, Kenneth, 47–8
Goddard, Kieran, 58–9, 61, 62
Gordon, Nada, 103–4
grand narrative, 64, 79; *see also* Jean-Francois Lyotard
Greenberg, Arielle *see* Gurlesque
Grobe, Christopher, 49–50
Gudding, Gabriel *see* Menippean satire
Gurlesque, 7, 49, 101–3

Haraway, Donna, 76, 81
Harlem Globetrotters, 110, 111

Handeyesque poetry, 41, 43, 49, *56*
hauntology, 78–9
Hill, Selima, 32, 39–42
Hinchliffe, Arnold, P., 8
Hollingsworth, Margaret, 2, 32
Holloway-Smith, Wayne, 94, 105
hooks, bell, 107
Howe, Sarah, 75
hyperfemininity, 104–5

Iglesias, Holly, 18, 28
Institute for Precarious Consciousness, 124

Jackson, Major, 92–3, 107
Jameson, Frederic *see* waning of affect
Jones, Owen, 56

Kaufman, Gloria, 33, 117, 124
Kaufmann, David, 47–8, 96, 100
Keller, Catherine, 72, 75
Kempf, Christopher, 44
Kennard, Luke, 12, 32, 42–3
Kharms, Daniil, 2, 70
Kilalea, Kate, 6
King, Amy, 102
Klein, Emily B. *see* New Feminist Absurd
Knox, Jennifer L., 33, 81, 85–7, 91–100, 103–12
Kraus, Kris, 50

Lehman, David, 5, 10, 12, 95, 97
Lerner, Ben, 43, 94, 95
Loden, Rachel, 111
Loffreda, Beth *see* Claudia Rankine
Logan, William, 93, 95, 98
Lowell, Robert, 49
Luckhurst, Roger, 133, 136, 145
Lumsden, Roddy, 7
Lyotard, Jean-Francois, 64

McDonald, Paul, 34, 42
McKee, Lucky *see The Woman*
MacNeice, Louis, 119
Magi, Jill, 4, 91, 155
Marso, Lori Jo, 57
masculinity, 61–6, 67
Masud, Noreen *see* flat style
meme, 59, 157
Menippean satire, 86, 96, 156
Merrett King, Caitlin *see* unsure theory
Moi, Toril, 16
Monson, Jane, 12
Mslexia, 36
Mullen, Harryette, 4
Murphy, Marguerite S., 12

New Audacity, 47–50
New Feminist Absurd, 2, 14, 15, 124
Newitz, Annalee *see* Matt Wray
New York School, 5, 10, 26, 95
Ngai, Sianne, 61, 82
Noel-Tod, Jeremy, 12
Nørth, Never Angeline, 72–4
Notley, Alice, 2, 102

Obama, Barack, 64–7
O'Hara, Frank, 10, 94
Ostern, 109–10

Palmer, Jerry *see* peripeteia
parable, 28, 119–20, 122
Park Hong, Cathy, 3, 26, 28, 102, 155
Parker, Morgan, 81–3, 85, 87
Parmar, Sandeep, 4, 7, 10, 20, 25–8, 32, 37, 75, 139, 155
Pedwell, Carolyn *see* confrontational empathy
Petit, Pascale, 13–14
peripeteia, 9, 19, 30, 62, 98
Perloff, Marjorie, 3, 9–10

Phillipson, Heather, 32, 34–6
Pickering, Jo, 104
Pioneer Day, 152
Place, Vanessa, 47–8
Plester, Barbara, 61, 62
post-internet poetry, 35, 45–6, 61
post-feminism, 128
prose poem, 8, 12, 17, 28, 29, 53

Railton, Diane, 108
Ramazani, Jahan, 26, 28
Rankine, Claudia, 3, 43, 91, 95–6
Reed, Anthony, 3, 102
respectability politics, 58, 65, 67
Rich, Adrienne, 140
Riviere, Sam, 6, 32, 35, 36–7, 45–6, 49
robot *see* cyborg
Rooney, Kathleen *see* Handeyesque poetry
Rosemont, Penelope, 9
Rosencrantz and Guildenstern are Dead, 70–1, 73, 78

Sad Girl, 113–18
  Asian Sad Girls Club, 117
  Instagram Sad Girl, 116
  Sad Girls Y Qué, 117
  Tumblr Sad Girl, 116
Silem Mohammed, K. *see* Rachel Loden
Skeggs, Beverley, 53–6, 57, 104
Sontag, Susan *see* camp
Southern Gothic, 143–5, 149
Sparks Lin, Meiya, 76, 78
Stoppard, Tom, 9, 70–1
The Stranger, 17–18
Sweeney, Gael, 95, 104, 106

Tate, James, 2, 14, 29, 31, 37, 41, 139
Techno-Orientalism, 76, 78

Thelandersson, Fredrika, 76, 113–16,
124, 132
Thring, Oliver, 74–5
Trump, Donald, 10, 66–7
Turing, Alan, 79
Tyga *see* Chris Brown

uncanny, 134, 136, 142
Uncreative Writing, 47–8
Underwood, Jack, 6
unheimlich *see* uncanny
universal, 4, 27, 35, 36, 43, 51,
95–6, 100, 139, 142, 149,
155
universality *see* universal
unsure theory, 46

Waiting for Godot, 119, 120–2
Walker, Nancy, A., 117
waning of affect, 49, 78–9

Watson, Paul *see* Diane Railton
Webb, Ralf, 6, 137
Welsch, J. T., 31–2, 94
Western film, 108–11
Wet-n-Wild, 153
Whalley, Charles, 6–7, 53, 58, 61,
103, 136
white trash, 91–3, 95–6, 104–7
Williams, Hannah, 113, 115–16
Williamson, Alan, 18
Winrow, Lucy, 40
Wollen, Audrey, 114, 116, 117
The Woman, 146–7
Wordsworth, William *see* Samuel
Taylor Coleridge
Wray, Matt, 72, 105

Yeh, Jane, 81, 83–5, 87
Yezzi, David, 51
Yu, Josephine, 91–2, 96